CIPS STUDY MATTERS

DIPLOMA IN PROCUREMENT AND SUPPLY

COURSE BOOK

Business needs in procurement and supply

Printed and distributed by:

The Chartered Institute of Procurement & Supply, Easton House, Easton on the Hill, Stamford,
Lincolnshire PE9 3NZ
Tel: +44 (0) 1780 756 777
Fax: +44 (0) 1780 751 610
Email: info@cips.org
Website: www.cips.org

First edition September 2012
Reprinted with minor amendments June 2016

Contents

Preface

Welcome to your new Study Pack.

For each subject you have to study, your Study Pack consists of two elements.

- A **Course Book** (the current volume). This provides detailed coverage of all topics specified in the unit content.
- A small-format volume of **Revision Notes**. Use your Revision Notes in the weeks leading up to your exam.

For a full explanation of how to use your new Study Pack, turn now to page xi. And good luck in your exams!

A note on style

Throughout your Study Packs you will find that we use the masculine form of personal pronouns. This convention is adopted purely for the sake of stylistic convenience – we just don't like saying 'he/she' all the time. Please don't think this reflects any kind of bias or prejudice.

The Office of Government Commerce

The Course Book refers several times to the UK's Office of Government Commerce (OGC). The OGC no longer functions in its original form and its responsibilities have been allocated to different areas within the UK Government, principally the Crown Commercial Service (CCS). However, the OGC's publications remain an authoritative source of guidance on best practice in procurement and definitions of terminology. It is perfectly valid to cite the work of the OGC in these areas when answering exam questions.

June 2016

The Unit Content

The unit content is reproduced below, together with reference to the chapter in this Course Book where each topic is covered.

Unit purpose and aims

On completion of this unit, candidates will understand practices that help achieve value for money solutions in procurement.

This unit explores a variety of elements that underpin the development of criteria. It also considers the options that should be explored when procurement and supply personnel are involved in defining requirements.

Learning outcomes, assessment criteria and indicative content

Chapter

1.0 Understand how to devise a business case for requirements to be sourced from external suppliers

1.1 Analyse how business needs influence procurement decisions

- Type of purchase such as new purchase, modified re-buy, straight re-buy — 1
- Implications of the business needs on the types of procurement — 1
- Procurement's role in developing a business case — 1

1.2 Explain how costs and prices can be estimated for procurement activities

- Types of market data that can provide information on costs and prices — 2
- Direct and indirect costs — 2
- Producing estimated costs and budgets — 2
- Approaches to total costs of ownership/total life cycle costing — 2

1.3 Explain the criteria that can be applied in the creation of a business case

- Examples of criteria typically applied in the production of a business case: costs, benefits, options, alignment with organisational needs and timescales — 1
- Benchmarking requirements — 6

1.4 Explain the operation of financial budgets for the control of procurements

- The purpose of financial budgets — 3
- Cost entries and timings of cashflows — 3
- Performance and control of budgets — 3
- Dealing with variances to budget — 3

4.0 Understand the main implications of outsourced work or outsourced services for procurement

How to Use Your Study Pack

Organising your study

'Organising' is the key word: unless you are a very exceptional student, you will find a haphazard approach is insufficient, particularly if you are having to combine study with the demands of a full-time job.

A good starting point is to timetable your studies, in broad terms, between now and the date of the examination. How many subjects are you attempting? How many chapters are there in the Course Book for each subject? Now do the sums: how many days/weeks do you have for each chapter to be studied?

Remember:

- Not every week can be regarded as a study week – you may be going on holiday, for example, or there may be weeks when the demands of your job are particularly heavy. If these can be foreseen, you should allow for them in your timetabling.
- You also need a period leading up to the exam in which you will revise and practise what you have learned.

Once you have done the calculations, make a week-by-week timetable for yourself for each paper, allowing for study and revision of the entire unit content between now and the date of the exams.

Getting started

Aim to find a quiet and undisturbed location for your study, and plan as far as possible to use the same period each day. Getting into a routine helps avoid wasting time. Make sure you have all the materials you need before you begin – keep interruptions to a minimum.

Using the Course Book

You should refer to the Course Book to the extent that you need it.

- If you are a newcomer to the subject, you will probably need to read through the Course Book quite thoroughly. This will be the case for most students.
- If some areas are already familiar to you – either through earlier studies or through your practical work experience – you may choose to skip sections of the Course Book.

The content of the Course Book

This Course Book has been designed to give detailed coverage of every topic in the unit content. As you will see from pages vii–ix, each topic mentioned in the unit content is dealt with in a chapter of the Course Book. For the most part the order of the Course Book follows the order of the unit content closely, though departures from this principle have occasionally been made in the interest of a logical learning order.

Each chapter begins with a reference to the assessment criteria and unit content to be covered in the chapter. Each chapter is divided into sections, listed in the introduction to the chapter, and for the most part being actual captions from the unit content.

All of this enables you to monitor your progress through the unit content very easily and provides reassurance that you are tackling every subject that is examinable.

Each chapter contains the following features.

- Introduction, setting out the main topics to be covered
- Clear coverage of each topic in a concise and approachable format
- A chapter summary
- Self-test questions

The study phase

For each chapter you should begin by glancing at the main headings (listed at the start of the chapter). Then read fairly rapidly through the body of the text to absorb the main points. If it's there in the text, you can be sure it's there for a reason, so try not to skip unless the topic is one you are familiar with already.

Then return to the beginning of the chapter to start a more careful reading. You may want to take brief notes as you go along, but bear in mind that you already have your Revision Notes – there is no point in duplicating what you can find there.

Test your recall and understanding of the material by attempting the self-test questions. These are accompanied by cross-references to paragraphs where you can check your answers and refresh your memory.

The revision phase

Your approach to revision should be methodical and you should aim to tackle each main area of the unit content in turn. Begin by re-reading your Revision Notes. Check back to your Course Book if there are areas where you cannot recall the subject matter clearly. Then do some question practice. The CIPS website contains many past exam questions. You should aim to identify those that are suitable for the unit you are studying.

Additional reading

Your Study Pack provides you with the key information needed for each module but CIPS strongly advocates reading as widely as possible to augment and reinforce your understanding. CIPS produces an official reading list of books, which can be downloaded from the bookshop area of the CIPS website.

To help you, we have identified one essential textbook for each subject. We recommend that you read this for additional information.

The essential textbook for this unit is *Purchasing and Supply Chain Management* by Kenneth Lysons and Brian Farrington.

Examination

This subject is assessed by completion of four exam questions, each worth 25 marks, in three hours. Each exam question tests a different learning outcome.

CHAPTER 1

Business Needs and Procurement Decisions

Assessment criteria and indicative content

1.1 Analyse how business needs influence procurement decisions

- Type of purchase such as new purchase, modified re-buy, straight re-buy
- Implications of the business needs on the types of procurement
- Procurement's role in developing a business case

1.3 Explain the criteria that can be applied in the creation of a business case

- Examples of criteria typically applied in the production of a business case: costs, benefits, options, alignment with organisational needs and timescales

Section headings

1 What are business needs?
2 The procurement cycle
3 The procurement context
4 Developing a business case
5 Criteria for the business case

Introduction

The first section of the syllabus focuses on the role of procurement in developing a robust 'business case' for sourcing requirements from external suppliers: that is, how procurement can demonstrate that a given sourcing exercise will be worthwhile and cost-effective, in order to justify the effort and expenditure that will go into implementing and managing it. This is an essential stage in the planning of procurements – but one that is often under-emphasised in the procurement cycle.

In this chapter we examine the nature of 'business needs', and how procurement functions define the business needs for a given sourcing exercise. We look at how business needs influence procurement decisions, in different contexts, according to the type of purchase, and the priority of the purchase in the procurement portfolio.

We then turn to the notion of the 'business case': justification of a procurement on the basis of how effectively and efficiently it meets identified business needs. We examine procurement's role in developing the business case for major purchases, and consider a range of criteria or factors which are typically used to make a business case.

In Chapters 2 and 3 we will develop the financial aspects of a business case, by exploring issues such as the estimating of prices and costs, and the use of financial budgets to control procurement expenditure.

1   What are business needs?

1.1   You should be broadly familiar with the concept of input needs or requirements, as the basis for procurement activity.

- An organisation needs certain inputs – materials, components, energy, machinery and equipment, supplies, services or skills – in order to perform its activities and pursue its objectives.
- The planners of business activities, and the users of inputs, typically notify the procurement function of these requirements, in various ways (eg using purchase requisitions, new product specifications, bills of materials generated by materials requirements planning systems and so on).
- The task of procurement is to fulfil the input requirements, by achieving what are often called the **five rights of procurement**: products of the right quality, supplied in the right quantity, to the right place, at the right time, for the right price.

1.2   We may say, therefore, that the functional and operational objectives of procurement are basically to provide the 'right' inputs to meet the operational needs of the organisation.

1.3   But organisations do not only have functional or operational objectives. At a higher level, they also have overarching **strategic and commercial objectives**, such as:

- To operate profitably, achieving value for shareholders (and return on shareholders' investment) – or, in the public sector, to achieve service delivery representing good value for money in the use of public funds
- To achieve and maintain competitive advantage over competitors in the organisation's product or service market, enabling the organisation to maintain or enlarge its market share (share of customers or sales in the market)
- To achieve and maintain cost leadership in a given market, by reducing and managing costs more effectively than competitors
- To achieve and maintain differentiation ('standing out') or leadership in a given industry or market, by developing distinctive capabilities in corporate social responsibility, quality, technology development, innovation, environmental sustainability, ethical trading – or other strategic areas
- To attract and retain high quality employees, supply partners and business allies, supporting continuous and sustainable learning, improvement and competitive advantage.

Increasing business focus of procurement

1.4   In recent decades, there has been a significant shift in the role of procurement functions, from a mainly administrative or clerical role (fulfilling technical or operational requirements) to a more **strategic, commercial and business-focused role**.

- The cost base of most manufacturing companies has changed dramatically in recent decades, owing to increasing automation (reducing the proportion of costs represented by labour). A significant proportion of turnover and total costs is now typically spent on the procurement of goods, services or works from external organisations. Procurement responsibility therefore extends to a larger proportion of the organisation's spending – and procurement decisions can make a significant impact on bottom line profit, in the crucial area of external expenditure.
- The adoption of world class manufacturing approaches – including just in time techniques, total quality management and lean production (the elimination of wastes from the supply chain) – have further enhanced the role of procurement and supply chain functions. It is now widely recognised that they have a strategic part to play in value addition and the securing of competitive advantage, through their value-adding roles in quality management, waste reduction, and supply chain innovation and development.
- The need to secure proactive, consistent, high-quality performance from supply chains has driven a shift towards strategic supplier relationships and supply chain management development. This is now

recognised as a key determinant of commercial and competitive success. Christopher *(Logistics and Supply Chain Management)* argues that, these days: 'The real competitive struggle is not between individual companies, but between their supply chains or networks... What makes a supply chain or network unique is the way the *relationships and interfaces in the chain or network are managed*. In this sense, a major source of differentiation comes from *the quality of relationships that one business enjoys, compared to its competitors.*'

1.5   This shift is reflected in a variety of models of the historical development of the procurement function. Reck & Long, for example, have classified the development of procurement into four stages.

- **Passive:** procurement has no strategic direction, and mainly reacts to the requests of other functions. Its function is mainly clerical.
- **Independent:** procurement adopts the latest procurement techniques and processes, and its own functional strategies. The focus is mainly on functional efficiency, with contribution measured in terms of cost reduction and supplier performance.
- **Supportive:** procurement supports the firm's competitive strategy by adopting techniques (such as just in time or lean supply) and products which strengthen its position. Its role is now that of a strategic facilitator, measured by contribution to competitive objectives.
- **Integrative:** procurement's strategy (along with those of other functions) is fully integrated into the firm's overall strategy. Its role is that of a strategic contributor, and is measured by strategic contribution. The emphasis is on cross-functional information exchange and understanding.

1.6   Increasingly, therefore, the role of procurement is not merely to fulfil operational or technical requirements (as expressed in requisitions or specifications), but to contribute to:

- The bottom line profit of the unit or enterprise
- The addition of shareholder value (return on the value of shareholders' investments) and customer value (customer satisfaction and the related willingness to pay for the product or service)
- The achievement of value for money solutions in conducting procurement exercises (securing an optimum balance of whole life costs and quality)
- The effective management of organisational cashflows, to ensure that the business maintains the 'liquidity' (available funds) to cover its short-term liabilities (eg paying employees and suppliers) and to maintain operations
- The fulfilment of other commercial and strategic objectives of the business or business unit (including competitive advantage and market share, sustainable production, corporate social responsibility, innovation and so on).

Business need and business case

1.7   The term 'business case' may be used for the justification of a procurement or sourcing project in terms of its identifiable business benefits, balanced against any recognised constraints, costs and risks involved in obtaining those benefits. The reasoning behind the need for a business case is that a significant commitment or consumption of organisational resources (including finance, time and effort) will only be justified if it is demonstrably *in support of an identified business need*.

1.8   In other words, procurement activity and expenditure with external suppliers should not be carried out 'for its own sake', or because it is embedded in organisational procedures, processes, customs or assumed technical requirements. Proposed procurements should be:

- Examined and challenged to **demonstrate how they contribute** to the commercial and strategic objectives of the business
- Planned and managed in such a way as to **maximise their contribution** to the commercial and strategic objectives of the business (eg through achieving value for money, minimising the cost of meeting required quality standards, minimising wastes and risks – and so on).

1.9 So, for example, a user or IT department might argue that a software upgrade would 'improve the performance of the IT system': a legitimate **technical benefit**. The purchasing department might agree that the upgrade would 'help improve supply chain co-ordination': a legitimate **functional benefit.**

1.10 However, the *business case* argument for the upgrade would have to show that improved IT system performance would offer a commercial or **business benefit:** by improving customer satisfaction, say, or shortening task processing times (improving productivity), or reducing system maintenance costs, or minimising data security risks.

1.11 Similarly, it might show that improved supply chain co-ordination would offer a commercial or business benefit: by reducing order cycle times (improving productivity and reducing inventory); reducing supplier management and transaction costs; offering competitive advantage (eg by supporting late customisation of products for customers); supporting lean supply and collaborative cost and waste reductions through the supply chain; or leveraging the value-adding potential of existing IT systems.

2 The procurement cycle

2.1 The main stages of a procurement process – depicted as a cycle – are shown in Figure 1.1. The process starts with the identification of the need. Note that in viewing the procurement process as a *cycle,* we are highlighting the fact that the business need will be periodically *reviewed,* to ensure that procurements are not simply renewed without modification, but have continuing justification on the basis of business benefits.

Figure 1.1 *A generic procurement cycle*

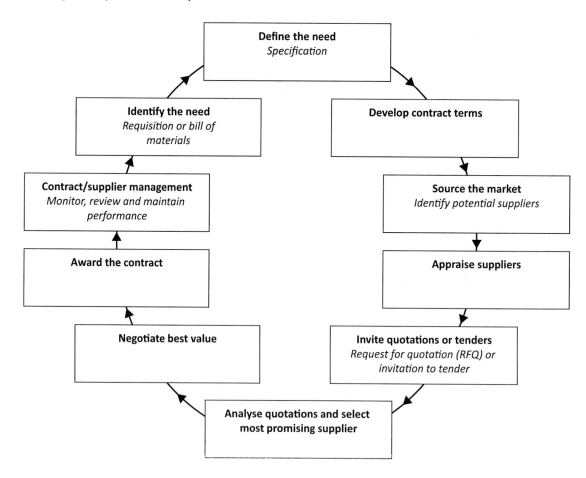

2.2 Business needs will be considered at *all* stages of the procurement cycle. For example:

- Suppliers will be appraised and pre-qualified on the basis of their ability to deliver the volume, quality and price required to meet the business need for value for money and competitive advantage (eg through quality differentiation or competitive pricing). Long-term supply partners will particularly be selected for strategic fit with the buying organisation, and potential to contribute to its business objectives: to support innovation, to provide competitive supply chain agility or quality, to minimise business risk (eg of supplier failure or under-performance) and so on.

- Supplier proposals, bids and quotations will generally be evaluated on the basis of lowest price or 'most economically advantageous tender': fulfilling the primary business need for competitive value for money.

- Contract and supplier management is intended to meet the business need for cost-effective performance of the contract; legal compliance; and, for longer-term relationship management, the potential to leverage collaboration for business benefits (such as waste reduction, continuous quality improvement, competitive innovation, competitive advantage through securing exclusive or preferential supply – and so on).

2.3 However, the earliest and main opportunity for a business case to be developed and presented is at the stages of identification and definition of sourcing or input needs. If business needs are *not* considered at this early stage:

- Unnecessary procurements may be made (eg where items already in stock could be used to meet the technical need) – wasting resources on the procurement process, the price and costs of ownership, and related problems of stock proliferation, underutilisation and obsolescence

- Procurements may be over-specified (eg where not all features requested by designers or users are necessary) – wasting resources on non-value-adding features and functionality

- Sourcing effort may be wasted by *subsequent* rejection or revision of the specification or project (eg during tender evaluation or negotiation with suppliers) due to the emergence of unevaluated costs or risks, or a negative cost/benefit analysis or feasibility study.

2.4 The syllabus therefore focuses primarily on the **identification, definition and communication of requirements,** embracing processes such as: specification of requirements, and the development of key performance indicators and express contract terms for inclusion in contractual arrangements made with suppliers. We will cover these issues in detail in Chapters 4–8.

2.5 Here, we will just give a brief overview of these stages of the procurement cycle, to set the context.

Identifying needs

2.6 Before any procurement exercise or transaction can begin, someone must notice that something is needed which is not currently available, and this need must be notified to the procurement function (or other staff responsible for procurements). The need may be identified by a user department: for example, a designer may recognise the need for new software. Or the driver for procurement may come from a stores department or warehouse: a check of inventory levels may reveal the need to replenish stocks of materials or components.

2.7 In either case, the normal procedure would be for the department concerned to issue a **requisition**: a form (or its electronic equivalents) which describes the item needed and initiates action by the procurement function. If the organisation operates a materials requirements planning (MRP) system, the identification of the need may instead be signalled by a **bill of materials** (BOM). Briefly, the approach is to forecast the manufacturing schedule for finished products, and to translate this into details of the materials and parts needed for production: the bill of materials. This can then be compared with stock files, where relevant, to establish which materials and parts will have to be procured.

2.8 Requisition and bill of materials forms will contain details of the required item(s) in a standardised form. However, the procurement function may at this point consider the business need for the procurement. It may be appropriate to refer the requisition back to the originator:

- To challenge over-specification or unnecessary variation (perhaps on the basis of systematic value analysis), or
- To suggest alternatives that will offer better quality or lower price than the item requisitioned.

2.9 This is a key potential source of added value in the procurement process, since it is designed to minimise waste in the form of unnecessary variation, features, quality or service levels – and associated unnecessary costs.

2.10 For more substantial procurements, a formal feasibility study, cost/benefit analysis or systematic business case may be requested by the budget holder, finance manager, procurement team leader or project sponsor – or may be required by organisational policy (eg for new procurements over a certain value threshold).

Defining needs

2.11 The process so far relates to the identification and description of the need *within* the buying organisation. The next step will be to establish a detailed description of the requirement which can be communicated to potential suppliers. Detailed descriptions may already exist (if the purchase is a re-buy, for example), but for new procurements, they may have to be drawn up, in the form of:

- Specifications (of various types)
- Service level agreements (added to the specification of services)
- Contract terms which set out the obligations of buyer and seller in relation to the fulfilment of the specification
- Key performance indicators, or performance measures which will be used to establish whether the requirement has been satisfactorily met.

3 The procurement context

Type of purchase

3.1 Three basic classifications of 'type of purchase' are highlighted by the syllabus.

- **Straight re-buy** of items already sourced from a supplier
- **Modified re-buy,** where some of the requirement has changed
- **New buy**, where the requirement has not previously been specified or sourced

3.2 Not every procurement will follow every stage of a systematic procurement process, or be subject to detailed business case justification. For some purchases, this level of analysis and decision-making will already substantially have been done – while for others, it will be particularly significant. The type of purchase therefore has implications for the extent to which systematic business case justification is required.

3.3 Business needs will still influence decisions about the purchase, however, and different types of purchase may prioritise different business needs.

Straight re-buy

3.4 If a procurement is a **straight re-buy** of items already sourced from a supplier:

- The buyer may already have a preferred supplier, and perhaps a standing purchase agreement or 'call-off contract' enabling stock replenishment orders without further investigation or negotiation

- It will not be necessary to establish a specification, or to survey and source the market, and it may not be necessary to invite quotations or select a new supplier
- A systematic justification of expenditure on the basis of business need may not be warranted.

3.5 In such a case, however, the priority in regard to business case may be to ensure the continuing suitability, value for money and competitiveness of the specification, supplier and supply contract. Circumstances and requirements may have changed. Different solutions, suppliers or products may have emerged which would offer better value for money or create new opportunities for improvement or differentiation. Established suppliers may have grown complacent and ceased to be competitive in their value offering.

3.6 For straight re-buys or inventory replenishments, therefore, business needs might influence procurement decisions by suggesting the need:

- To **optimise inventory replenishment methods**, to minimise inventory (and associated costs) while securing adequate service levels and minimising the risks and costs of stockouts and bottlenecks. So, for example, procurement might investigate options for pull or demand-led supply (such as just in time methods) for dependent demand; or might utilise economic order quantity calculations to optimise stock replenishment for independent demand; or might evaluate its stock replenishment systems (eg periodic review or fixed order quantity) to ensure that they are optimally efficient.
- Periodically to **review existing specification and arrangements** against supply market developments, to ensure that they still represent the optimum solutions
- Periodically to **re-open existing long-term contracts to competition**, to ensure that existing suppliers remain competitive
- To **secure additional business benefits in repeat or renewed contracts**, eg by entering into continuous improvement agreements with suppliers (setting increased quality or delivery targets year on year), or providing contractual incentives to improve cost or quality performance (eg by negotiating a capped price for the contract which *decreases* year on year, giving the supplier an incentive to reduce wastes in order to preserve its profit margins).
- To collaborate with engineering, quality, marketing and user departments in systematic **value analysis of products**: looking critically at all the elements that make up a product or service and investigating whether they are really necessary, and whether they could be done more efficiently or cheaply. (In other words, investigating whether a 'straight re-buy' *should* be a straight re-buy, or whether it might be modified in order to better meet business needs.)

Modified re-buy

3.7 If a procurement is a modified re-buy, in that some of the requirement has changed:

- It may be necessary to re-specify the need or re-negotiate the contract, while using the same supplier (or *vice versa*: the specification may stay the same, but a new supplier will be sought, in order to provide more innovative or better value solutions)
- A business case justification of the modification may be required, for high-value, strategically important or high-risk procurements
- Modification of the requirement may represent an *opportunity* to revisit specifications or contracts, in order to seek to meet business needs more efficiently or effectively.

3.8 For modified re-buys or re-specifications, therefore, business needs might influence procurement decisions by suggesting the need or opportunity:

- To **review existing specifications and arrangements** against supply market developments, to ensure that they still represent the optimum solutions
- To **challenge modified specifications** put forward by engineering, design or user functions, in order to promote commercial considerations such as value (eg avoiding over-specification); standardisation or variety reduction (to reduce inventory costs); environmental sustainability; the leveraging of supplier relationships and expertise (eg by keeping specifications 'open' to diverse supplier solutions)

- To **re-open existing contracts to competition**, to ensure that existing suppliers remain competitive
- To **justify specification or contract modification** on the basis of identified business benefits: avoiding unnecessary risks and costs of re-specification, variety and stock proliferation, supplier switching, learning curves and 'teething problems' and so on. Modifications should not be made unless there is a business case justification for change, such as lower-cost production, variety reduction (reduced costs of inventory), improved customer satisfaction (as a result of product improvement) or a prolonged product lifecycle for additional sales revenue (as a result of product or brand refreshment).
- To **re-negotiate contract terms** to build in additional business benefits, such as quality improvements, collaborative waste or cost reductions, or additional KPIs (such as environmental or social sustainability standards).

New purchase

3.9   If a procurement is a new buy, which has not been specified or sourced before:

- Procurement activity is more likely to conform to the full, systematic procurement process
- An in-depth business case justification of the modification may be required, especially for high-value, strategically important or high-risk procurements
- New identification and specification of requirements represents a key opportunity to build in business benefits at the product, service or project development stage.

3.10   For new purchases, therefore, business needs might influence procurement decisions by suggesting the need or opportunity:

- To engage in systematic **purchasing research:** 'the systematic study of all relevant factors which may affect the acquisition of goods and services, for the purpose of securing current and future requirements in such a way that the competitive position of the company is enhanced' (van Weele). This includes:
  — *Demand analysis,* aimed at accurate demand forecasting for high-value, high-usage, high-risk materials, in order to minimise sourcing and inventory waste and risks. Accurate demand forecasting will be particularly important in estimating and managing materials and inventory costs, for example.
  — *Vendor analysis:* evaluating the capability of potential suppliers and the performance of current suppliers to optimise supplier value and minimise supplier risk; and analysing supplier cost structures to support cost management and price negotiation
  — *Supply market analysis:* appraising conditions in the supply market, in relation to factors such as: likely availability and the risk of shortages or disruptions to supply; market prices, price fluctuations and trends; and environmental factors affecting supply or demand.
- To engage in proactive **value engineering:** value analysis applied at the design, development and specification stage of product development, in order to eliminate wastes, over-specification and non-value-adding features and processes from the outset.
- To promote **early buyer involvement** (EBI) in product and specification development, in order to ensure that commercial and supply market considerations are taken into account at an early stage, when they can make the greatest whole-life impact.
- To promote **early supplier involvement** (ESI) in product and specification development, in order to ensure that solutions take into account supply market expertise, technology and innovation.
- To **develop specifications, supplier performance measures (KPIs) and contract terms** which will maximise business benefits and value to the buying organisation – as discussed in Chapters 4–8.

Procurement categories

3.11   Similar considerations might be applied to the nature or categories of the items being procured. (Note that this is another interpretation of the phrase 'types of purchase'. If this phrase is used in the examination, you will need to state clearly your assumptions about what is being referred to.) Different business needs may be a priority for procurement decision-making about different categories of purchase.

3.12   For **capital procurements** (the procurement of assets with a long usage life and high acquisition cost, such as buildings, plant and equipment, computer systems or vehicles), the priority business need for procurement decisions is likely to be whole life value for money. This might encompass issues such as:

- Systematic appraisal of the benefits, costs and risks of the investment, and likely 'payback' period of the investment (the length of time it will take for the business benefits to outweigh the cost). Because of their high value, capital procurements are most likely to be the subject of systematic formal business case justification.
- Robust comparison of alternative assets or options, to reach the optimal solution: balancing the whole life costs and performance, functionality and quality of the asset
- Negotiation, specification and contracting with the chosen supplier for a total 'package' of benefits sought over the asset's lifecycle (eg including installation, user training, finance, maintenance, warranties and/or technical support)
- Analysis and management of lifecycle costs: not just the price, but ongoing costs of acquisition, operation, maintenance and disposal over the years of the asset's useful life
- Management and maintenance of the asset in such a way as to prolong its useful life and maximise its residual value on disposal (eg for recycling or re-sale).

We will look specifically at the business case for capital assets, when we look at whole life costing (WLC) in Chapter 2.

3.13   For the procurement of **production materials** (such as raw materials, components and assemblies), the priority business need for procurement decisions might be the achievement of operational objectives including the five rights. Operational efficiency may be best served by the timely and secure flow of inputs (of specified quality) to production processes, in order to minimise the risks and costs of bottlenecks or disruption to production.

3.14   For the procurement of **maintenance repair and operating** or MRO supplies ('all goods and services, other than capital equipment, necessary to transform raw materials and components into end products', such as paint, lubricants, packing materials, cleaning products and industrial clothing), the priority business need for procurement decisions might be:

- The need to avoid stock proliferation: an increase in the range and variety of items, models or brands over time, as different users specify different items – without considering whether an item already in stock, or a generic item, would do the job. Some estimates suggest that a reasonably large manufacturing plant will carry in excess of 10,000 MRO stock lines: although usage of any particular part may be relatively low, the potential for incurring high procurement and stock-holding costs is clearly high. Opportunities for rationalisation – reducing duplication and variation – would have a strong business case.
- The opportunity to manage costs by establishing optimum stock levels, based on accurate usage data and replenishment systems
- The need to enforce sound procurement disciplines in MRO procurements (rather than letting users purchase on a 'maverick' or *ad hoc* basis) eg by using call-off contracts
- The opportunity to minimise prices (eg by consortium buying or demand aggregation for bulk discounts and negotiation leverage).

3.15   For the procurement of **commodities** (raw materials such as textile, food and beverage crops and minerals such as coal or iron ore, for incorporation in products), the priority business need for procurement decisions might be securing supply (minimising the risk of scarcity or supply disruption) and price/cost management. Commodities are often sourced from international markets, creating a complex set of costs and risks (including currency exchange risk, transport risk, and differences in legal jurisdiction for contract disputes). They are also subject to significant and unexpected fluctuations in price, due to variable supply and demand. It is important for buyers to monitor relevant commodity supply market factors carefully. A business case may be made for solutions such as:

- Forward buying (deliberately over-stocking in order to take advantage of low prices – a business benefit which must be weighed against the costs of storing and insuring the additional stock)
- The use of commodity market tools such as futures contracts (acquiring rights to buy or sell a specified quantity of a commodity in the market: hedging the contract by ensuring that movements in price have a self-cancelling or off-setting effect).

3.16 In the purchase of **goods for re-sale** (eg purchases by a retailer, wholesaler or brokerage for sale onwards to customers or consumers), the priority business need for procurement decisions might be the selection of goods for which there will be sufficient market demand to secure profitable trading. Wholesalers and retailers are generally not adding much value to the products they sell, and their margins are therefore somewhat tight: buyers must focus on buying what will sell at a good profit margin – and acting swiftly on market feedback (what is selling and what isn't) to adapt the portfolio.

Procurement priority

3.17 You may have gathered, from our coverage so far, that the need for – and justification of – a robust business case analysis also depends on the importance, priority, value or 'criticality' of the item being purchased.

- For routine, low-value items, it may be worth an informal periodic re-considering of costs and benefits – in the interests of incremental or 'small step' value improvements. However, a full-scale business case analysis would probably not be justified: the costs of such an exercise would probably outweigh any future cost savings, efficiency gains or quality improvements that could be obtained.
- For strategically important, high-value or high-risk procurements, however, a systematic business case may be required to minimise risk and ensure value.

3.18 In addition, different business needs may be a priority for procurement decision-making, according to the importance of the procurement.

3.19 Several tools have been developed to segment an organisation's procurement portfolio according to priority. Peter Kraljic (1973) developed a tool of analysis that seeks to map:

- The importance to the organisation of the item being purchased (related to factors such as the organisation's annual expenditure on the item, and its profit potential through enabling revenue earning or cost reductions) against
- The complexity of the supply market (related to factors such as the difficulty of sourcing the item, the vulnerability of the buyer to supply or supplier failure, and the relative power of buyer and supplier in the market).

3.20 The Kraljic matrix (or procurement portfolio matrix) therefore has four quadrants, as follows: Figure 1.2.

Figure 1.2 *The Kraljic procurement portfolio matrix*

Complexity of the supply market

	Low		High	
High	**Procurement focus** Leverage items	**Time horizon** Varied, typically 12-24 months	**Procurement focus** Strategic items	**Time horizon** Up to 10 years; governed by long-term strategic impact (risk and contract mix)
	Key performance criteria Cost/price and materials flow management	**Items purchased** Mix of commodities and specified materials	**Key performance criteria** Long-term availability	**Items purchased** Scarce and/or high- value materials
Importance of the item	**Typical sources** Multiple suppliers, chiefly local	**Supply** Abundant	**Typical sources** Established global suppliers	**Supply** Natural scarcity
	Procurement focus Non-critical items	**Time horizon** Limited: normally 12 months or less	**Procurement focus** Bottleneck items	**Time horizon** Variable, depending on availability vs short-term flexibility trade-offs
	Key performance criteria Functional efficiency	**Items purchased** Commodities, some specified materials	**Key performance criteria** Cost management and reliable short-term sourcing	**Items purchased** Mainly specified materials
Low	**Typical sources** Established local suppliers	**Supply** Abundant	**Typical sources** Global, predominantly new suppliers with new technology	**Supply** Production-based scarcity

3.21 Examining each of the quadrants in turn:

- For *non-critical or routine items* (such as common stationery supplies), the business need for **functional efficiency** will be met by low-maintenance routines to reduce procurement costs. Arm's length approaches such as vendor managed inventory, blanket ordering (empowering end users to make call-off orders against negotiated agreements) and e-procurement solutions (eg online ordering or the use of purchasing cards) will provide routine efficiency.

- For *bottleneck items* (such as proprietary spare parts or specialised consultancy services, which could cause operational delays if unavailable), there will be a primarily operational business need for control over the **short-term continuity and security of supply**. This may suggest approaches such as negotiating medium-term or long-term contracts with suppliers; developing alternative or back-up sources of supply; including incentives and penalties in contracts to ensure the reliability of delivery; or keeping higher levels of buffer or 'safety' stock.

- For *leverage items* (such as local produce bought by a major supermarket), the business need for **cost/price management** will be met by using the buyer's power in the market to secure best prices and terms, on a purely transactional basis. This may mean taking advantage of competitive pricing; standardising specifications to make supplier switching easier; and using competitive bidding and/or buying consortia to secure the best deals.

- For *strategic items* (such as core processors bought by a laptop manufacturer), a more complex set of business needs (for **strategic alignment, lifetime cost and value, long-term security of supply and competitive supply**) will be met by developing long-term, mutually beneficial strategic relationships with suppliers.

4   Developing a business case

4.1   As we introduced it earlier, the term 'business case' is used for the justification of a procurement or sourcing project in terms of its identifiable business benefits, balanced against any recognised constraints, costs and risks involved in obtaining those benefits.

4.2   **Business benefits** may take the form of increased revenue, reduced costs, enhanced profitability or value for money (especially in public sector contexts); increased capacity or capability; improved performance; enhanced shareholder value; competitive advantage; and so on. (We will discuss potential business benefits in more detail below.)

4.3   Remember that we are talking about '*business* needs' – not just technical or operational needs. It is worth noting that a procurement or project may be a 'technical success' (ie it conforms to specification in terms of deliverables and products) but a 'business failure' (ie it fails to achieve the wider contribution specified in the business case). For example:

- A construction project may be completed on-budget, on-time and to specification – but may still fail to deliver planned business benefits (eg enhanced shareholder value, enhanced corporate image and reputational capital, learning and capability development, partnership development – and so on).
- A technical success in developing and launching a new product may be a business failure if planned financial and commercial benefits (product adoption, revenue, return on investment, profitability, market share, brand development) are not realised.

The business case process

4.4   The main objectives of a formal business case process (developing and presenting the business case for a procurement, proposal or project) include the following.

- Fostering **strategic, business-focused thinking**: requiring people with the authority to recommend projects or proposals to pre-evaluate their value, risk and priority
- Improving the **efficiency and quality of decision-making** by weeding out (or 'self-culling') proposals that cannot demonstrate business value
- Enabling management to evaluate proposals for feasibility, suitability and acceptability
- Enabling management to **compare alternatives and options** on objective business cost/benefit criteria
- Establishing measurable **yardsticks** by which the subsequent performance, deliverables or outcomes of projects can be evaluated at key review points.
- Is the project or asset achieving the business case benefits anticipated?
- Are the assumptions made in the business case turning out to be accurate?
- Is the business case justification for the project still valid?

4.5   The formulation of business case is also a basic skill of influencing, motivation and 'upward management' (Boddy): if you want senior managers, internal customers and clients or project sponsors to agree to a proposal, you have to give them a reason that makes sense to *them*, in terms of the fulfilment of *their* priorities, needs and goals. Senior managers want to know how a plan or proposal will further the strategic objectives of the business, just as project sponsors will want to know how it will deliver the target business objectives of 'their' project.

4.6   As we suggested earlier, a full-scale formal business case development (potentially a time-consuming and costly exercise) may not be justified in all circumstances, depending on the size, value and risk of the proposal, project or procurement.

4.7   A full-scale exercise may be preceded by a **project feasibility study**, which considers high-level objectives and possible options, with ballpark estimated figures for costs and benefits. Such a feasibility study will be used to assess whether the initial proposals are robust enough, and have sufficient potential, to take forward to developing a full-scale business case.

Contents of a business case

4.8 A **brief, informal analysis**, report and/or presentation may be devoted to low-value, low-risk procurements. An exam case study scenario, for example, would probably only contain sufficient data for a brief informal report, based on interpretation and analysis of fairly 'broad brush' data, and structured according to relevant criteria and issues.

4.9 A simple framework for the kind of business case you might be able to formulate in an exam might include the following sections: Table 1.1.

Table 1.1 *Informal business case structure*

Introduction/ background	• Overview of the business need: the objective to be met, problem to be solved, threat to be countered or opportunity to be exploited • Priority of the need or issue (eg using Kraljic analysis) • The current situation: what has given rise to the need for a business case analysis, and what (if anything) has been done so far
Options	• Options considered (if any), with reasons for rejecting or carrying forward each option
Business benefits	• Expected outcomes of the proposed solution, and their associated business benefits (both quantifiable and qualitative) • Alignment of the proposed solution with business objectives, strategies, policies and values
Costs and risks	• Estimated costs of the proposed solution • Anticipated risks of the proposed solution • Anticipated impacts on activities and relationships (both internal and in the external supply chain) • Anticipated risks and costs of not pursuing the proposed solution (or doing nothing)
Recommendation	• Net (on-balance) cost/benefit assessment • Return on investment or payback period (if data is available)
KPIs (if data is available)	• Target costs and results which will be used to evaluate performance at key decision points in the project or procurement lifecycle, to indicate that anticipated business benefits are being realised.

4.10 A more comprehensive, formal and highly structured business case may be required for high-risk, high-value projects or capital procurements. The systematic formulation and approval of business case is an important part of procurement authorisations in the public sector, for example, and project management methodologies place considerable emphasis on definition of the business case of a project, at the project initiation stage. Organisations are forced to focus on doing the right projects, at the right times, for the right reasons, by making the start of a project and its continued existence (at review stages) dependent on a valid ongoing business case, and delivery of business case outcomes.

4.11 A comprehensive formal business case for a project might include the following elements.

- Executive summary
- Reference: project name or reference, background and current status
- Context: business objectives and strategic alignment, threats and opportunities, and the priority of the project
- Value proposition: the desired business outcomes or deliverables; business benefits (by outcome); quantified or monetised value of the benefits; cost estimates; financial modelling and return on investment calculations; risks and costs of *not* proceeding; and risks of the project (project risks, business risks, risks of the benefits not being realised)
- Scope: the problem or solution scope, assumptions and constraints, options identified and evaluated, assessment of scale and complexity
- Deliverables: outcomes, deliverables and benefits planned (with KPI measures against which results can be evaluated at key review or decision points)
- Impacts: functions, activities and relationships impacted (internally and within the supply chain); key stakeholders; dependencies

- Work planning: approach; project stage definitions; workload estimate or breakdown; sourcing or project plans and schedules; critical path analysis
- Resource requirements: managerial and team resources; funding or budget allocation
- Risk management and contingency plans
- Commitments: project controls and reporting processes, schedule of deliverables, financial budget

5 Criteria for the business case

Business benefits

5.1 The commercial or business benefits of a given procurement, proposal or project may take any of the following forms.

- Fulfilment of a specific **business objective** or furtherance of a specific business strategy (eg improving quality, where the organisation's competitive strategy is one of quality leadership; or harnessing the innovation capability of a supplier, where the organisation has the objective of new product development)
- Increased **revenues** (eg through increased customer satisfaction, brand loyalty and product sales as a result of improved performance or product quality; or the licensing of products or processes to external producers)
- Reduced **costs** (eg through the elimination of wastes; increased efficiency and productivity; price leverage through negotiation or competition; collaborative supply chain cost reductions; reduced inventory – and so on)
- Enhanced **profitability** (as a result of increased revenue and/or reduced costs)
- Enhanced **value for money** (especially in public sector contexts), as a result of reduced costs without compromise on quality or service delivery standards
- Enhanced **shareholder value**, or return on shareholders' investment in the organisation (through enhanced profits, which might be returned to shareholders in the form of dividends; the enhanced value of organisational assets)
- **Competitive advantage**, enabling the organisation to capture market and sales or revenue share from competitors (eg through cost leadership, enabling competitive pricing; product and brand differentiation on quality, customisation, delivery; or gaining preferential or exclusive access to quality suppliers)
- **Leverage** of key resources such as technology or supplier relationships: maximising the value added by the resource (ie not wasting opportunities for synergy and added value
- Increased **capacity, capability or flexibility** (eg through developing quality suppliers and supply chains), which in turn offer potential for enhanced profitability (greater production volumes, responsiveness to fluctuations in demand) and competitive advantage (more capable performance, innovation and design capability, late customisation etc).
- Improved **brand or reputational equity** (eg through consistent quality performance, corporate social responsibility, ethical sourcing and trading, environmental sustainability and so on)

5.2 These benefits can broadly be characterised under the headings of 'added value' and 'competitive advantage'. You may well be familiar with these concepts from your other studies, but we will very briefly re-cap their nature here.

Added value

5.3 Value can be seen simply as the 'worth' of the product or service, which may be measured in two ways: what it costs the organisation to produce or provide, and what customers are willing to pay for it. The term 'added value' thus essentially refers to the addition of greater value or worth to a product or service, as a result of all the processes that support its production and delivery to the customer: marketing, design, production, customer service, distribution, maintenance and so on.

5.4 According to Michael Porter *(Competitive Strategy)*, the ultimate value a firm creates is measured by the amount customers are willing to pay for its products or services *over and above* the cost to the firm of carrying out all its value-creating activities. A firm is profitable if the realised value to customers (what they are prepared to pay) exceeds the cost of value creation.

5.5 The main focus for procurement is that value can be added either by cutting costs (without loss of quality or product features) *or* by securing operational efficiency (enabling superior quality or features at no additional cost). A strong business case on the basis of added value can be made for any activity that achieves both of these objectives: improving the quality and/or quantity of output, while maintaining or reducing costs. Such a business case might be made, for example, for proposals to develop a supplier partnership (potential for collaborative cost reductions and quality improvements); or to implement e-procurement (improved productivity and reduced transaction costs).

Competitive advantage

5.6 Competitive advantage may be defined as the ability (gained through the development, protection and leverage of distinctive competencies and resources) to deliver value to customers more efficiently or effectively than one's competitors.

5.7 Essentially, according to Porter, a business can achieve competitive advantage by performing strategically important activities more cheaply or better than its competitors.

- Providing comparable value to the customer more efficiently than competitors (cost leadership), *or*
- Performing activities at comparable cost but in unique or distinctive ways, creating more value for customers than competitors, and potentially commanding a premium price (differentiation).

5.8 Success in securing competitive advantage – or successful competition – is measured mainly by **market share**: that is, the proportion of sales volume or value in a given market that is gained by a given provider. An organisation might also measure sales growth (in volume or value) – but this would not necessarily indicate *competitive* success: any increase in sales may be a result of the growth of the market, rather than securing customer preference over competitors.

Costs

5.9 The other side of the value proposition, to be balanced against benefits, is the estimated costs of a proposal. These may be:

- Financial costs (eg purchase price, costs of acquisition and ownership, fees and charges, and the costs associated with risk events eg failure costs, 'teething trouble' costs and contingency plan costs)
- Non-financial costs (eg operational disruptions and learning curves as a result of change; impacts on other functions and the supply chain; reputational damage; loss of knowledge or capability; damage to supplier relationships and goodwill).
- Opportunity costs of choosing one option over another (ie the benefits that will be forgone by devoting resources to one plan rather than an alternative plan).

5.10 We will be looking in detail at the identification and estimation of procurement and project costs in Chapter 2.

Risks

5.11 The business case for a given plan will need to take into account a range of internal and external risks.

- Risks arising *from* (or as a result of) the proposed project or procurement, and the associated costs of those risks if they occur. Some procurement proposals may be inherently risky (such as outsourcing, single sourcing and international sourcing) – and it will be necessary to balance the risks and associated costs against the benefits of the proposal.

- Risks which might *affect* the proposed project or procurement, and which might jeopardise the anticipated benefits. Exchange rate fluctuations and transport risks, for example, might reduce the cost advantages anticipated from sourcing from low-cost labour countries. The financial instability of a key supplier might place at risk all the benefits of a procurement, in the event of supplier failure. The risk of system breakdown or data theft would similarly jeopardise the benefits of ICT development.

5.12 Risks will have to be assessed for likelihood (probability of occurrence) and impact (severity of adverse consequence if the risk event occurs, expressed as a quantified cost if possible). The costing of the business case should include the costs of:

- Risk management: identification, assessment and mitigation (eg insurances, monitoring and control)
- Risk events occurring (if they are highly probable and cannot be adequately mitigated): such costs, if significant, may deter the organisation from pursuing the proposal
- Contingency planning (for high impact risks, however improbable): that is, alternative or back-up arrangements to be implemented if risk events occur. There may be costs of maintaining back-up supplier relationships, for example, or off-site storage facilities.

Cost/benefit (or net benefit) analysis

5.13 Cost/benefit analysis is a fairly simple technique for deciding whether or not to pursue a particular plan or procurement. However creative and potentially effective your preferred solution to a business need may be, it will not be 'worth' implementing (in quantitative terms) if the costs of doing so are greater than the benefits that will accrue.

5.14 Put simply, cost-benefit analysis involves putting a monetary value to the benefits of a course of action, and deducting the costs associated with it. However, this may not be as simple as it sounds.

5.15 The benefits of a given plan may not be completely, or easily, quantifiable as a monetary value. Direct financial benefits (such as cost savings or revenue earnings) may be easy to calculate, but putting a financial value on intangible benefits may be highly subjective. (What value can be put on greater employee satisfaction or creativity, say, or the minimising of environmental impacts through better waste management?)

5.16 Similarly, costs may be difficult to analyse.

- Direct costs are those incurred directly as a result of carrying out the plan.
- Indirect costs are those which may be attributed to the plan, but would have been incurred by the organisation whether or not the plan had been carried out: management time, office space and so on.
- Opportunity costs are revenue-earning opportunities lost as a result of implementing the plan.

5.17 There are also intangible costs, which are harder to quantify: what is the cost of environmental damage, or an increase in employee stress, say? The term 'externalities' has been coined by economists to describe costs which are not absorbed in a product or service and not paid for directly by the customer, but are borne by the wider community (such as the costs of pollution control). With increasing pressure for corporate social responsibility (CSR), there is a greater interest in quantifying these kinds of costs.

5.18 As one more complicating factor, costs may be incurred, and benefits received, on an ongoing basis, over time – rather than 'up front' when a plan is implemented. Various techniques can be used to calculate the whole life costs of an asset in today's values: these will be discussed in Chapter 2.

5.19 The essence of cost/benefit analysis is that if benefits exceed costs, the procurement can be justified as worthwhile – while if costs exceed benefits, the procurement proposal will be rejected. It is possible to express this in the form of a benefit/cost ratio.

- If the ratio is significantly less than 1, benefits are less than costs. Conclusion: reject the project.

- If the ratio is significantly greater than 1, benefits are greater than costs. Conclusion: proceed with the project.
- If the ratio is close to 1, benefits and costs are approximately equal. Conclusion: further investigation is needed into the non-financial factors that might influence a decision.

5.20 Figure 1.3 shows a very simple cost benefit analysis for the introduction of a new e-procurement system. The manager making this decision believes that a new system will offer cost savings, enhance the efficiency of stock management and expediting, and enhance supply chain relationships – but is it *worth* doing, from a business case point of view?

Figure 1.3 *Specimen cost benefit analysis*

COSTS	$
Computer equipment:	
8 PCs @ $1,000	8,000
1 server @ $1,200	1,200
2 printers @ $400	800
Installation and technical support	1,800
Purchasing management software	3,200
Staff training:	
Introductory computing (6 people × $200)	1,200
Purchasing management system (8 people × $400)	3,200
Other costs:	
Lost time (20 person days @ $100 per day)	2,000
Cost of errors/wastage through initial inefficiencies (estimate)	5,000
Total cost	**26,400**
BENEFITS (estimate, per year)	$
Improved efficiency of ordering and expediting	20,000
Improved supplier selection and management	10,000
Improved planning and control through supply information	15,000
Total benefit (per year)	**45,000**

Benefit/cost ratio: 45,000/26,400 = 1.70 (positive)

Payback time: 26,400/45,000 = 0.59 year = approximately 7 months

Options or alternative solutions

5.21 The business may be required not only to show that a proposed solution is a 'good' solution (presenting a positive net benefit), but that it is the 'optimum' solution (presenting the *highest* net benefit out of a number of alternative solutions or options).

5.22 Note that the aim is not to identify or compare *all* conceivable options for a decision: even if this were possible, the gathering and evaluation of information would be prohibitively costly and time-consuming, and the organisation would run the risk of 'analysis paralysis'. Especially in an exam case study scenario, where you typically have little information to go on, it should be sufficient for a business case argument to compare the benefits, costs and risks of the proposed plan or procurement with those of:

- Other options which have been considered (eg if alternative proposals are presented in the scenario, or if there is a choice between Suppliers A, B and C)
- Other options which might be considered, perhaps representing typical procurement choices (eg single-sourcing versus multi-sourcing, make/do versus buy, buying versus leasing, or international vs local sourcing).

5.23   As an example, various options may be evaluated as an alternative to the purchase of a capital asset.

- The advantages and disadvantages of outright purchase and leasing can be compared as in Table 1.2. Note that these are sound business case arguments, addressing business needs for cost optimisation, value for money, well-managed cashflow (to minimise liquidity or insolvency risks), competitive performance (eg in regard to the up-to-dateness of technology) and so on.
- The organisation may consider a *hire purchase* agreement, under which, after all the rental payments have been made, the user has the option of becoming the outright owner of the equipment. This enables the latest technology to be hired, but interest rates on the financing may make this a less financially effective approach than either leasing or purchase.
- There may be other options which avoid capital expenditure altogether, in order to minimise large up-front investment and protect cashflows. For example:
  - Equipment could be rented for the duration of a particular short-term project, avoiding the costs of ownership if the asset is likely to be underutilised in future
  - An IT system might be upgraded one unit or application at a time, over an extended period, instead of commissioning a large-scale project to replace the entire system.

Table 1.2 *The lease or buy decision*

ADVANTAGES OF OUTRIGHT PURCHASE	DISADVANTAGES OF OUTRIGHT PURCHASE
Total cost is low, compared to rental	High initial expenditure ties up capital: impact on cashflow, and opportunity cost of capital (what the purchase price would earn if used for other purposes)
The user has total control over the use of the asset	User bears all costs and risks of maintenance, operation and disposal
The asset may have residual re-sale value at the end of use	Risk of technological obsolescence (especially in rapidly changing environments): eroding value, requiring upgrade expenditure
Capital allowances may be set against tax, and government grants may be available	Wasteful, if equipment is needed only for a short period (eg a particular project)
ADVANTAGES OF LEASING	**DISADVANTAGES OF LEASING**
No initial investment to tie up capital	Long-term commitment to pay instalments: may be difficult in recession
Protects against technological obsolescence: ease of upgrade and replacement	User does not have total control of asset: lacks flexibility (and prestige) of ownership
Costs are known and agreed in advance	Total cost may be higher than purchase
Fewer complex tax and depreciation calculations	Large organisations may get better terms by securing their own finance to purchase (benefiting from capital allowances)
Hedge against inflation, as payments are made in 'real' money terms	Contract terms may favour the lessor (eg limitations to use, liability for risks and costs)

Alignment with strategic objectives

5.24   One of the key qualitative business benefits of a project or procurement is its alignment or 'fit' with strategic objectives, or in other words:

- How the proposal will further a strategy, or contribute to the achievement of a strategic objective (such as profitability, market share, diversification or innovation)
- How the proposal 'fits' with the policy and values of the organisation (eg in terms of corporate social responsibility, ethics, sustainability or customer focus).

5.25   It is imperative for procurement and supply chain activities to align with business and corporate strategies: firstly, to support and enable their achievement (by securing the right resources at the right place at the right time at the right price); and secondly, to justify and reinforce Procurement's strategic role and business contribution.

5.26 As a simple example, imagine that an organisation's overall corporate strategy of quality leadership includes a commitment to total quality management. The procurement function might justify a proposal to rationalise the supplier base and develop partnership relations with key suppliers on the basis of its contribution to total quality management.

5.27 Specific areas where corporate objectives and purchasing objectives can be clearly seen to be interlinked are shown in Table 1.3, which adapts a list published by the UK government.

Table 1.3 *Links between corporate and purchasing objectives*

BUSINESS OBJECTIVES	PURCHASING OBJECTIVES
Maintain or increase market share	Provide supplies to match customer needs; assure quality; reduce delivery lead time; reduce cost
Improve profits, cashflow, and return on capital	Reduce stocks; improve reliability; more frequent deliveries
Shorten time to market	Early supplier involvement
Eliminate non-core activities	Develop effective make-or-buy policy; integrate purchasing and capacity planning
Introduce continuous improvement	Reduce supplier base; partnership approaches; reduce product complexity; increase accuracy and reliability
Become world class supplier	Work with suppliers to establish world class standards; improve flexibility of response to market conditions; liaison with technological sources

5.28 *Johnson, Scholes and Whittington* identify three key evaluation criteria for strategic options, but the same framework could be used to present the business case for procurements or project proposals.

- **Suitability**. Does the proposal fit the strategic objectives and circumstances of the organisation? Does it solve the business problem or meet the business need?
- **Feasibility**. Can the proposal be implemented? Will it work in practice? Do the benefits outweigh the costs?
- **Acceptability**. Will the strategy be acceptable to key stakeholders?

Sustainability

5.29 Sustainability has become an extremely important aspect of procurement policy in both the public and private sectors in recent years, and 'social and environmental' criteria are highlighted in later sections of the syllabus (relating to defining the business need in specifications). The term 'sustainability' is often used interchangeably with 'corporate social responsibility' and/or environmental responsibility. More specifically, however, it describes strategies designed to balance economic viability with considerations of environmental and social responsibility (Profit, Planet and People – sometimes referred to as the 'Triple Bottom Line').

5.30 CIPS has adopted the definition of sustainable procurement used by the UK's Sustainable Procurement Task Force (SPTF) in its influential report, *Procuring the Future*.

'[Sustainable procurement is] a process whereby organisations meet their needs for goods, services, works and utilities in a way that achieves value for money on a whole life basis in terms of generating benefits not only to the organisation, but also to society and the economy, whilst minimising damage to the environment.'

5.31 The 'Triple Bottom Line' concept argues that businesses should measure their performance (and develop business case arguments) not just on the basis of profitability, but on the basis of:

- **Economic sustainability (Profit)**: profitability, sustainable economic performance – and its beneficial effects on society (such as employment, access to goods and services, payment of taxes, community investment and so on)

- **Environmental sustainability (Planet):** sustainable environmental practices, which either benefit the natural environment or minimise harmful impacts upon it.
- **Social sustainability (People):** fair and beneficial business practices towards labour, suppliers and the society in which the business operates.

5.32 It may not appear that such measures fall into the 'business benefits' category, but a strong business case can be made for environmentally and socially sustainable supply, on the basis of factors such as:

- Ensuring that the organisation retains its 'licence to operate' from stakeholders
- Contributing to the reputational capital and revenue-earning potential of the business, by creating a positive sustainable brand (which increasingly appeals to consumers)
- Minimising the risk (and associated costs) of reputational damage as a result of unethical or irresponsible conduct (or association with the unethical or irresponsible conduct of suppliers)
- Preserving scarce and non-renewable resources for the future
- Reaping value for money and cost benefits (eg through recycling, and minimising resource wastage, packaging and use of energy and fuel)
- Minimising failure costs (eg 'polluter pays' taxes, penalties for non-compliance with law and regulation, rectification orders, lost sales, product recalls and so on).

Alignment with tactical objectives and timescales

5.33 In addition to the broader strategic objectives and values of the organisation, the business case must demonstrate that the project, proposal or procurement will meet the immediate tactical and operational objectives set for it, including the five rights of procurement. For a business case to be made, the proposal must, for example:

- Secure supply within the timescales required by wider production, marketing or project plans
- Secure adequate levels of performance and process control (eg for the implementation of new systems, processes or supply arrangements, or the correction and improvement of supply problems) within the timescales required by wider organisational and project plans (eg schedules and milestones)
- Be feasible within existing resource constraints (eg expenditure budgets, managerial time, skills or production capacity, given existing commitments)
- Be capable of fulfilling agreed specifications and achieving agreed objectives, standards, targets and KPIs.

Chapter summary

- In recent years, procurement functions have become increasingly strategic in their scope. Analysing business needs and preparing a business case are now often parts of the purchasing remit.
- The main stages in a typical procurement can be represented by a cycle of activities. This begins with identification of a business need and ends with management of the contract and the supplier until the need is satisfied.
- Not all stages of the cycle apply to all purchases. In particular, straight re-buys are much simpler. But modified re-buys, and (even more so) new buys, will go through most or all of the stages.
- Preparation of a business case promotes strategic thinking. The business case will take account of all expected benefits and costs/risks of the proposed procurement.
- Key strategic objectives concern added value and competitive advantage. If the business case suggests that these can be obtained, while minimising risks and costs, a procurement is likely to go ahead.

 ## Self-test questions

Numbers in brackets refer to the paragraphs where you can check your answers.

1   Explain why procurement has become a more strategic function in recent years. (1.4)

2   What objectives can a modern procurement function help to achieve? (1.6)

3   List the main stages in a typical procurement cycle. (Figure 1.1)

4   What is a bill of materials? (2.7)

5   Why may a buyer return a requisition to the originator? (2.8)

6   Distinguish between straight re-buy, modified re-buy and new buy. (3.1)

7   What steps should a buyer take in relation to a modified re-buy? (3.8)

8   Explain EBI and ESI. (3.10)

9   Sketch Kraljic's matrix. (Figure 1.2)

10   What are the objectives of preparing a business case for a procurement? (4.4)

11   Suggest the main contents of a business case. (Table 1.1)

12   List possible business benefits of a proposed procurement. (5.1)

13   How, according to Michael Porter, can a business achieve competitive advantage? (5.7)

14   Explain the use of a benefit/cost ratio. (5.19)

15   How might a procurement function contribute to an objective of increasing market share? (Table 1.3)

CHAPTER 2

Estimating Costs and Prices

Assessment criteria and indicative content

 Explain how costs and prices can be estimated for procurement activities

- Types of market data that can provide information on costs and prices
- Direct and indirect costs
- Producing estimated costs and budgets
- Approaches to total costs of ownership/total lifecycle costing

Chapter headings

1. Market data on costs and prices
2. Understanding supplier pricing
3. Understanding costs
4. Lifecycle costing
5. Cost estimates and budgets

Introduction

In Chapter 1 we noted that an estimate of the *costs* of a procurement or project is a key component in the development of the business case.

In this chapter we explore the methods by which costs and prices can be established or estimated for procurement activities. This information will be useful management information for a range of purposes.

- Developing the business case for procurement and projects on the basis of cost/benefit analysis
- Understanding suppliers' costs and pricing mechanisms, as the basis for price evaluation, comparison and negotiation when sourcing from external suppliers
- Understanding costs in the internal and external supply chains, as the basis of plans for cost reduction and management
- Preparing cost budgets and cashflow management plans for procurement activities, as the basis for controlling actual expenditures and ensuring that business case targets are met.

The operation of financial budgeting and budgetary control, as a tool for controlling purchase expenditure, is discussed in detail in Chapter 3. In this chapter we will focus on how costs and prices can be researched, estimated and understood.

1 Market data on costs and prices

1.1 It may seem like an obvious point, but let's start this chapter by distinguishing clearly between 'price' and 'cost'. This is an important distinction – especially when reading exam questions.

- **Price** is what a seller charges for a package of benefits offered to a buyer.
- **Cost** is what the buying organisation pays to acquire the goods or services purchased. As we will see, this may be much more than just the purchase price paid to the seller: it will also include a range of acquisition, installation, maintenance, operating, insurance and disposal costs. It is also worth noting that the seller also has costs: the finance and resources it expends in producing and providing goods

and services. And a buyer cannot routinely expect the (purchase) price of goods to be the same as their cost (of production) – otherwise, the supplier would not make a profit, and would be unlikely to survive.

1.2   It should be clear just from this brief definition that finding out about *prices* and finding out about *costs* are two different things.

Obtaining prices from suppliers

1.3   There are various methods by which suppliers can communicate prices to buyers, or by which buyers can ascertain the price of the goods they are interested in.

- Suppliers may have a *standard price list* or *price schedule,* available in printed form, or posted online, or published within a catalogue. This is common with standard articles and industrial components. Discounts on 'list price' are often available for bulk purchase, or for prompt or early payment; to secure the business of an attractive or high-status client; or to stimulate demand (eg 'off-season' discounts, promotional discounts and special offers).
- Prices may be *quoted on request*: based on an internal price list (not seen by buyers) or on specially prepared estimates for the proposed contract. Quotations may be included in a sealed bid or tender by the supplier, as part of a competitive bidding process. Historical data on past quotations (and the price bases and discounts used to calculate them) should be retained as the basis for future price estimates and comparisons.
- Prices may be arrived at through *negotiation* between the supplier and the buyer, based on price and cost analysis (discussed a bit later).
- Prices may be determined by *competition*, in an auction (where buyers bid for goods offered for sale, and the highest bid wins) or reverse auction (where suppliers bid to supply goods advertised as wanted, and the lowest bid wins). Historical data on the value of past winning bids may be available as a guide to the price of similar goods and contracts.
- Prices may be determined by the *market* eg for commodities and other materials which are traded in market exchanges: 'market prices' are published on the exchange, and in the national press and trade journals. Major commodities markets include the market for precious metals (Comex) in New York, the New York Mineral Exchange (Nymex) and the Chicago Board of Trade, where grain, rice and soya are traded. Major markets in the UK include the London Metal Exchange, with dealings in metals such as copper, zinc, tin and aluminium, and the International Petroleum Exchange. Historical data will help to identify trends and fluctuations in market prices, which can be used (with caution) to extrapolate future prices.
- *Economic indices* are published for various price data (including commodity prices) and cost data (eg labour costs) indicating changes and trends in average data over time.

1.4   The more specialised or customised the buyer's requirement, the less likely there is to be a 'standard' price or price list, and prices are more likely to be estimated and negotiated by buyer and supplier on the basis of the requirement.

Price and cost research

1.5   In-depth supply market research is expensive and time-consuming. It should therefore be focused on procurements that are most strategically critical to the business, which can be identified using risk assessment and prioritisation tools such as the Kraljic matrix (discussed in Chapter 1).

1.6   A number of sources of market data may be consulted to gather information on market prices and average costs, and factors and trends affecting prices and costs.

1.7   **Primary data** are data collected especially for a particular purpose, directly from the relevant source: the 'horse's mouth', whoever that may be (eg supply chain partners or industry analysts). Primary research is usually 'field research', involving surveys, interviews, questionnaires or observations. Here are some primary sources of market data on costs and prices.

- *Communication with suppliers*: eg via requests for information or price enquiries; 'Meet the Buyer' events; online supplier/buyer forums; networking at trade conferences and exhibitions; non-negotiatory dialogues (with existing or prospective suppliers); and so on.
- The buyer's *database of market data*, including historical records of supplier prices and cost schedules; market price movements; competitor and industry analyses; price trends analyses; spend analyses; and so on. One of the main bases for future cost estimates is historical costs, as we will see in Section 4 of this chapter.
- The *marketing communications* of suppliers: advertising, brochures and catalogues, visits from sales representatives, websites and so on. Catalogues (and their electronic equivalents) may be particularly helpful, with detailed product descriptions, trading terms, price lists and so on.
- *Online market exchanges*, auction sites and supplier/buyer forums, which may also allow the posting of requests for quotation and other exchanges
- *Advisory and information services,* including relevant professional institutions (such as CIPS)
- *Trade fairs, exhibitions and conferences*, which may provide opportunities for visitors to meet supplier representatives, gather relevant catalogues, and hear expert industry analysis and reports.
- *Informal networking* and information exchange with colleagues, other purchasing professionals and suppliers.

1.8 **Secondary data** are data which have already been gathered and assembled for other purposes, general reference or publication. They are generally accessed by 'desk research', which can literally be carried out from the researcher's desk (given appropriate reference sources). Here are some secondary sources of data on costs and prices.

- *Financial and trade or industry press* (newspapers, magazines, journals and bulletins) and specialist procurement journals (such as *Supply Management* or *Procurement Professional)* which may carry market analysis, statistical digests on cost/price trends and so on.
- *Published economic indices* such as the retail price index (RPI), the labour market index and various commodity price indices. Commodities indices track the weighted average of selected commodity prices, and are designed to be representative of a broad commodity asset class or a subset of commodities (such as energy, metals or agriculture). Examples include the World Bank Commodity Price Index, the Goldman Sachs Commodity Index, the Thomson Reuters/Jefferies CRB Index, the S&P Commodity Index, and the Merrill Lynch Commodity Index eXtra (MLCX).
- *Published and online market analysis,* in the form of searchable databases and reports provided by organisations such as Gallup, MORI, Euromonitor and Mintel.
- *Published statistical surveys* compiled by the government, such as:
  — *Economic & Labour Market Review* (monthly)
  — *Statistical Bulletins (*published by the Office for National Statistics, giving detailed information about various industries)
- *Price listing and price comparison websites,* which allow the gauging of market prices. In some cases (eg for commodities) market prices will be directly quoted on market exchanges such as The London Stock Exchange.

1.9 Much of the above-listed secondary published material is accessible and inexpensive to gather – although it may need processing and analysis in order to produce sufficiently targeted and meaningful information to support accurate cost estimates.

2   Understanding supplier pricing

Factors in suppliers' pricing decisions

2.1   A wide range of factors may be taken into account by suppliers when setting or negotiating prices, and any given pricing decision will be a combination of factors, both internal and external: Table 2.1.

Table 2.1 *Factors in supplier pricing decisions*

EXTERNAL FACTORS	INTERNAL FACTORS
Prices charged by competitors: the need to stay competitive to win business – while avoiding potentially damaging price wars	Costs of production and sales, which must be matched by sales revenue in order to earn profits
Extent of competition (market structure): with little competition, the supplier can charge what it likes; with lots of undifferentiated competition, 'the market' decides the price	How badly the supplier needs the business at a particular time (eg to cover fixed costs, cover the costs of research and development of a new product, gain cashflow, reassure shareholders)
The nature of competition in the market, which may (or may not) be based on price	Risk management: eg making provision in the price to cover unforeseen costs or changes
Market conditions: levels of demand and supply, dictating the price that the market will bear. If demand exceeds supply, prices rise; if supply exceeds demand, prices fall.	How attractive a particular customer is to the supplier: pricing low to win or retain good customers, or high to penalise unattractive (eg late-paying, low-volume) customers
Customer perceptions of value: different perceptions of value for money; willingness to pay a premium for 'quality' and so on	Financial position and product portfolio, which may (or may not) allow the supplier to accept occasional losses to secure business
Price elasticity of demand: the extent to which market demand rises or falls with changes in price	Where the product is in its 'lifecycle': eg new products need higher prices to cover the costs of research and development.
What a particular (desirable, powerful) customer is prepared to pay	Shareholders' expectations and managerial objectives in regard to profit margins
Environmental factors affecting the cost of raw materials (eg weather, disrupted supply, shortage of raw materials)	The strategic objectives of the organisation: positioning as a 'value for money' or 'premium' provider; increasing market share (by competitive pricing); and so on.
Environmental factors affecting demand and affordability: eg economic recession reducing spending; government price watchdogs	

Supplier pricing strategies

2.2   Suppliers' pricing strategies are likely to be based on either (a) costs or (b) market factors.

2.3   Essentially, **cost-based pricing** allows the supplier to cover its costs (which may be calculated in various ways) and allow for an extra sum to secure a reasonable profit. Cost-based pricing approaches include the following.

- **Full-cost pricing**. The supplier calculates the total cost of a product, adds a mark-up to produce a profit, and the result is the selling price. This method is often used for non-routine work which is difficult to cost in advance, such as the provision of complex services.
- **Cost-plus or mark-up pricing**. The supplier calculates the direct costs of a product, and adds a mark-up which incorporates both an amount to cover indirect costs (overheads) and a profit element.
- **Marginal pricing**. The supplier fixes a price that will yield a predetermined profit margin (percentage of the quoted price).
- **Rate of return or 'target return' pricing**. The supplier bases the profit on the desired return on the investment – rather than the estimated product cost (which may not include costs such as R & D, administration and marketing).

- **Contribution pricing**, where the price is less than the full cost of the product, but covers variable costs, in order to keep plant running. This avoids the costs of shutting down plant and machinery, and laying off staff. Buyers may take advantage of such prices – but should be cautious in doing so: (a) because this is not a 'normal' price that can be expected in future and (b) because the supplier may try to cut corners on quality in order to maximise its earnings from the job.

2.4 A range of **market-driven pricing** approaches can be explained briefly as follows.

- **Price volume**: the supplier uses cost-volume-profit (or breakeven) analysis to determine a volume of production which will be most economical (spreading overhead costs over a larger number of units), and will allow it to offer quantity discounts to buyers to increase sales.
- **Market share pricing** (or **penetration pricing**): the supplier sets low introductory prices that will win customers and/or discourage or eliminate competition (because of the low profit margins available in the market). The aim may be (a) to stimulate the growth of a market, by getting people to try a new product or (b) to increase the supplier's share of the market (a strategy of 'market penetration'). As the supplier's market share and sales volume increase, it is able to produce more, at a lower cost per unit, and therefore reap better profits. It may be able to raise prices later (taking advantage of customer loyalty and discouraged competition) and still dominate the market.
- **Market skimming**: the supplier sets a *high* introductory price, to attract buyers who (a) have a strong desire to get the product early (while it is innovative and may present a competitive advantage for them); and (b) can afford it. In other words, the supplier maximises its short-term profits early on ('skims the cream off the top'): gradually reducing prices over time to attract further 'layers' of buyers, who are more price sensitive. This also enables the supplier to recoup some of the costs of research and development, and the costs of marketing a new product.
- **Current revenue pricing** (or **contribution pricing**): the supplier aims to cover its operating costs, rather than earning profits. It may accept an order at or below cost because, without the order, the lack of demand or work will necessitate shutting down part of its production, incurring lay-off costs, shut-down and re-start costs and so on.
- **Promotional pricing**: the supplier offers a discount for a specific, limited period, in order to boost short-term sales. (This is common in consumer markets.)
- **Market segment pricing** (also called **differential pricing** or **price discrimination**): the supplier sets different prices for different market segments, depending on the price they will bear – and the different value received by different customers. You can see this in the difference between 'peak' and 'off-peak' travel or telephone charges, for example.
- **Competition pricing** (or **dynamic pricing**): the supplier 'bids' competitively to win a contract, eg in a reverse auction, by setting the highest price that is lower than competitors' prices.

Factors in buyers' decisions on price

2.5 So far, we have talked about how suppliers go about deciding what prices to charge. However, we might also mention how buyers go about deciding what prices to accept. Here are some of the factors in such a decision.

- The buying organisation's relative bargaining power in the market and relationship. (A monopoly supplier may have power to set prices as it wishes – but if a buyer represents a large proportion of a supplier's business, he will be in a strong position to negotiate favourable prices.)
- The number of suppliers in the market and the possibility of substitute products (enabling the buyer to exploit competition to force prices down)
- The type of purchase. For non-critical or routine products, for example, a buyer will want to secure best price by competitive purchasing, while for critical or strategic products, he may pay more for service and security of supply.
- The prices paid by competitors (if this information is available), so that the buyer keeps his materials costs competitive

- The total package of benefits offered for the price, and whether 'value' is better at a higher price (given the need for quality, delivery, supplier relationship and so on)
- What the buyer can afford, given the quantities likely to be involved over a given period
- What is a 'reasonable' price, based on price analysis
- What is a 'fair' (ethical and sustainable) price from the buyer's and supplier's point of view

Price and cost analysis

2.6   When considering the prices quoted by a supplier, or offered in negotiation, there are two basic approaches that a buyer can use to decide whether 'the price is right'.

- Price analysis
- Cost analysis.

2.7   **Price analysis** simply seeks to determine whether the price offered is a fair and appropriate price for the goods. The 'right' price in this sense may be one which is advantageous or reasonable compared to: the prices offered by other suppliers (competitive tenders or quotations); the prices previously paid by the buyer for the same goods or services; the market or 'going' rate; and/or the price of any alternative or substitute goods.

2.8   **Cost analysis** is a more specialised technique, often used to support price negotiations where the supplier justifies its price by the need to cover its costs (cost-based pricing, which we will explain further below). Cost analysis looks specifically at how the quoted price relates to the supplier's cost of production. Suppliers may be asked to include cost breakdowns with their price quotations, so that:

- Differences between the supplier's cost breakdown and the buyer's own analysis or estimate of the supplier's costs can be examined to arrive at an agreed cost figure
- Buyers can identify when suppliers are claiming higher-than-average or unjustifiable profit margins
- Buyers can calculate a target price or price range for use in negotiation (based on suppliers covering their costs plus a reasonable profit margin).

Accessing supplier cost information

2.9   In a close, long-term supply relationship, there may be a policy of:

- **Open book costing**, where suppliers provide information about their costs to buyers, in order to reassure them that they are getting value for money. In principle, such an approach is helpful in agreeing cost-based prices, and can enable the buyer to help the supplier to identify potential for cost savings. In practice, however, it is unlikely to appeal much to suppliers, because the flow of information is all one way – and to the buyer's advantage.
- **Cost transparency**, where both buyer and supplier share cost information, in order to collaborate in joint cost reduction initiatives. This is arguably a fairer and more mutually advantageous approach than open book costing – but it does demand a high level of trust, which may only exist within long-term partnership relationships.

2.10   In most cases, therefore, buyers will not easily be able to discover details of a supplier's cost structure. However, they may be able to derive some information from a supplier's tender (if a competitive bidding approach has been used), or may be able to estimate the cost of a supplier's products from their own knowledge of the industry.

2.11   If buyers can ascertain the supplier's cost structure, the information will be useful in several ways.

- Cost analysis can keep prices realistic (ie no unreasonably large profit margins), especially in the absence of competition – for example, where there is a preferred supplier.
- It focuses attention on what costs ought to be involved in producing the goods or services, which acts as an incentive for cost control and reduction, and which may in turn lead to cost savings passed on to the buyer.

- It identifies the minimum price the supplier can afford to charge for sustainable supply.
- It also enables the buyer to estimate how valuable the business or contract will be to the supplier, in terms of profitability, which will help to determine negotiating strength – and to manage dependency issues in the relationship.

2.12 We will look at some key concepts and tools for cost analysis in Section 3 of this chapter.

3 Understanding costs

Components of the cost base

3.1 There are three major areas in which a manufacturing business incurs costs. (If an exam question refers to different 'types' of cost or 'components' of costs, this is probably what the question is referring to – although you might also choose to discuss 'direct and indirect' or 'fixed and variable' costs, which we will cover a bit later.)

- **Raw materials** (and/or components, subassemblies and consumables): the 'inputs' to the manufacturing process
- **Labour:** the wages or salaries of workers employed by the organisation
- **Overheads:** expenditure which cannot be directly identified with the output of any particular production item, but is associated with keeping business processes up and running. Overheads may be sub-divided into production or manufacturing overheads (eg electricity, maintenance and set-up costs); administration overheads (eg office expenses and management costs); and selling and distribution overheads (eg marketing, advertising and sales force costs, and storage, transport and logistics costs). *Marketing* and *logistics* may be considered as separate categories of cost.

3.2 It is worth emphasising that the supplier's *profit* (or profit margin) is not a cost – although, along with costs, it is a component in price, or in the supplier's pricing decision. Successive Senior Assessors' reports have complained of this mark-losing misconception: beware the pitfall!

3.3 Of course, these same cost components will apply to the *purchasing* organisation as well as to the supplier. The buyer may need to analyse the costs of its own organisation, in order to ascertain how profitably it is selling its own products; how the procurement function can contribute to profitability by reducing the cost of materials for the organisation; or what the cost and profitability of a given procurement proposal will be, for the purposes of formulating a business case.

Direct and indirect costs

3.4 One common way of classifying costs is to distinguish between direct and indirect costs.

- **Direct costs** are costs which can be directly identified with a specific saleable unit of output. So, for example, the direct costs of producing the textbook you are reading include: direct materials (such as paper, ink and glue); direct labour (wages paid to employees working on the production of the book); and direct expenses (eg costs of royalties payable to the author of the book, on a per-copy basis).
- **Indirect costs (or overheads)** are expenditures on labour, materials or other items which cannot be identified with a specific saleable unit of output. For example, the indirect materials costs of this book might include the oil used to lubricate the printing press; and indirect labour costs might include the salaries of the shift supervisor and sales staff. (These costs contribute to all jobs performed by the printing press – not just this one.) Such costs are often classified as production overheads, administration overheads and selling and distribution overheads.

3.5 We can therefore build up an overall picture of a manufacturing operation's costs as follows: Figure 2.1

Figure 2.1 *Total costs*

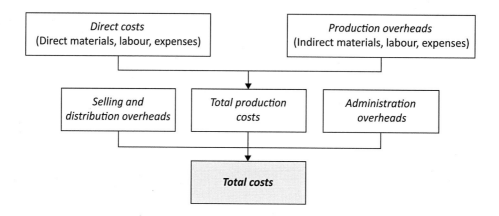

Fixed and variable costs

3.6   **Cost behaviour** is the way in which the costs of output are affected by fluctuations in the level of activity: the volume of production, say, or the level of sales.

- Some costs do not vary at all as the volume of sales or production changes. If an organisation is paying rent on a factory, or paying employees a salary (not based on output), it will have to pay the same amount for a given period, whether the factory is operating or not, and however much it is producing. This type of cost is called a **fixed cost**.
- Some costs vary as the volume of sales or production increases. If an organisation uses raw materials to produce widgets, say, at a cost of $0.40 per widget, production of 10,000 widgets costs it $4,000 – but production of 20,000 widgets costs it $8,000. This type of cost is called a **variable cost**.

3.7   Fixed and variable costs are illustrated in Figure 2.2.

Figure 2.2 *Fixed and variable costs*

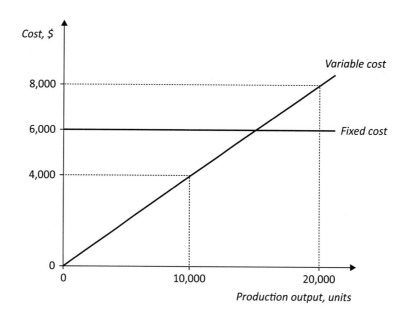

3.8   The way in which costs behave as production output changes is a key element in the way prices are set by suppliers. The supplier's sales force will always be seeking to generate at least enough business to cover fixed costs: the costs incurred by the business whether they produce anything or not. If the cost structure of the supplier includes a high proportion of fixed costs, there will be strong pressure to achieve high sales volume – and this may result in competitive, incentive-level pricing.

3.9 Similarly, the business case for a procurement proposal will need to take fixed costs into account. As we will see in Chapter 9, this is a key consideration in the decision to outsource production or service activities previously carried out within the firm (a make/do or buy decision). The organisation *may* benefit from ceasing to manufacture a given item in house if an external supplier's price is *less* than the firm's own direct or variable cost to produce the same number of units. But if it does buy in the item, it may still be incurring a significant proportion of its *fixed* or overhead costs – while at the same time having idle production capacity (incurring fixed costs but not earning revenue).

3.10 Understanding fixed and variable costs can help the procurement function in various ways.

- Calculating a supplier's cost structure can help to determine the parameters for negotiation on price (and other issues, such as cost reduction targets or supplier development).
- Establishing cost per unit can help in making direct comparisons between different suppliers.
- Understanding variable costs can help to determine economic order quantities, minimum order units, and potential for economies of scale.
- Understanding variable costs can also help a buyer to assess the reasonableness of a supplier's proposed price increases (eg on the basis of raw material cost rises).
- Understanding fixed costs can help in understanding the supplier's resistance points and walk-away position in negotiation, because of the supplier's need to cover fixed costs.
- Understanding fixed costs can also indicate the level of profit a supplier is seeking. Once the supplier has covered fixed costs, any price in excess of variable costs will be sufficient to make a contribution to profit, so the buyer may hope to negotiate movement on price.

Different approaches to calculating costs

3.11 There are two main approaches that may be adopted in calculating the costs of operations and products or services, whether for a supplier, or for the buying organisation.

- A **marginal costing** approach uses only the marginal cost of producing additional units: basically, using only variable costs to derive a unit cost. Marginal cost is the cost of one unit of product or service which would be *avoided* if that unit were not produced or provided. Variable costs are included in the unit cost, but fixed costs are not: they are treated as a 'period cost' and deducted, as a total amount, from total contribution to profit for the period, in the firm's profit and loss account.
- An **absorption costing** approach attempts to calculate the total cost of producing products. In addition to variable cost, a 'fair' proportion of fixed costs is allocated to (or 'absorbed into') each unit of output, as a fixed cost per unit. This may be done by determining the amount of some measurable resource consumed in a production period (say, labour or machine hours) and the overhead cost of that resource (eg total fixed overhead costs *divided by* labour or machine hours = overhead absorption rate per hour). Alternatively, a more accurate approach may be used, called activity based costing: fixed costs are allocated to products on the basis of the cost of the activities used in creating them.

Profit

3.12 Profit is the difference between the selling price of a product (or the total revenue earned from selling a product) and the cost of producing the product. In other words, it is the gain or surplus left over after the manufacturer (or service provider) has paid all its costs. Profitability is the primary objective of most businesses.

3.13 Both buyers and suppliers seek to make a profit for a number of reasons.

- Profit means that the business has covered its costs, and is not 'bleeding' money in losses. This is important for the business to survive in the long term.
- Profit belongs to the owners (or shareholders) of the business, as a return on their investment: a share of profits is paid to them in the form of a 'dividend' on their shares. Strong and consistent profits are therefore important to encourage shareholders to continue to invest in the company, and

to maintain the share capital of the company through a high share price (reflecting market demand for the shares).

- Profits which are not paid to shareholders ('retained profits') are available for reinvestment in the development of the business, enabling the business to acquire assets, meet long-term borrowings, update plant and equipment and build up reserves for future contingencies – without the cost and risk of borrowing funds for these purposes.

3.14   While a buyer will want to maximise its profits for all these reasons, it is also important to allow suppliers to make a reasonable profit:

- In order to protect the security of supply: not creating financial instability for suppliers, or driving them out of business by squeezing their profit margins
- In order to protect the quality of supply: allowing suppliers the revenue and retained profits they require to maintain quality and develop their business (potentially, to the benefit of their customers)
- In the interests of corporate social responsibility (CSR) and sustainability: allowing suppliers reasonable profits in order to protect employment and supplier diversity, develop sustainable supply chains and so on.

Mark-ups and margins

3.15   Costs, profit and selling price are related in the following fairly obvious way (using illustrative figures for clarity).

	$
Total costs incurred by the supplier	80.00
Plus profit earned by the supplier	20.00
Equals selling price charged by the supplier	100.00

3.16   It is often convenient to indicate the profitability of a particular business, or a particular product, by expressing the profit as a percentage. We may choose to express the profit as a percentage of total costs, or as a percentage of selling price.

- When we express the profit element as a percentage of cost, we refer to it as a *mark-up*. In our example above, the mark-up is 25% on cost (because $20 is 25% of $80).
- When we express the profit element as a percentage of selling price, we refer to it as a *margin*. In our example, the margin is 20% on selling price (because $20 is 20% of $100).

Contribution and breakeven analysis

3.17   **Contribution** is the difference between sales revenue and the *variable cost* of making the sales.

3.18   Another way of putting this is to say that it is the amount of selling price left over after variable costs have been paid for. It is this amount which must be sufficient to cover fixed costs and, perhaps, to make a profit. (In fact, 'contribution' is a short-hand expression for: 'contribution to covering fixed costs and making a profit'.) Suppose that the unit selling price of a widget is $1.00, and its variable cost is $0.40. Every time we sell a widget, we earn a contribution of $0.60 towards covering fixed costs and making a profit.

- If we sell only a few widgets, our total contribution will not be sufficient to cover fixed costs and we will make a loss.
- If we sell very many widgets our total contribution will more than cover fixed costs and we will make a profit.
- Somewhere in between there is a sales level such that our total contribution exactly matches our fixed costs. In this case we make neither profit nor loss: we break even.

3.19   **Breakeven point** is the point at which a supplier sells a sufficient volume of product to cover its costs exactly: it 'breaks even', neither making a loss nor a profit. Any additional sales will tip the balance over into profit. Suppose that our widget maker has annual fixed costs of $60,000. If each widget earns a contribution of $0.60, the business needs to sell $60,000/$0.60 = 100,000 widgets per year, to cover its fixed costs. For each additional widget sold, the company will be making a profit of $0.60.

3.20 Instead of giving the monetary amount of $0.60, we could have expressed contribution as a percentage of the selling price: $0.60 = 60% of $1.00. We could then have calculated the breakeven point (in $) as $60,000 ÷ 60% = $100,000. At a selling price of $1.00 per unit, this equates to a breakeven sales volume of 100,000 widgets per year.

3.21 If asked to calculate a breakeven point from data given, the simplest way is to plug the data into the following simple formula.

$$\text{Breakeven point (in units)} = \frac{\text{Fixed costs}}{\text{Selling price } \textit{minus} \text{ variable cost per unit}}$$

You can then multiply this number of units by selling price (per unit) to get a breakeven point in sales revenue terms.

3.22 Breakeven analysis has some important implications for buyers. For one thing, suppliers will be conscious of the need to reach breakeven point, and their sales staff will be under pressure to obtain sufficient business to reach the required sales volume. Automated manufacturing plants are particularly 'hungry' in this respect: the use of machines reduces variable costs (cost of direct labour) while increasing fixed costs (capital and running costs of machinery). So automated plants have to keep production and sales volume high to cover their costs – and their sales staff may be prepared to offer tight selling prices to capture additional business.

3.23 On the other hand, once such a supplier has passed breakeven point, every additional unit produced and sold represents profit. The supplier may not have to press too hard for optimum prices: even a comparatively low selling price will cover the (relatively low) variable costs and so add contribution to profit. In the case of our widgets, any sales achieved at prices in excess of the $0.40 variable cost will add to profits: there is a wide gap between $0.40 and the current selling price of $1.00 for buyers to target in negotiation.

4 Lifecycle costing

4.1 There is a vital difference between the purchase price of an article and its **total cost of ownership**. Total cost of ownership includes not just the price of the items being purchased, but also:

- Various transaction costs, such as taxes, foreign exchange rate costs and the cost of drawing up contracts
- Finance costs (if capital has to be borrowed to pay for the purchase, say)
- Acquisition costs: costs of delivery, installation and commissioning
- Operating costs, such as energy, spares, consumables, maintenance and repair over the useful life of the purchase (eg for equipment and machinery), operator training, supplier support and so on
- Costs of storage and other handling, assembly or finishing required
- Costs of quality (inspection, re-work or rejection, lost sales, compensation of customers etc)
- End of life costs, such as decommissioning, removal and disposal (*minus* some 'negative cost' if the asset has sufficient residual value for re-sale).

4.2 Baily, Farmer, Jessop and Jones suggest that there is a 'price/cost iceberg' for any purchase (not just long-term assets), of which purchase price is only the most obvious or visible 'tip': Figure 2.3.

Figure 2.3 *The price-cost iceberg*

4.3 Some or all of these costs may be included in the price quoted by a supplier, and a purchaser will need to bear this in mind when comparing two quotations: does a lower price reflect competitive pricing – or a lesser total package of benefits?

4.4 More generally, there is a *trade-off* between the purchase price and the total package of benefits. 'It is an obvious fact, yet a commonly ignored one, that a low price may lead to a high total acquisition cost' (Baily *et al*). A lower price may reflect poorer quality, for example, and this will not necessarily be better value for money: the purchase price may be lower, but the total cost of acquisition and ownership may be higher, because of the need for more rigorous quality inspection, the number of rejects and reworks due to poor quality, lost sales through customer disappointment, and so on.

4.5 'Best value' may therefore be defined as the lowest whole life cost which meets the purchaser's complex package of requirements (for quality, service, ongoing partnership with the supplier and so on).

Whole life costing (WLC)

4.6 A capital asset such as a building, vehicle, plant or machinery is expected to be used for a number of years, and over that time, it will give rise to many costs, in addition to the cost of purchase, lease or hire. In choosing between one asset and another, or in justifying the procurement of an asset, procurement staff must take into account the costs arising over the whole useful life of the asset.

4.7 **Whole life costing** (also called **lifecycle costing** or **through-life costing**) can be defined as 'economic assessment considering all agreed projected significant and relevant cost flows over a period of analysis, expressed in monetary value. The projected costs are those needed to achieve defined levels of performance, including reliability, safety and availability'. (ISO 15686 Whole Life Costing Standard)

4.8 The CIPS Australia Knowledge Club notes that WLC has traditionally been associated with high-value procurement decisions, but 'there is no reason why it should not be applicable to relatively low-value purchases' – other than, perhaps, the high cost of a large-scale WLC exercise itself.

Discounted cashflow (DCF)

4.9 The long time period involved in the use of capital assets, combined with the subjectivity of estimates for most of these elements of cost, make it difficult to assess lifetime costs. One technical difficulty is that the relevant cashflows occur in years to come: such cashflows are not easy to evaluate in today's terms, even if they are known with certainty.

4.10 The process of evaluating future cashflows in today's terms is referred to as 'discounted cashflow' (DCF): by applying this technique to all the costs and benefits associated with capital assets we can calculate, compare and evaluate the 'net present value' (NPV) of the asset.

4.11 The basic technique of DCF is as follows.

- The buyer makes assumptions about the level of costs that will arise *in each year of the asset's useful life,* including the initial purchase price (in year 0) – but also ongoing costs of acquisition (delivery, installation and commissioning); operation (eg energy, spares, maintenance and repair) and end of life (eg decommissioning, removal and disposal).
- This can be broken down into two basic processes.
  — Analysing the **cost structure**: identifying and recording each of the elements or components of cost
  — **Cost estimating**: calculating the likely cost for each category or element of cost, as accurately as possible.
- At the same time, the buyer attempts to quantify the benefits that will arise from the ownership of the asset (in consultation with users and other stakeholders) – and to allocate them, similarly, to each year of the asset's useful life.
- **Discounted cashflow calculations** (invariably computerised) are then used to express future costs and benefits, and therefore total costs, *in today's values*. A selected discount rate should be developed enabling each future cost to be adjusted and valued at the point at which the procurement decision was made.
- Annual costs, in today's values, can also be calculated to allow comparison of assets or proposed asset purchases, even if they have different life spans.

Payback or recovery period

4.12 A purchaser may also calculate the **payback (or recovery) period** of the investment: calculating the time it takes for the benefits of a procurement to 'pay back' the initial total outlay. (If a machine is being bought for $1 million, say, and it is estimated that it will generate annual revenues or cost savings of $150,000 for 10 years, the payback period is calculated as $1 million *divided by* $150,000 = 6.6 years.)

4.13 In general, an investment that pays back in a relatively short period is preferable to one that takes many years to pay back, but the basic question is whether the payback period is acceptable to the organisation.

Accounting rate of return (ARR)

4.14 It is also possible to identify the accounting rate of return or **return on investment** of a purchased asset. In the above example, the asset generates revenue over 10 years of $1,500,000: a profit of $500,000 over 10 years, or $50,000 per annum. The accounting rate of return, in its simplest form, is therefore $50,000/$1,000,000 or a 5% return on investment. Again, the organisation has to judge whether this is an acceptable rate.

Benefits and limitations of WLC

4.15 The point of calculating whole life costs is to identify options that cost least over the long term – which may not be apparent from the purchase price. Here are some benefits of carrying out a systematic WLC exercise.

- Enabling the fair (like-with-like) comparison of competing options
- Enabling realistic budgeting over the life of the asset
- Highlighting, at an early stage, risks associated with the purchase
- Promoting cross-functional communication on cost and asset management issues, and improving awareness of total costs
- Supporting the optimisation of value for money.

4.16 There are, however, some key limitations to the use of WLC.

- It is not an exact science, and future cost estimates are inevitably subjective. They tend, for example, to be based on sales forecasts – which are typically over-optimistic.
- Many costs are incurred through the life of a product or asset, and not all of these will be easy to forecast (eg development costs, marketing and advertising, re-design and replacement, repair and maintenance).
- A wide range of intervening factors may affect costs over the lifecycle of a product or asset, including supply market changes (eg supplier failure), fluctuating prices, new technology development (shortening the product lifecycle) and so on.
- A systematic WLC exercise can be time-consuming, labour-intensive and costly, even if a computerised system is used.

5 Cost estimates and budgets

Estimating costs

5.1 The main principle involved in controlling costs is to estimate in advance what the costs are expected to be; compare the estimate with actual outcomes; and investigate any significant discrepancies or variances. This is the process of **budgetary control**, discussed in detail in Chapter 3.

5.2 To get started on the process of estimating costs we need a good understanding of cost behaviour. Specifically, we need to know which costs are variable (because the level of these costs will depend on the estimated level of activity), and which costs are fixed (and will be unaffected by the level of activity) – as discussed earlier in the chapter.

5.3 Fixed costs are easy, as they may be known or routine costs, and will not vary in line with sales volume. Once we have forecast a level of sales for the budgetary period, it should be possible to estimate the costs that depend on sales volume.

Dealing with mixed costs

5.4 Some costs include a mix of fixed and variable elements. These are sometimes called **semi-variable costs**, or mixed costs. For example, the cost of heat and light will to some extent be fixed, because the premises must be heated and lit during normal working hours. However, there may also be a variable element in this cost, perhaps because additional hours are being worked as overtime.

5.5 In these cases, it is necessary to determine the amount of the fixed element included in the mixed cost. A common technique for achieving this is the **high-low method**. This is based on looking at the total cost at a time when activity is at a *high* level and comparing it with the total cost at a time when activity is *low*.

5.6 As an example, suppose that a particular cost amounted to $3,100 in a month when sales volume was 300 units, while in another month the cost amounted to $2,400 and sales volume was 200 units. Clearly this cost is not fixed, but neither is it wholly variable (because if it was, the cost level at 200 units would be exactly two thirds of the cost level at 300 units, and this is not the case).

5.7 So we are dealing with a mixed cost. The difference in the total amount ($3,100 – $2,400 = $700) must be the variable element associated with the additional 100 units. This indicates that the variable cost per unit is $7 – and the *variable* cost of 200 units is therefore $1,400. Since the total cost of 200 units is $2,400, this means that the *fixed* element included in this particular cost is $1,000 per month.

5.8 We can check this by looking at the total cost for 300 units. According to our calculations this should comprise a fixed element calculated at $1,000, plus a variable element of $7 per unit or $2,100 in total. Our calculations therefore indicate a total cost at the 300 unit level of $3,100, which is indeed the case.

Statistical techniques for cost estimation

5.9   Predictions and estimates of cost are generally made by using the following sources of information.

- Historical data
- Current data and information (such as that available from suppliers)
- Market research and environmental monitoring, to identify 'what is happening' within the supply market (affecting costs and prices).

5.10   Various statistical techniques can be used to extrapolate from historical data to forecast future costs: Table 2.2.

Table 2.2 *Statistical forecasting techniques*

Simple moving average	This technique assumes that costs of a given material for a coming period will be 'average', that is an average of the costs recorded in recent past periods. So if costs for a given item from January to June ran at $450, $190, $600, $600, $420 and $380 respectively, we might anticipate that July's cost would be an average of these six months: $2,640/6 = $440. The reason this is called a moving average is that each month we move along by one step: in forecasting August's costs, for example, we would take an average of costs in February to July; in forecasting September's costs, an average of costs in March to August. This isn't a very accurate method, as it doesn't take into account the fluctuations hidden by the average: in our example, actual monthly costs could be anywhere from $190 to $600.
Weighted average (or exponential smoothing)	This technique recognises that older data is generally less reliable as a guide to the future than more recent data, and therefore gives extra weight to more recent data in calculating the average This adds some sophistication and accuracy by reflecting more recent trends, such as price inflation or supply shortages. Continuing our earlier example, we might base an estimate of costs for July on just the four previous months (March to June). We could recognise the higher importance of recent months by giving a weighting of 0.4 to the June figure, 0.3 to May, 0.2 to April and 0.1 to March (or whatever appropriate weightings will give a total weighting of 1). The estimate for July would therefore be calculated as: $(0.4 \times \$380) + (0.3 \times \$420) + (0.2 \times \$600) + (0.1 \times \$600) = \$458$.

Time series (trend) analysis	This method works by examining past data in chronological order, identifying underlying trends (consistent upward or downward movements over time) and projecting or 'extrapolating' these trends into the future. This is a more subjective, broad-brush approach. Historical data may show:
	  — *A steady trend*: an increase or decline in costs, moving with a predictable pace that can easily be forecast (eg in the case of general price inflation and labour costs)
	  — *A fluctuating trend*: rises or falls in cost or price are volatile or unstable, and reliable predictions are hard to achieve (eg in the case of commodities)

Regression analysis	This method works by identifying connections or 'correlations' between certain measured variables (such as the price of oil and transport and logistics costs) and modelling the effect of changes in one variable (oil prices go up) on the other (transport prices go up by a greater or lesser proportion). This may involve complex modelling, and is often done using computerised spreadsheet or scenario analysis programmes.

5.11   Statistical methods are unlikely to take into account all the various environmental factors which may cause fluctuations in costs. A number of more subjective or 'qualitative' methods may therefore be used, based on the knowledge, experience and judgement of expert users, buyers, suppliers or consultants.

- **Supply market research** and market engagement can be used to ascertain likely supplier costs, pricing decisions and market price levels and trends.
- **Expert opinion** is the gathering of views, judgments and opinions from people regarded as knowledgeable and experienced in relevant business areas, markets and disciplines (such as cost analysis).

Who should be involved in cost estimation?

5.12 Procurement staff will be involved in relation to many categories of costs, and for all costs involving bought-in materials and services. They are likely to be most aware of the prices that they have been obtaining from the suppliers of such goods, and of any likely changes (arising, perhaps, from newly negotiated agreements with the suppliers).

5.13 Finance and accounting staff will also be involved. Estimates of costs are very much their province, and they have ready access to historical cost trend data, which are often an important starting point in estimating future cost levels.

5.14 Marketing staff will also be involved, since they are in the best position to forecast the likely level of sales, which is usually the 'principal budget factor', because it dictates the level of variable costs. The level of sales has a knock-on effect on many cost areas – most notably on production costs, because the level of production will depend mainly on the level of expected sales.

Procurement budgets

5.15 Business case goals are usually captured in budgets. A **budget** has been defined as 'a plan quantified in monetary terms, prepared and approved prior to a defined period of time, usually showing planned or estimated income to be generated and/or expenditure to be incurred during that period, and the capital to be employed to attain a given objective'.

5.16 The first step in budget preparation for a procurement or project is to ascertain the **projected sales demand** for a product or service (in collaboration with the sales and marketing function) and **projected usage** of materials, components and other supplies (in collaboration with production and other client functions) in order to estimate input requirements. It is important to be realistic at this stage, as one of the key causes of problems is the optimistic overestimation of demand.

5.17 Historical demand, sales or stock usage data may be used, but it is also essential to consider factors such as: the organisation's sales and promotion plans; competitor activity; changes in market demand or customer preferences; changes in utilisation efficiency (eg due to quality management or machine operation); and macro-economic factors that might dampen or stimulate demand (such as economic recession or recovery).

5.18 The next step is to **estimate or predict costs**.

- What are the direct or **variable costs** of sales (which change in accordance with changes in the level of output), including the costs of materials, components, staff overtime or commission payments, and/or subcontractors to make the product or supply the service? The sales forecast or budget will be used to project variable costs. A separate 'materials budget' may be used to list materials and components required over the budgetary period (usually time-phased on a week-by-week or month-by-month basis), and their known or estimated costs.
- What are the indirect or **fixed costs or overheads** (which are unaffected by changes in the level of output)? For the business as a whole, these may be broken down by type, to include:
  — Premises costs (rent or mortgage payments, business rates, service charges)
  — Labour and staff costs (pay and benefits)
  — Utilities (eg electricity, water, telecommunications)
  — Printing, postage and stationery (office and administration costs)
  — Equipment costs (eg consumables, repair and maintenance)
  — Fleet and vehicle costs (eg staff vehicles and petrol allowances, transport and logistics fleet or service costs)
  — Advertising, promotion and sales activities

— Financing costs (eg loan interest payments)
— Legal and professional costs (including insurance).

- What are the **one-off capital costs** for the period or project (eg purchases of computer equipment or systems development, plant or premises)?

5.19 If historical cost or price information is available, this may be used as a guide for estimation, but again, it will be necessary to consider the effect of factors such as:

- Under- or over-supply, changes in supply and risk factors that might raise prices by creating scarcity or supply disruption
- Changes in supply market structure or competition, and the relative bargaining power of suppliers and buyers on price
- The effect of fluctuations in exchange rates (for international purchases)
- Pricing trends in the market
- The general rate of price inflation.

5.20 Additional information will generally be sought for cost estimates (as outlined in Section 1 of this chapter), including quotations from suppliers for specific planned procurements. A number of statistical forecasting techniques may also be used to project historical data accurately, as discussed above.

5.21 A procurement expenditure budget can be formatted quite simply, with:

- A list of anticipated cost or expenditure items or categories
- A column for the budgeted amounts of costs or expenditures for each item
- A column for actual amounts of costs or expenditures for each item (with dates of payments, and identification of the payees, if the budget operates at this level of detail).

Cash budgets

5.22 A cash budget (or **cashflow projection**) is designed to project the future cash position of the firm or project for the short-term budgetary period, on a month-by-month basis. In other words, it is a *time-phased* income and expenditure budget.

5.23 This is particularly important for small and medium-sized enterprises (SMEs), which may not have significant cash reserves to cover their short-term liabilities. It may also be particularly important for capital procurements, which typically involve significant 'up front' investment and potentially long timescales before the asset begins to generate revenues.

5.24 In general terms, however, if the business is not managing its cashflow (the balance and timing of cash coming in and going out), or is experiencing a strong cash 'drain' from the business, it may find it difficult to meet its short-term debts and expenses. There is a saying that 'cash is like oxygen': if you run out of it, you don't survive long. Being *profitable* does not necessarily mean that the business has sufficient cash resources available to pay debts when they fall due. It may need to seek short-term financing (eg in the form of extended credit terms from suppliers, a bank overdraft or short-term loan) to cover planned expenditures.

5.25 Firms need to ensure that they time incoming and outgoing cashflows, so that at any given time they have sufficient cash resources to maintain operations: the process of **cashflow management.** The cash budget should be reviewed and updated at least monthly, to ensure that the firm manages its cashflow position, so that it has working funds to pay its bills, buy materials and pay workers.

5.26 A cashflow forecast or budget is designed to identify the sources and amounts of cash inflows, and the destinations and amounts of cash outflows, over a given budgetary period (say, the following quarter or month, usually divided into weeks). As with a cost budget, there are normally two columns: one for *budgeted* dates and amounts and one for *actual* dates and amounts. The budget should list:

- The bank or cash balance at the start of the period
- Receipts (money due or forecast to come in during the period)
- Payments (money due or estimated to go out during the period)
- The anticipated bank or cash balance at the end of the period.

5.27   We will look at the operation of both cost and cash budgets in detail, in the next chapter.

Chapter summary

- A buyer can determine a supplier's price from published information (eg a catalogue), or from discussion with the supplier (eg a request for quotation, a negotiation process, or an auction).
- Price and cost research may involve reference to both primary and secondary data.
- A supplier may fix his prices by reference to his costs (to which he will add a mark-up for profit) or by reference to market factors.
- In a close, long-term relationship buyer and supplier may adopt open book costing or cost transparency.
- Direct costs can be identified directly with a unit of output; indirect costs cannot.
- Variable costs increase or decrease in line with the level of activity; fixed costs do not.
- Contribution is the difference between sales revenue and variable costs. If total contribution equals total fixed costs the organisation breaks even.
- The purchase price is just one element in the total lifecycle costs of a procurement.
- There are numerous methods for estimating costs, both statistical and subjective.
- A cash budget projects the future cash position of a firm or a project.

 ## Self-test questions

Numbers in brackets refer to the paragraphs where you can check your answers.

1 List methods by which a buyer can determine a supplier's price for a purchase. (1.3)

2 List sources of (a) primary data and (b) secondary data. (1.7, 1.8)

3 Describe different methods of cost-based pricing. (2.3)

4 Distinguish between price analysis and cost analysis. (2.7, 2.8)

5 Give examples of (a) a direct cost and (b) an indirect cost. (3.4)

6 Give examples of (a) a fixed cost and (b) a variable cost. (3.6)

7 Distinguish between a profit mark-up and a profit margin. (3.16)

8 List elements of cost that might form part of a total cost of ownership. (4.1)

9 Describe the process of discounted cashflow. (4.9ff)

10 Summarise what is meant by 'budgetary control'. (5.1)

11 Describe the use of a simple moving average in cost estimation. (5.10, Table 2.2)

12 List the main items in a cash budget. (5.26)

CHAPTER 3

Operating Financial Budgets

Assessment criteria and indicative content

 Explain the operation of financial budgets for the control of purchases

- The purpose of financial budgets
- Cost entries and timings of cashflows
- Performance and control of budgets
- Dealing with variances to budget

Section headings

1   The purposes of financial budgets
2   Preparing the budget
3   Performance and control of budgets
4   Dealing with budget variances
5   Operating the cash budget

Introduction

In this chapter we continue our exploration of the business case, focusing on a key method by which managers can monitor actual costs against estimated costs, in order to check that the promised balance of business benefit and cost is in fact being achieved.

Of course, there are many ways in which business case outcomes may not accrue as anticipated. A higher than anticipated number of risk events may occur, incurring costs and constraining benefits. Variation from the plan may embrace schedules and timescales, or output or quality standards, as well as cost variances (although such variations will often have cost implications).

The syllabus deals specifically with financial budgets, as a tool to control purchases. Having estimated and justified the costs of a procurement or project, it will be crucially important to monitor and check that actual costs are in line with the estimates; to investigate the reasons for variances (both positive and negative: why is the procurement more expensive or cheaper than anticipated?); and to correct negative variances (cost 'blowouts').

In Chapter 8, we will look at various contractual methods for anticipating, preventing or adjusting for changes in supplier costs and prices. In this chapter, we will explore the use of financial budgets in procurement, how they are operated and controlled, and how variances can be dealt with.

1   The purposes of financial budgets

Budgets and budgetary control

1.1   Business case goals are usually captured in budgets. As we have seen, a **budget** has been defined as 'a plan quantified in monetary terms, prepared and approved prior to a defined period of time, usually showing planned or estimated income to be generated and/or expenditure to be incurred during that period, and the capital to be employed to attain a given objective'.

1.2 Budgets are set for specific periods of time. A procurement budget might be set for the coming year or (in an exam case study scenario, say, to avoid the manipulation of large volumes of data) for a month or quarter (three months). A procurement budget might also be set for the duration of a particular project, or for stages or periods within a long-term project.

1.3 **Budgetary control** is a process involving:

- The establishment of budgets for a particular policy or plan, allocated as the responsibility of a manager or team
- The continuous comparison of actual results (income or costs) with budgeted results
- The identification of variances or deviations from the policy or plan, so that *either* action can be taken to bring performance back into line with the policy or plan, *or* so that the policy or plan itself can be revised in order to reflect more realistic expectations and current circumstances. Significant divergences between budgeted and actual results should be reported to the appropriate managers so that the necessary action can be taken.

The purposes and benefits of budgeting

1.4 The objectives of preparing a budget are as follows.

- To express organisational objectives as operational targets
- To communicate plans and targets to stakeholders throughout the organisation (especially responsible managers and teams)
- To motivate people to attain performance and cost targets (especially if targets are realistic but challenging)
- To motivate managers to identify risks and problems (eg cashflow difficulties, or the need to raise additional finance) before they arise
- To measure unit or project performance, by comparing target results (income and costs) with actual results
- To help evaluate managerial performance
- To pre-authorise estimated levels of expenditure for procurement activities (which can thereafter be controlled mainly via 'reporting by exception' in the event of variances)
- To co-ordinate operations (since there will be interlocking or co-ordinated budgets for sales, engineering, operations, inventory and procurement, for example, on multi-functional projects and processes)
- To control procurement activities and costs (by highlighting areas where business case benefits may be at risk owing to unexpected or unmanaged costs or cost levels, triggering corrective action)

Limitations of budgeting

1.5 As with any management technique there are limitations to budgeting.

- A comprehensive and co-ordinated budgeting system can be cumbersome to establish and maintain.
- Budgeting and budgetary control requires managerial time that could arguably be used for more directly value-adding activities.
- The political aspects of budgeting (eg competing for funds with other functions within the organisation) can waste managerial time, create inter-functional conflicts and result in dysfunctional behaviours (such as unnecessarily 'spending up' to budgeted expenditure limits, in order not to have targets lowered in the following period).
- Budgets involve income and cost estimation, which means that they will invariably be inaccurate and unreliable to a greater or lesser degree. Additional inaccuracies may be added through lack of care in preparation, or because of 'padding' for contingencies. Managers must be prepared to recognise that budgets are not always a perfect guide to planning operations.
- Budgeted data may become swiftly outdated, inaccurate and irrelevant because of unforeseen changes in the internal or external environment.

- Managers may over-rely on budgets and variance analysis, and might under-utilise alternative tools such as the use of key performance indicators and service level agreements to control procurement operations.
- Where managers are judged against departmental budgets, they are likely to take decisions that benefit their department, regardless of the impact on the organisation overall (a problem known as 'sub-optimal' behaviour).
- Where managers focus their efforts on, and are evaluated by, budgetary measures, there may be a tendency to focus on short-term, purely financial performance factors – at the expense of longer-term value and business benefits, with longer pay-back periods (such as sustainability, innovation and learning). This will especially be the case if the budget does not take whole life costs into account.

Co-ordinated budget preparation

1.6 As we saw in Chapter 2, budget preparation generally flows from the forecasting of sales for the product or service on which variable costs depend. The process for overall co-ordinated corporate budgeting would therefore be depicted as follows: Figure 3.1.

Figure 3.1 *Corporate budget preparation*

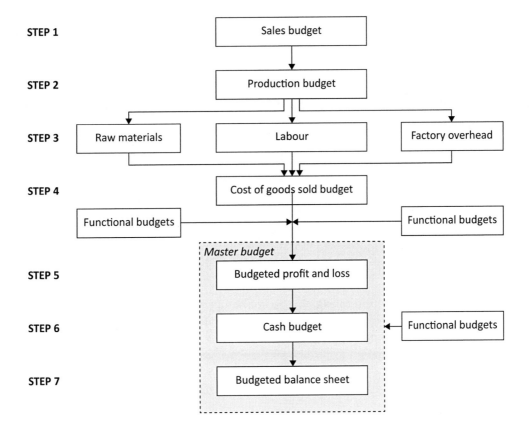

Types of budget

1.7 There are various ways of establishing budget targets.

- With an **incremental budget** we begin by looking at the actual figures for the previous period. We then adjust in line with known changes to arrive at a budget for the current period. (For example, we might add a percentage to the last period's procurement costs, to reflect average cost rises, or pricing trends in the supply market.)
- With a **zero-based budget** we ignore previous periods and start completely from scratch. (For example, we might estimate costs and prices for the procurements planned in the new period.)

1.8 Whichever of these methods is used, it is important to keep the budget up to date. Two techniques are worth mentioning in this context.

- A **rolling budget** is usually maintained. For example, a 12-month budget may be constructed for the period January to December. At the end of January, we update this by adding figures for the following January. Our revised budget then still covers a 12-month period, from February to January inclusive.
- At intervals during the year it is common to revisit the budget and update it in line with new information. This is sometimes referred to as producing a **forecast**.

Fixed and flexible budgets

1.9 It is clear that the budget process will involve the prediction of future costs. To do this effectively it is important to understand the nature of the costs in question, and in particular whether the cost is fixed, variable, or a mixture of the two. (Analysis of costs incurred in the past will help with this.)

1.10 A **fixed budget** is based on a particular estimate of activity levels. For example, it may assume that sales volume will be 200,000 units in the coming year. The revenue and costs shown in the budget will all be based on this assumption – and a problem arises when the assumption turns out to be wrong.

1.11 Suppose that an unexpected opportunity arises to increase production by 50,000 units because of a sudden surge in sales demand. This is obviously good news for the business, but it means that the fixed budget is no longer much use as a control tool. For example, it is likely that procurement will be out-spending all of its estimates of materials costs. While this would normally cause concern, in this case it is an inevitable consequence of increased production – and not detrimental to planned business benefits. The budget simply signals 'overspending', whereas in fact, the procurement department is meeting the business need effectively.

1.12 To cope with this problem, many businesses instead use **flexible budgets** which, by recognising different cost behaviour patterns, are designed to *change as the volume of output changes*. In the example above, as soon as we know that sales are ahead of target, all the variable costs of sales are automatically revised in the budget. Fixed costs, of course, are not altered. That is one reason why it is important to be able to distinguish fixed from variable costs: recap our discussion in Chapter 2 if you need to.

2 Preparing the budget

2.1 The following data will be used to explain the technique of budget preparation.

2.2 Hash Ltd has the following opening stock and required closing stock of its two products: the PS and the TG.

	PS units	TG units
Opening stock	100	50
Required closing stock	1,100	50

2.3 You are also given the following data about the materials required to produce PS and TG and the whittling and fettling processes involved in production.

	PS	TG
Finished products		
Kilos of raw material X, per unit of finished product	12	12
Kilos of raw material Y, per unit of finished product	6	8
Direct labour hours per unit of finished product	8	12
Machine hours per unit – whittling	5	8
Machine hours per unit – fettling	3	4

	Raw material	
	X	Y
Direct materials		
Desired closing stock in kilos	6,000	1,000
Opening stock in kilos	5,000	5,000
Standard rates and prices		
Direct labour	$6.20 per hour	
Raw material X	$0.72 per kg	
Raw material Y	$1.56 per kg	
Production overheads		
Variable	$1.54 per labour hour	
Fixed	$0.54 per labour hour	
	$2.08 per labour hour	

The sales budget

2.4 The sales budget represents the plan in terms of the quantity and value of sales. In practice this is often the most difficult budget to calculate.

2.5 Hash Ltd makes two products – PS and TG. Sales for next year are budgeted at 5,000 units of PS and 1,000 units of TG. Planned selling prices are $65 and $100 respectively. The sales budget would be as follows.

	Total	PS	TG
Sales units	6,000	5,000	1,000
Sales value	$425,000	$325,000	$100,000

The production budget

2.6 The next step is to produce the production budget. This is usually expressed in quantity and represents the sales budget adjusted for opening and closing finished stocks and work in progress.

	PS units	TG units
Sales budget	5,000	1,000
Budgeted stock increase		
(1,100 – 100)	1,000	
(50 – 50)		–
Production in units	6,000	1,000

2.7 The production budget must next be translated into requirements for: raw materials; direct labour; machine utilisation; production overheads; closing stock levels. We look at each of these in turn below.

The raw materials budget

2.8 Hash Ltd is going to produce 6,000 units of PS and 1,000 units of TG.

	X Kilos	Y Kilos
For production of PS		
6,000 × 12 kilos	72,000	
6,000 × 6 kilos		36,000
For production of TG		
1,000 × 12 kilos	12,000	
1,000 × 8 kilos		8,000
	84,000	44,000
Increase/(decrease) in stock		
(6,000 – 5,000)	1,000	
(1,000 – 5,000)		(4,000)
Raw materials required	85,000	40,000

	$	$
Budgeted value		
X $0.72 per kilo × 85,000	61,200	
Y $1.56 per kilo × 40,000		62,400

The direct labour budget

2.9   We can now prepare the direct labour budget.

	Hours		$
For PS: 6,000 × 8 hrs	48,000		
For TG: 1,000 ×12 hrs	12,000		
	60,000	@ $6.20	372,000

The machine utilisation budget

2.10   We can now prepare the machine utilisation budget.

	Whittling hours	*Fettling hours*	*Total hours*
For PS			
6,000 × 5 hrs	30,000		
6,000 × 3 hrs		18,000	
For TG			
1,000 × 8 hrs	8,000		
1,000 × 4 hrs		4,000	
	38,000	22,000	60,000

Production overheads

2.11   We can now calculate the production overheads.

	$
Variable costs: 60,000 hours × $1.54	92,400
Fixed costs: 60,000 hours × $0.54	32,400
	124,800

Other budgets

2.12   Depending on the requirements of management, additional budgets may be prepared for any or all of the following.

- Purchasing – consolidates purchases of raw materials, supplies and services in raw materials and expense budgets, analysed to show when the goods are received (for control of supply) and also when they are paid for (for cash budget).
- Personnel (manpower) – shows detailed requirements, month by month, for production and administration personnel.
- Stocks – itemises quantity and value, month by month, of planned stock levels for raw materials, work in progress and finished goods.

3 Performance and control of budgets

Actual income entries

3.1 For a project, business unit or corporate budget, budgetary control would involve the comparison of actual income with the sales or revenue budget.

- Entering actual income or revenue figures against estimates (eg for each category or product, for each week or month)
- Analysing the reasons for lower than expected turnover (eg lower than expected sales volumes, low market demand, under-performing products, competitor activity or reputational crisis)
- Analysing the reasons for higher than expected turnover (eg unplanned promotional opportunities, or targets set too low)
- Taking action to prevent further shortfalls, or revising the budget to reflect more realistic expectations

Actual cost entries

3.2 The main component of a procurement or project cost budget will, as we have seen, be estimated costs on purchases and procurement activities. Budgetary control will therefore involve comparison of actual expenditures against the cost budget.

- Entering actual costs or expenditures as they occur against the budgeted amounts for the relevant item
- Analysing how fixed costs differed from the budgeted amount. The accuracy and fairness of the function's estimation or apportionment of fixed costs may need to be improved – or higher than estimated fixed costs may need to be investigated and reduced
- Verifying that variable costs were in line with the budget (and/or in line with actual sales volume, in a flexible budgeting system)
- Analysing any reasons for changes in the relationship between costs and turnover. (Has there been an increase in cost efficiency and profitability: achieving the same or higher turnover at reduced cost? Or, conversely, were costs cut, or prices squeezed, so far as to compromise quality and customer satisfaction, for example?)
- Analysing any differences in the *timing* of actual and budgeted expenditures. (Is the project running behind schedule? Did the supplier deliver on time? Was the supplier's invoice paid according to agreed payment terms?)

3.3 The differences between the budget and actual values are known as **variances**. Where they relate to costs (rather than revenue), if the actual cost is less than the budget cost the variance is described as 'favourable'; if the actual cost is greater the variance is said to be 'adverse'.

Budget example

3.4 The following example illustrates the comparison of actual and budget results in a basic expenditure budget.

3.5 Bug Ltd manufactures one uniform product only. The following statement shows the departmental overhead budget based on an average level of activity of 20,000 units of production per four week period, and the actual results for four weeks in October.

	Budget average for four week period $	Actual for 1–28 October $
Indirect labour	20,000	19,540
Consumables	800	1,000
Depreciation	10,000	10,000
Other overheads	5,000	5,000
	35,800	35,540

3.6   The variances would be calculated as follows.

	Average four week budget $	Actual results $	Variances favourable/ (adverse) $
Indirect labour	20,000	19,540	460
Consumables	800	1,000	(200)
Depreciation	10,000	10,000	—
Other overheads	5,000	5,000	—
	35,800	35,540	260

4   Dealing with budget variances

4.1   As the name implies, variance analysis is based on a comparison of what something **should have cost** with what it **actually did cost**.

Standard costing and variance analysis

4.2   In its usual form, variance analysis is based on the use of **standard costs**. Managers determine in advance what a unit of output should cost by drawing up standards for each of the cost elements comprised in it. For example, a company might determine that the standard cost of producing one blodgit is $4.40, made up as follows.

	$
Raw material X, 1.2 kilos @ $2.00 per kilo	2.40
Grade A labour, 20 minutes @ $6.00 per hour	2.00
Total	4.40

4.3   Suppose now that on a particular day 120 blodgits were produced, with costs incurred as follows.

	$
Raw material X, 150 kilos	285.00
Grade A labour, 35 hours	217.00
Total	502.00

4.4   Based on standard costs, we would expect 120 blodgits to cost $528.00 (ie 120 @ $4.40). In fact it has cost us less than that (good news). Variance analysis enables managers to pinpoint why.

4.5   The basic idea is to examine each input resource (in this case, raw material X and Grade A labour) and to compare actual results with standard, both in terms of the amount of resource used and in terms of the cost per unit of resource.

4.6   In relation to raw material X, the analysis is as follows.

120 blodgits should use	144 kilos
but actually used	150 kilos
Usage variance (bad news)	6 kilos

At a standard cost of $2 per kilo, the excess usage means bad news of $12.

	$
150 kilos should cost	300.00
but actually cost	285.00
Price variance (good news)	15.00

We have paid less than expected for each kilo of material.

4.7 Overall, the good news on material X (the purchase price) outweighs the bad news (the excess usage) by $3. Sure enough, in producing 120 blodgits we would expect to spend $288 on material X (ie 120 @ $2.40), whereas in fact we spent $3 less than that ($285).

4.8 A similar analysis applies to Grade A labour.

120 blodgits should take	40 hours
but actually took	35 hours
Efficiency variance (good news)	5 hours

At a standard cost of $6 per hour, the improved efficiency means good news of $30.

	$
35 hours should cost	210.00
but actually cost	217.00
Labour rate variance (bad news)	7.00

We have paid our labour force $7 more than expected for the number of hours they have worked.

4.9 Overall, the good news on Grade A labour outweighs the bad news by $23. Sure enough, in producing 120 blodgits we would expect to spend $240 on labour (ie 120 @ $2.00), whereas in fact we spent $23 less than that ($217).

4.10 The advantages of standard costing are chiefly to do with the improved management control it offers. Each product's costs are carefully analysed and listed out, and an expected amount allocated. In addition, budgeted figures for expected production are calculated, so altogether the standard costing system has encouraged the organisation to plan very carefully. Once activities commence, standard costing requires regular and systematic comparison of actual with estimate so that variances are calculated. This should provide early warning signals regarding specific issues such as prices, efficiency and utilisation, which might go unregarded for a longer period were it not for standard costing.

4.11 The problems presented by standard costing are generally to do with the fact that the system is expensive to install and run effectively. In addition, a product's or service's standard costs can quickly become out of date, which renders the variances meaningless. Finally, while the system should mean that managers take more responsibility for the variances under their control, often the interdependence of variances means that direct responsibility cannot be taken on board by individual managers in quite such a straightforward way.

Causes of budget variances

4.12 Reasons for budget variances should be investigated, to establish whether there is a cause for concern which can be corrected, or whether the budget itself requires adjustment to reflect more realistic or up-to-date assumptions.

4.13 The actual prices of bought-in materials or other items, for example, may be higher or lower than anticipated, because of:

- The skill of the buyer's negotiating team, and the relative strength of its bargaining position at the time of contracting

- Fluctuations in commodity prices, due to supply and demand factors
- Fluctuations in the exchange rate, affecting the value of the price in the buyer's currency
- Quantity discounts lost by buying smaller than anticipated volumes – or gained by buying larger than anticipated volumes (eg through a consortium)
- Opportunistic spot buying at lower prices
- The purchase of different or substitute goods (eg owing to non-availability or supply disruption)
- The purchase of additional quantities of goods (eg owing to increased production volume, under-estimated usage rates or higher than anticipated wastage and scrap rates)
- The incurring of late payment or other price penalties.

5   Operating the cash budget

5.1   As we saw in Chapter 2, a cashflow forecast (or cash budget) is a detailed budget of income and cash expenditure. The objective of a cash budget is to anticipate cash shortages or surpluses and allow time to make plans for dealing with them.

5.2   The steps in preparing a cash budget are as follows.

- Forecast sales.
- Forecast the time-lag on converting debtors to cash, and hence forecast the dates of actual cash receipts from customers.
- Determine purchase requirements.
- Forecast the time-lag on paying suppliers, and hence forecast the dates of actual cash payments to suppliers.
- Incorporate other cash payments and receipts, including such items as capital expenditure and tax payments.
- Collate this information so as to find the net cashflows.

5.3   A tabular layout should be used, with columns for months and rows for receipts and payments. We will use an example to illustrate the procedure.

Cashflow budgeting example

5.4   Here is a company's profit and loss account for the three months to 30 September. We assume that all revenue and costs accrue evenly over the three months. The task is to convert the profit and loss account into a cash budget.

	$000	$000
Sales (cash received one month in arrear)		1,200
Purchases (paid one month in arrear)	1,044	
Depreciation	72	
		1,116
Budgeted profit		84

5.5   The company's capital expenditure and receipts budget for the three month period is as follows.

	$000
Payments for new plant	
July	12
August	25
September	13
Increase in stocks, payable August	20
Receipts: new issue of share capital (September)	30

5.6   Current assets at 1 July include debtors of $210,000 and cash of $40,000. Liabilities at 1 July include trade creditors of $160,000, dividends payable in August of $24,000 and tax payable in September of $30,000.

5.7 The cash budget can be prepared as follows. You should work carefully through this solution to ensure you can establish where each figure comes from. The trickiest figures are those relating to payments from debtors and to suppliers, because of the one month delay.

CASH BUDGET FOR THREE MONTHS TO 30 SEPTEMBER

	July $000	August $000	September $000
Cash receipts			
From debtors	210	400	400
Share capital			30
Total	210	400	430
Cash payments			
To creditors	160	348	348
Purchase of plant	12	25	13
Increase in stock		20	
Tax			30
Dividends		24	
Total	172	417	391
Surplus/(deficit)	38	(17)	39
Opening balance	40	78	61
Closing balance	78	61	100

The timings of cashflows

5.8 In the **cost budget**, it may be important to analyse the differences in the *timing* of actual and budgeted expenditures.

- Does a later than expected expenditure mean that the project is running behind schedule, or that the supplier delivered late?
- Was the supplier's invoice paid according to agreed payment terms? (If early, this may represent inefficient cashflow management – or the buyer may be eligible for an early payment discount. If late, this may create contract compliance, trust and relationship issues with the supplier.)

5.9 In addition, the **cash budget** will, as we saw in Chapter 2, allow the manager to monitor the timing and amount of money flowing into and out of the business each month, and to ensure a balance of inflows and outflows. Cash includes money, bank balance and unused overdraft facilities that can quickly be converted into cash to pay debts. It does not include money owed by debtors, or stock or other assets, which cannot always be readily converted to cash to pay staff and suppliers.

5.10 Ideally, the business will have built up a cash balance or cash reserve to deal with immediate and short-term costs. However, cash inflows (eg payments from customers for goods and services) often lag behind cash outflows (eg payments to staff and suppliers to produce the goods and services for sale), so it will be important to monitor and manage the cash position. The aim will generally be:

- To speed up cash inflows. In the words of Emmett *(Supply Chain in 90 Minutes):* 'make it faster, move it faster, get paid faster'! Other remedies to boost cash receipts might be raising an overdraft or bank loan, increasing sales (eg by promotional activity), reducing customer credit terms, or encouraging prompt payment by customers (eg by offering prompt payment discounts).
- To slow down cash outflows, eg by:
  - Reducing purchases from suppliers, perhaps by running down stock levels
  - Making more frequent, smaller orders in preference to aggregating demand (although the cashflow gain is off-set by a value for money loss in higher transaction costs)
  - Avoiding large up-front procurement costs on capital items by using leasing, hire purchase or short-term rental options

— Negotiating instalment payments with suppliers, rather than payment of the full contract amount on delivery (spreading out cash commitments)

— Negotiating extended credit terms with suppliers (or simply paying suppliers late – although this has contractual, ethical, relational, reputational and sustainability down-sides...).

5.11   Credit periods are an issue for cashflow, for both the buyer and the supplier. The buyer may want to pay as late as possible, in order to retain cash (or earn interest on banked funds), but the supplier will want to be paid as early as possible, to obtain those same benefits – especially since it has already incurred the cost of supplying the product or service.

5.12   Cash outflows that might be entered in a procurement function cash budget include:

- Purchases
- Staff salaries or wages and benefits, rents and daily operating expenses
- VAT, National Insurance contributions, corporation tax and similar payments
- Loan repayments (if these come within the procurement function's budget).

Some of these (such as salaries, rents, tax and loan repayments) will be committed for payment on regular, fixed dates.

5.13   Entries of actual inflows and outflows in the cash budget should clearly indicate where there is an excess of outflows to inflows: in other words, where the project or function is in a **negative cashflow position**. This might indicate an urgent need to speed up planned cash inflows (eg by stronger debt collection efforts) or to secure a short-term injection of finance (such as additional overdraft facilities, a short-term loan, or drawing on a contingency fund).

5.14   The cash budget will have to be reviewed regularly, in order to:

- Identify potential future cashflow problems, and take steps to minimise the risks in advance
- Ensure that there are sufficient cash reserves or planned positive cashflows before making major financial commitments (including large procurement contracts, up-front payments or instalment payments)
- Adjust cashflow forecasts to take account of changes in actual sales, purchases and labour costs, interest and exchange rates, tax changes and so on.

Chapter summary

- A budget is a plan expressed in monetary terms. Budgetary control involves continuous comparison of actual results with budgeted results, and taking action to remedy any variances.
- It makes sense to use a flexible budget which is automatically adjusted in line with changes in activity levels.
- There is a logical sequence in which budgets should be prepared. For a manufacturing company the order would normally be sales budget, production budget, raw materials budget, direct labour budget, machine utilisation budget, and overheads budget.
- Variances from budget are often computed in relation to standard costs. This enables managers to identify what has gone wrong, which helps in deciding on remedial action.
- A cashflow budget may give advance warning of an adverse cash position. To remedy this, a firm will try to speed up cash inflows or slow down cash outflows or both.

 ## Self-test questions

Numbers in brackets refer to the paragraphs where you can check your answers.

1   Summarise the process of budgetary control. (1.3)

2   List possible limitations of budgeting. (1.5)

3   Why is a fixed budget an inadequate tool for budgetary control? (1.10)

4   What is meant by a favourable cost variance? (3.3)

5   What is meant by a standard cost? (4.2)

6   List possible reasons for a materials price variance. (4.13)

7   List the steps in preparing a cash budget. (5.2)

8   Suggest methods of boosting cash inflows. (5.10)

9   List categories of cash outflows that might appear in a cash budget. (5.12)

CHAPTER 4

Specifying Requirements

2.1 Assess different types of specifications used in procurements of products or services

- Definitions of specifications
- Examples of specifications such as drawings, samples, branded and technical
- Conformance based specifications
- Output or outcome based specifications

2.2 Explain the content of specifications for procurement

- Typical sections of a specification

Section headings

1 What are specifications?
2 Types of specification
3 Conformance specifications
4 Performance specifications
5 Specifying services
6 Sustainable specification

Introduction

One of the key steps in procurement activity, as we saw in Chapter 1, is 'description of the need'. Two assessment criteria are devoted to the development and analysis of specifications: statements of the requirements to be satisfied in the supply of products and services.

We have split our coverage of the topic into two chapters. In this chapter, we look at the basic definitions and types of specifications, and why they are important. We also examine the particularly tricky area of specifying services – and why it is so tricky.

In Chapter 5, we get down to the 'nuts and bolts' of the topic: how specifications are developed, and what information and decisions are required. We also focus on some particular areas in which company policies may influence the content of specifications, such as standardisation and variety reduction, social and environmental sustainability, and issues of data security and knowledge management.

In Chapter 6 we go on to look at the processes and criteria by which *performance* or fulfilment of the specified need can be measured, including the development of key performance indicators (contractual performance measures) and service level agreements.

1 What are specifications?

1.1 As we have seen, it is one of the key functions of procurement to specify and document the business requirements for supply. This activity is designed to support the overall corporate strategy and objectives of the organisation: if executed in an efficient and effective manner, supply specification can provide value to other functional areas within the organisation, and contribute to the flow of value towards the end customer (eg by helping to ensure product and service quality).

1.2 The overall procurement objective is to obtain the right goods and services for the best value for money: that is, the optimal balance of quality (to meet customer requirements) and life-time costs. The formulation of effective product and service specifications is a prerequisite to achieving this objective. It will usually engage procurement staff in cross-functional collaboration with internal and external stakeholders (as discussed in Chapter 5) to gain appropriate inputs of knowledge and expertise.

Specifications

1.3 A specification can be simply defined as a systematic statement of the requirements to be satisfied in the supply of a product or service.

1.4 As part of the procurement cycle, the role of a specification is as follows.

- **To define the requirement** – encouraging all relevant stakeholders (including the purchasers and users of the supplied items) to consider what they really need, and whether what they think they need is the only, most cost-effective or most value-adding solution
- **To communicate the requirement** clearly to suppliers, so that they can plan to conform – and perhaps also use their expertise to come up with innovative or lower-cost solutions to the requirement 'problem': in other words, so that you get what you need.
- **To provide a means of evaluating the quality or conformance** of the goods or services supplied, for acceptance (if conforming to specification) or rejection (if non-conforming) and improvement planning. For this purpose, specifications are generally used alongside contractual performance measures, such as key performance indicators – discussed in Chapter 6.

1.5 A specification is often thought of in terms of the 'right product or service' of the 'right quality' – but it may also include other aspects of the 'five rights of procurement' in defining the requirement, including the quantity required, and when and where delivery is required: Table 4.1.

Specifications and tolerances

1.6 It is generally recognised that a supplier cannot match all the requirements of a specification exactly, all the time, so some 'leeway' – or room for variation – is usually built into the specification. The term *tolerance* is used to describe a statement or measure of how much variation from specification will be acceptable, in the assessment of quality.

1.7 Tolerances will vary according to the nature of the work being specified. Consider a specification for an engineered component, for example: because such a component would have to fit within a complex assembly, and perform to a fine degree of accuracy, it would typically have an extremely small tolerance. The dimensions of such a component might be expressed as specification 'plus or minus' (+/−) 1 millimetre: if the specified dimension was 500mm, there would be leeway for the component to measure 499 or 501 millimetres.

1.8 Different sorts of tolerances might be set for services. A call centre might be required to answer incoming calls 'within five rings' (ie a tolerance of 1–5). A cleaning service might be required to have its employees on the premises and starting work 'between 7.00 pm and 7.30 pm' (ie a tolerance of 30 minutes).

Table 4.1 *Key questions when drawing up specifications*

Product	• Performance objectives: functionality, outputs, outcomes • Process needs and input parameters • Features • Aesthetics • Compatibility • Reliability • Durability • Maintainability • Ease of use
Price	• Purchase price • Life time costs (maintenance, operating, disposal)
Quantity	• One-off or scheduled ongoing requirement • Forecast demand: supplier production and delivery capacity to supply
Quality	• Desired level of quality: best?; most appropriate to user needs and usage context?; lowest pricing point • Acceptable tolerances (range of variance)
Timing	• Time-phased requirements (daily, weekly or monthly schedule) • Acceptable tolerances (range of variance)
Place	• Delivery address(es) • Delivery requirements (eg breaking of bulk, or consolidation) • Packaging requirements • Transport requirements (mode preference, special conditions)

1.9 The concept of **zero defects** (or 'get it right first time') is a cornerstone of radical quality management philosophies such as total quality management (TQM). It means, among other things, that a buyer relies on its suppliers to achieve 100% quality in their deliveries. This refers to all aspects of the buyer's orders: the supplier is expected to deliver exactly the right quantity, at exactly the right time and place, and exactly in line with the buyer's specification.

1.10 Zero defects has implications for many aspects of a buyer's work.

- **Specifications:** exact requirements will have to be set out (defining right quality), with very low or zero tolerance for variation, or for number of defects in an order.
- **Supplier pre-qualification, selection and appraisal:** buyers will have to ensure that suppliers have (and maintain) the capabilities required to meet specification reliably, dependably and consistently.
- **Quality control:** even if a supplier has been fully audited and certified as having excellent quality assurance (defect prevention) systems, the buyer will still wish to inspect the first few deliveries to ensure that quality assurance processes are working as effectively as they should be.
- **Costs:** the costs of assuring quality, or preventing defects, are significant – but generally *less* than the costs of poor quality or quality failure (repeated inspections, scrap, re-work, damage to machinery, returns and recalls, compensation to customers, lost sales and goodwill and so on).
- The **buyer's quality management**: the focus of zero defects is not just supplies from outside the organisation. Internal controls must work towards zero tolerance for defects in their own production processes, with the overall aim of delivering faultless product to the external customer.

1.11 In the present context, however, the main point about a zero defects approach is that it builds quality in at the design stage of product development – in other words, as early as possible in the value chain. There is an old saying in information technology: 'garbage in, garbage out' (GIGO). The same applies to production processes. If defects are to be prevented (as opposed to detected once they have already occurred), it is necessary to get the inputs right – and accurate low-tolerance or zero-tolerance materials specifications are a key contributing factor.

1.12 So why wouldn't every specification provide for extremely small or zero tolerances, if the buyer knows exactly what it wants and sees the benefit of zero defects?

- Some work is difficult to specify accurately or prescriptively, so wider tolerances may be required within a 'looser' specification. This is often the case for service specifications, for example, as we will see later in the chapter.
- Tight tolerances are more costly to achieve, because of the more advanced machinery and skills required, extra time taken, and the cost of scrapping production that does not conform to specification.

Why are specifications important?

1.13 Specifications are said to be **the heart of the contract** between a buyer and seller, because (as we will see in later chapters) contract law provides that:

- Goods supplied must *conform to any specification of requirement* included in the contract
- Goods supplied must be of *satisfactory quality* and *fit for their purpose* – mostly, as defined by specification.

1.14 A contract is formed when one party makes an 'offer' and the other party unconditionally 'accepts' it: a specification is **part of the offer to buy**, and if the supplier accepts the contract, it is contractually bound to fulfil the specification in full (within any specified tolerances). In a landmark legal case (*Moore v Landauer*, 1927), the parties had a contract for tinned fruit to be delivered packed in cases of 30 tins each. The correct number of tins was delivered – but in cases varying between 24 and 30 tins each. The court held that the contract had not been properly fulfilled, even though the market value of the goods was the same: the specification had not been met. The buyer could reject all the goods and not pay.

1.15 In addition, under contract law, if a buyer tells a supplier **the purpose for which a purchased item is to be used**, the item delivered must effectively fulfil that purpose. Steve Kirby (a CIPS chief assessor) uses the example of a bucket. If you specify a 5-litre bucket and the supplier delivers a 3-litre bucket, the item delivered is not fit for its purpose: it will not hold five litres of water. Adding to this example, if you tell the supplier that you want to use the bucket to hold a chemical (when the bucket is usually used for water), and the supplier accepts the order, the bucket must be able to hold the chemical (without being damaged or causing a safety hazard) – otherwise it is not fit for its purpose.

1.16 An effective specification removes any doubt, ambiguity or misunderstanding in the supplier's mind as to what is required, and therefore what constitutes satisfactory quality and fitness for purpose.

Advantages and disadvantages of specifications

1.17 The main *advantages* claimed for using specifications are as follows.

- The process of drawing up specifications is a useful discipline. It forces careful consideration of needs and possible alternative ways of satisfying them. This can lead to other benefits, such as innovation and cost savings.
- If items are to be purchased from more than one source, the use of conformance specifications (specifying exactly what is to be supplied) may be essential to ensure uniformity.
- Specifications provide useful criteria for measuring the quality and acceptability of purchases once delivered.
- Specifications provide evidence, in the event of a dispute, as to what the purchaser required (and the supplier agreed to provide) as part of the contract.

1.18 Effective specifications can specifically support **value for money** procurement by:

- Specifying requirements clearly and in non-technical language, allowing for ease and speed of use, understanding and evaluation
- Enabling potential bidders for contracts to 'self-select' (eg with a concise introductory summary of the requirement): avoiding wasted time on further specification analysis and bidding
- Enabling supplier flexibility and innovation in coming up with value-for-money solutions (eg by

using functional or performance-based specifications, rather than more prescriptive conformance specifications, as discussed in the next section of this chapter)

- Avoiding over-specification, building in unnecessary features or specifying excessively high quality/ variance tolerances, which are unnecessarily costly to fulfil, without adding corresponding value
- Avoiding under-specification, leaving uncertainties, or potential for conformance problems, which will lead to later delays, variations, disputes, quality costs and so on
- Avoiding the use of brand specification, which (as we will see a bit later in the chapter) tends to reduce the potential for value for money arising from supplier choice, competitive pricing and flexible solutions to the requirement.

1.19 The main *disadvantages* of using specifications are as follows.

- Detailed specification is an expensive and time consuming process, and almost certainly uneconomic for routine and small-value purchases.
- The costs of inspection and quality control are greater for complex specifications than if simple specification is used (eg by a brand name and model, for which conformance is easily established).
- Specifications can become too firmly embedded: they need to be regularly reviewed, to ensure that the latest design decisions, and the latest developments in the supply market, and the latest reassessment of the business need and business case, are being taken into account.
- Specifications can create a temptation to over-specify, adding cost (without necessarily adding value) and increasing stock variation and proliferation (a widening range of items held, reflecting potentially minor differences in specification, rather than 'rationalising' the range of inventory by utilising generic or already-stocked items).

Consequences of poor specification

1.20 The consequences of *ineffective* specification processes are potentially costly for the organisation.

- There may be misunderstandings with suppliers over requirements and expectations (eg if the specification was vague, inaccurate or overly technical), leading to rejection of deliveries, lost production time, legal disputes and damaged supplier relationships.
- There may be misunderstandings with other stakeholders over requirements and expectations (eg if the specification did not take into account users' needs), leading to internal conflict, resistance to use of the product and loss of credibility for purchasing.
- There are more likely to be quality defects in the goods supplied, and these are costly in terms of lost time, scrapped goods, rework, additional inspections and controls, and so on. If defects reach the customer, there may be additional serious consequences of lost customer loyalty, lost business, the adjustment of complaints and so on.
- Poorly defined specifications may mean that, even if the procured materials or services conform to specification, they may fail to function as they should (or to meet the business need): the risk and cost of such a failure is borne by the buyer.
- Goods and services may be over-specified: related to some 'ideal' standard rather than a robust business case: without reference to users' actual needs, the cost of higher standards, or the added value actually contributed by higher standards.

2   Types of specification

2.1 Two main categories of specification are **conformance specifications** (also known as technical or design specifications) and **performance specifications** (also known as functional specifications, output or outcome specifications). You need to be able to distinguish clearly between the two.

- With a *conformance* specification, the buyer details exactly what the required product, part or material must consist of. This may take the form of an engineering drawing or blueprint, a chemical formula or 'recipe' of ingredients, or a sample of the product to be duplicated, for example. The supplier may not know in detail, or even at all, what function the product will play in the buyer's operations. The supplier's task is simply to *conform to the description* provided by the buyer.

- With a *performance* specification, the buyer describes: what it expects a part or material to be able to achieve, in terms of the functions it will perform and the level of performance it should reach; or what outputs or outcomes (results) it expects to be delivered by a service. It is up to the supplier to furnish a product or service which will *satisfy these requirements*: the buyer specifies the 'ends', and the supplier has relative flexibility as to 'means' of achieving those ends.

Evaluating the use of conformance specifications

2.2   Conformance specifications are generally becoming less common, for a number of reasons.

- It can be very difficult, time-consuming and costly to draft a comprehensive description of exactly what is wanted.
- The buyer bears the risk of the design not performing to expectation: suppliers who conform to the letter of the description are safeguarded in law, even if the product supplied does not perform its intended function. In other words, if the specification is limited, vague, inaccurate, or incompatible with other elements of the buyer's process, the work may conform to specification, but not be of 'right quality' (or 'fit for purpose').
- Conformance specifications may restrict the potential supplier base. A tight specification may be capable of fulfilment only by a small number of suppliers: in effect, the capabilities of other potential suppliers have been 'specified away'.
- The prescriptive nature of the specification may restrict innovation and the range of solutions to problems. This is a particular problem if the specification details the *means* by which the supplied items should be manufactured: the buyer potentially closes itself off from manufacturing developments of which it may be unaware – especially in supply markets where technology is developing quickly. In addition, the buyer may be ignoring 'off-the-shelf' solutions to the requirement, and incurring unnecessary costs for a 'bespoke' solution. This drawback heightens the need for pre-specification market dialogue, discussed in Chapter 5.

2.3   However, there may be circumstances in which a conformance specification is most appropriate.

- A *technical or design specification* (such as an engineering drawing, design or blueprint) may be necessary where technical dimensions, weights or tolerances are critical for functional, operational or safety and quality reasons. They are typcially used in engineering and construction or architecture environments, which require a high degree of technical accuracy and very low tolerances (because of the complexity of assembly and machine function).
- A *composition specification* (specifying chemical or physical make-up or properties required) may be appropriate in contexts such as the production of chemicals, manufactured materials (such as plastic or metal alloys), engineering or construction. It may be particularly important where certain physical properties (eg strength, flexibility, durability) are important for safety and/or performance – as in the case of the metal used in car manufacture. It may also be a compliance issue, where materials are restricted by law, regulation or codes of practice, for health, safety or environmental reasons – as in the case of lead in paint, for example, or the composition of medical and pharmaceutical formulations (where the 'recipe' must be followed precisely).

Evaluating the use of performance specifications

2.4   Conversely, there are a number of advantages to a performance, functional, output or outcome based approach to specification, which have made them increasingly common.

- Performance specifications are easier and cheaper to draft, compared to a more detailed, prescriptive (conformance) approach.
- The efficacy of the specification does not depend on the technical knowledge of the buyer. Suppliers may well know better than the buyer what is required, and how it can best be manufactured.
- Suppliers can use their full expertise, technologies and innovative capacity to develop optimum, lowest-cost solutions.

- A greater share of specification risk is borne by the supplier: if the part supplied does not perform its function, or a process or service does not achieve its target outcome, the buyer is entitled to redress (whereas, with a conformance specification, the specifier bears responsibility for the functionality of the finished result).
- The potential supply base is wider than with a conformance specification. If the task is to supply something – anything – that will perform a particular function or achieve a given outcome, the expertise of different suppliers could potentially provide a wide range of solutions.

2.5 It is particularly appropriate to use performance specifications in the following circumstances.

- Suppliers have greater relevant technical and manufacturing expertise than the buyer – so that the best knowledge is being used and leveraged. (It should also be noted that the buyer will be highly reliant on the supplier's expertise, putting pressure on the effectiveness of its supplier pre-qualification and selection.)
- Technology is changing rapidly in the supplying industry – so that the buyer is not in a position of specifying yesterday's methodologies, but gets the best out of suppliers' innovation capacity and technological development.
- There are clear, objective criteria for evaluating alternative solutions put forward by suppliers competing for the contract. These should be clearly communicated to potential suppliers, who may invest considerable time and resources in coming up with proposals, and will want to be assured that the selection process is fair, transparent and genuinely competitive.
- The buyer has sufficient time and expertise to assess the potential functionality and outcomes of suppliers' proposals and competing alternative options (particularly if the supplier is using technology with which the buyer is unfamiliar). The potential complexity of the evaluation process is the major disadvantage of the performance specification approach.

2.6 With performance specifications, quality is measured by the extent to which the supplied goods are able to do what the buyer asks or expects them to do: that is, fitness for purpose. However, it is worth noting that the goods may *still* be incompatible with the buyer's true requirements in other ways: difficult or costly to use, say, or incompatible with the buyer's other systems – or perhaps quickly rendered outdated and obsolete by technological change. Again, such goods would arguably not be of the 'right quality' from the buyer's point of view, even though they conformed to specification.

2.7 The May 2008 *Purchasing Operations* exam gave the example of an organisation buying an expensive scanning machine. Neither the user nor the purchasing team were consulted when the specification was drawn up, and it did not take the user's needs and concerns into account. So although the purchased scanner conformed to specification, it was not what the end-user required and was difficult to use. In short, it offered 'conformance', but not fitness for purpose. The organisation incurred added costs of upgrading the scanner, obtaining training for staff and so on.

2.8 Let's now look in more detail at the different types and methods of specification.

3   Conformance specifications

Technical or design specifications

3.1 A technical specification or design specification may take the form of engineering drawings, designs or blueprints, or detailed descriptions. Such a specification is a highly prescriptive written specification or drawing giving a fully detailed definition of what is required.

3.2 A technical specification would typically include content such as the following.

- The scope of the specification (its objectives and content)
- Definitions: explanation of any technical or specialised terms used

- The purpose of the equipment or material that is the subject of the specification
- Reference to any related documents (such as standards or legislation) which apply
- Materials requirements (including approved or excluded materials), properties (eg dimensions, strength, recyclability), tolerances and permissible variability
- Desired appearance, texture and finish requirements of the finished product, including any identification marks, operating symbols, safety instructions and so on
- Drawings, samples or models of the required product (where available)
- Conditions under which the item or material is to be installed, used, manufactured or stored
- Maintenance and reliability requirements
- Specification of packaging (including any special conditions in transit) and protection
- Information to be provided by the supplier for users, such as instructions, or advice on installation, operation and maintenance.

3.3   Designs, technical drawings and blueprints are commonly used in engineering and construction or architecture environments, which require a high degree of technical accuracy and very low tolerances (because of the complexity of assembly and machine function).

3.4   Technical specifications have the following advantages.

- Allowing a large amount of technically precise and detailed information to be conveyed
- Supporting fair competition between suppliers, since the same plans can be sent to a number of potential suppliers for quotation
- Offering a precise standard against which deliveries can be measured, by comparison with the detailed technical specifications
- Minimising risk, and taking best advantage of situations in which the buying organisation has more design or technical expertise than prospective suppliers.

3.5   The *disadvantages* of design specification are those identified for conformance specifications in general. In particular, engineering drawings and blueprints are time-consuming and costly to produce, with a need for highly-qualified professional input.

Specification by chemical or physical properties

3.6   'Composition' specifications are the equivalent of technical specifications for different types of product, such as chemicals and manufactured materials (eg plastics), engineering or construction: they specify the chemical or physical make-up required. This may be particularly important where:

- Certain physical properties (eg strength, flexibility, durability) are important for safety and/or performance: so, for example, the metal used in car manufacture must have certain properties of shock absorption or crumpling, for safety purposes.
- Certain materials are restricted by law, regulation or codes of practice, for health, safety or environmental reasons: for example, some of the heavy metals in batteries, lead in paint, non-recyclable packing and so on.

3.7   The advantages and disadvantages of composition specifications are similar to those of technical specifications.

Specification by brand

3.8   A buyer may specify what it requires by means of a brand name. If you are familiar with a particular product on the market, and it meets your criteria, you can simply order the required quantity of that brand, usually supported by a particular model name or number.

3.9   There are some *advantages* to this approach.

- It is simple, quick, easy and cheap to administer. Provided the buyer is satisfied that the specified brand or model will fulfil the requirement, he can simply order it by name and there is no ambiguity about what he will receive. This may be important if the quantities required, or their total value, do not justify a costly specification process – which is why the method is common in small business and consumer purchases.

- Branded products will tend to be of good quality and consistency: the manufacturer will have invested heavily in building up the brand name and will protect its value by doing everything possible to ensure that customers are satisfied – which implies concentrated attention to quality issues.
- Branded products should be easy to source, since, again, the manufacturer will have invested in building up the brand and will therefore ensure that it is readily accessible to the market.
- If the brand is well known, it may be a selling point when the buyer's own product is finished and offered for sale. 'Our products include the industry standard Component X.'
- Purchasing by brand name may be essential if a particular part, material or technology is patented (and not licensed to other manufacturers), and therefore exclusively available in the form of a single brand.

3.10 However, there are also *disadvantages* to this approach.

- For the very reasons already mentioned – high quality, reliability, well known name and image – branded items are often more expensive than unbranded equivalents.
- There may be restricted choice of branded products in a market, and perhaps only one supplier for a given product.
- The supplier may alter the specification of its product, without changing the branding or notifying customers: ordering by brand alone may not therefore conform to the requirement.
- Branded products may be 'fakes' (products of low quality passed off under the brand name), and generic products claimed as identical equivalents to branded products (common in the pharmaceuticals industry, for example) may not be genuinely identical. This may be a particular hazard in consumer purchases.
- Manufacturers may tend to assume, without proper testing, that branded materials or components will be satisfactory, but cutting corners on quality assurance is always a risk.

Specification by sample

3.11 If the purchaser knows exactly what he wants, because he already possesses an example of the item (eg produced by another supplier, or 'prototyped' by the research and development function), he can simply send a sample or prototype to the supplier, requiring the supplier to *duplicate* the features and performance of the sample.

3.12 It is also common in some industries for *suppliers* to provide samples (eg the swatches of materials provided by upholsterers, and sample pots of paints provided by paint manufacturers): the buyer can then simply specify the model to be duplicated.

3.13 The main advantages of a sampling approach are as follows.

- If a buyer relies on a sample provided by the supplier, it is legally entitled to receive goods which correspond with the sample (under the Sale of Goods Act 1979).
- Some samples can be used or tested to assess suitability, prior to purchase.
- Samples are a quick and easy method of specifying requirements, without having to describe features in detail.
- If a supplier is asked to produce a sample, the buyer can be assured that it has developed the required capabilities and processes to produce the item (although he must also ensure that it can do so consistently and cost-effectively in bulk, according to the business need).

3.14 The main disadvantage of specification by sample is that it may be difficult to measure the product supplied against the sample: is it really the same, other than in obvious observable measures such as colour or size? If deeper testing is required to establish the product's compliance with criteria such as chemical composition, strength, flexibility, functionality and so on, it might be preferable to specify those characteristics. Also, it is necessary to have some assurance that a good quality sample is not merely a 'one off', done to secure the order: the supplier must be able to produce the same quality dependably.

Specification by market grade

3.15 Some materials, especially commodities such as steel and wool, are subject to a grading system, in which qualities such as purity, strength or flexibility are standardised. Buyers in the relevant industries are familiar with what is implied by each grade and can specify what they want simply by ordering '1,000 tonnes of Grade X'.

3.16 This has the virtue of simplicity and wide acceptance within an industry, but it does not necessarily specify the full range of parameters that may be relevant to a purchase.

Specification by standards

3.17 Standards are documents that stipulate or recommend minimum levels of performance and quality of goods and services. Like market grades, they offer a 'short-hand' method of specifying common requirements for common products and services – and for the processes used in their production and delivery (eg environmental management and quality management). The buyer can simply specify that supplies be compliant with a given standard, or that the supplier's processes be accredited under a given standard scheme.

3.18 Standards may relate to various aspects of product quality.

- *Standard terms and symbols* (harmonising the 'language' used in specification: British Standard 308, for example, sets conventions for technical drawings)
- The *dimensions* of items (encouraging interchangeability and variety reduction)
- The *performance or safety requirements* of items, with acceptable tolerances
- Environmental requirements (eg on pollution control or waste disposal)
- *Codes of practice*, giving guidance on best practice in relation to engineering and construction techniques, installation, maintenance, provision of services and so on
- *Methods of testing*, as a standard way of measuring the values of product characteristics and behavioural standards.

3.19 Standards are produced at different levels and by different bodies.

- Corporate standards and codes of practice, setting out standard specifications and tolerances for a range of bought-out items, can be produced by various functions as a guide to design, purchasing, manufacturing and marketing operations.
- Trade or industry standards are produced by trade associations and professional bodies.
- National standards are produced in most countries, for example by the British Standards Institution (BSI) in the UK. You might be aware of a range of technical standards, relevant to your industry, under the 'BS' designation. The BSI also offers independent quality assessment and certification for firms, under its Kitemark and CE schemes (which will be discussed further in Chapter 5).
- International standards are produced by organisations such as the International Standards Organisation (ISO) and the European Committee for Standardisation (CEN) in Western Europe. You may be familiar with the ISO 9000 series of standards on quality management systems, for example, or ISO 14001 on environmental management systems.

3.20 Lysons & Farrington urge purchasing staff to be aware of the major trade, national and international standards applicable to their industry and the items they buy regularly. The *advantages* of using standards are as follows.

- Clear specifications, no uncertainty or ambiguity as to requirement – and therefore less potential for error and conflict with suppliers
- Saving of the time and cost of preparing company specifications and related explanations and discussions
- Reduced time-to-market of finished product, because of reduced design time
- Accurate comparison of quotations, since all potential suppliers are quoting on the same specifications
- A wider range of potential suppliers, and less reliance on (more costly) specialist suppliers, because of the general application of the standard
- Saving of inventory and purchase costs, as a result of standardisation (in the sense of 'variety reduction'). The organisation may, where possible, use 'generic' or standard items instead of multiple lines of own-design or variant items: this should reduce stockholding, and enable the aggregation of orders (rather than multiple small orders of variant items), for bulk discounts and reduced transaction and materials handling costs.

3.21 The main *disadvantage* of using standards, however, is that – like any generic specification – they may not accurately reflect the buyer's requirements. They may also fail to reflect the very latest technology or practices, since it takes some years for standards to be developed and updated. Full harmonisation of standards internationally has not yet been achieved, so there may be complexities in using British or European standards in Asia, for example.

4 Performance specifications

4.1 A performance or functional specification is a relatively brief document (compared to a conformance specification) that defines the functionality, performance, outputs or outcomes to be achieved, including details of key input parameters. It does *not* (unlike a conformance specification) prescribe *how* the functionality, performance, outputs or outcomes are to be achieved (in terms of materials, designs and processes).

4.2 A performance specification would typically include the following content.

- The functionality, performance, capabilities, outputs or outcomes to be achieved, within specified tolerances
- The key process inputs which will contribute to performance, including available utilities (electricity, solar power and so on)
- The operating environment and conditions in which the performance is to be achieved (and extreme or unusual conditions in which it is *not* expected)
- How the product is required to interface with other elements of the process
- Required quality levels (including any relevant standards)
- Required health and safety levels and controls (including any relevant standards)
- Required environmental performance levels and controls (including any relevant standards)
- Criteria and methods to be used to measure whether the desired function, performance or outcomes have been achieved

4.3 The advantages and limitations of performance specifications were discussed in Section 2 of this chapter.

Output based specifications

4.4 The term 'output' or 'output-based' specification may be used to describe a functional or performance specification where the buyer wishes to specify the outputs of a system or process, such as:

- The deliverables of a project (eg in consultancy) or
- The outputs of a process.

4.5 Output specifications are commonly used in the procurement of IT projects (such as software or systems design and development) and systems (such as hardware and software). The specified outputs in such cases would typically consist of the kinds of data reports that users would be able to see (on screen) or print out when using the system. Similarly in a consultancy project, the specification might set out the scope of reports and analysis desired at the end of the process.

Typical sections of a specification

4.6 To ensure that specifications are developed in an efficient, comprehensive and consistent manner, **standard specification templates** are often used. For example, in the UK these are based on the British Standard 7373 series. This series covers the following aspects.

- BS 7373–1: Product specifications: Guide to preparation
- BS 7373–2: Product specifications: Guide to identifying criteria for a product specification and to declaring product conformity
- BS 7373–3: Product specifications: Guide to identifying criteria for specifying a service offering

4.7 BS 7373–1 recommends a basic structure for specifications: Table 4.2. Note that these are suitable for a major, complex specification document (such as might be appropriate for the procurement of equipment or engineering works): you wouldn't be expected to reproduce these in an exam.

Table 4.2 *A structure for developing specifications*

ITEM	CONTENT
Identification	Title, reference number, authority, designation, issue number and date
Circulation	Distribution list of the specification
Contents	List of parts, clauses, illustrations and annexes
Foreword	Reasons for writing the specification
Introduction	Summary of the business need and technical aspects of objectives
Scope	Range of objectives and content
Definitions	Terms used with special meanings in the text
Main body of the specification	Requirements, guidance and methods
Annexes	Additional detailed technical information and examples
Index	Alphabetical index
Bibliography	Details of internal and external standards and publications referred to in the specification

Specification in different industry sectors

4.8 The industry sectors in which different types of specification are most commonly used may be summarised (from a previous CIPS syllabus) as in Table 4.3.

Table 4.3 *Types of specification by industry sector*

TYPE OF SPECIFICATION	SECTORS IN WHICH COMMONLY USED
Blueprint/design	Engineering, projects, construction
Brand name	Small businesses, consumers
Sample	Textiles, commodities
Market grade	Commodity trades
Standards	Engineering, manufacturing
Performance/functional	Manufacturing, electronics and most sectors
Chemical/physical properties	Chemical engineering, engineering, construction
Outcome	Services, projects
Outputs	IT, consultancy and projects

4.9 Responsibility for specification, and the types of specification used, may vary in different contexts.

- *Manufacturers* will have a design or engineering section, producing product designs which include specifications for the parts and materials required to make the product. In assembly operations, these will mainly be technical specifications of various kinds, because many components or assemblies may be made or adapted especially for incorporation in a particular product. In other manufacturing contexts, composition specifications may be used.

- In *service* industries (insurance, banking, hotels and so on), requirements are set down in service specifications, incorporating service level agreements. (This is discussed in more detail below). The same would apply for manufacturing firms which outsource or buy in service functions (such as catering, logistics, IT support or premises management).

- *Distributive* industries (eg retailers and wholesalers) will specify the finished goods they require for sale to consumers. Finished goods might be specified by the distributor's marketing department by brand name or sample. Increasingly, however, major retailers specify detailed requirements for the production of own-branded products: these may be technical, sample or composition specifications (eg the ingredients to be used in food brands, their taste and appearance properties and so on).

5 Specifying services

Why services are different

5.1 So far, when we have discussed the sourcing requirements of organisations, we have lumped together products and services. But the fact is that, in many ways, they are not the same.

5.2 A service may be defined as 'any activity or benefit that one party can offer to another that is essentially intangible and does not result in ownership of anything' (Kotler). Some obvious examples include call-centre, cleaning, transport and logistics, and IT services: something is 'done for you', but there is no transfer of ownership of anything as part of the service transaction. (It is also worth remembering that some form of service is part of the 'bundle of benefits' you acquire when you purchase materials and goods: sales service, customer service, delivery, after-sales care, warranties and so on.)

5.3 Services (and service elements) present buyers with problems additional to those that arise in purchasing materials or manufactured goods, when it comes to specifying requirements.

- Goods are tangible: they can be inspected, measured, weighed and tested to check quality and compliance with specification. Services are *intangible*: specification of service levels – and subsequently checking whether or how far they have been achieved – is therefore fraught with difficulty. As Steve Kirby notes: 'How clean is clean? How long should it take to repair a computer? What is the definition of a well-cooked meal?'

- Goods emerging from a manufacturing process generally have a high degree of uniformity, which also simplifies their evaluation. Services are *variable*: every separate instance of service provision is unique, because the personnel and circumstances are different. It is hard to standardise requirements.

- Goods can be produced, purchased and stored in advance of need, for later consumption. Services are *inseparable* and *perishable*, provided in 'real time': they can't be provided first and consumed later. Transport, accommodation and catering services, for example, are only relevant when they are needed. Specifications therefore need to include the time of provision, so that the supplier can schedule provision accordingly.

- Goods can often be used anywhere, once purchased. Many services can only be performed in particular locations (eg accommodation provided at a hotel premises, cleaning provided at the buyer's offices). The service specification may therefore need to include explicit understandings about where the service is to be provided, the access required and related issues (such as confidentiality, if suppliers are working on the buyers' premises).

- The exact purpose for which a tangible good is used will usually be known, and its suitability can therefore be assessed objectively. It is harder to assess the many factors involved in providing a service: what weight should be placed on the friendliness or smart appearance of the supplier's staff, say, compared with the efficiency with which they get the job done?
- Goods are usually purchased for more or less immediate use, such as incorporation in a larger product, or onward sale. A service may be purchased for a long period, during which requirements may change from the original specification.

5.4   It is harder to draft accurate specifications for services than for goods, because of their intangible nature – and yet this makes it even more important, otherwise buyer and supplier could argue interminably as to whether the service was exactly what was asked for, or of an adequate standard. An advertising agency or architect might submit a design which meets all the client's stated criteria in regard to aims, inclusions, style and budget – but the client may still find it is not what he wanted or 'had in mind'. Who, if anyone, is at fault – and who pays for the second attempt?

Developing service specifications

5.5   The more work that can be done at the pre-contract stage, the better. This means agreeing service levels, schedules and the basis for charges in as much detail as possible before the contract is signed: disputes often stem from differing expectations on the part of buyer and supplier.

5.6   This is particularly vital if the organisation is outsourcing service functions currently performed by in-house staff. The organisation will typically seek to close down its internal service provision, disposing of equipment, redeploying or shedding staff and so on. Once this has been done, the supplier is in a strong position – and shouldn't be given the opportunity to renegotiate the contract on the basis that the original agreement was vague on details of the service to be offered.

5.7   The specification of services requires professional purchasing input, but it is equally important to involve user and beneficiary departments. For one thing, they are ideally placed (as customers) to help determine the level of service they require or expect; for another, involvement will help to secure 'buy in' and minimise later disputes.

5.8   Supplier management is also an important ingredient in successful service buying. Often the level of service agreed upon is expressed in terms which are difficult to measure: it is not like purchasing steel rods, which indisputably are – or are not – of the diameter or length specified. It is vital that from the earliest stages, the supplier is made aware of exactly what the buyer regards as satisfactory performance and exactly what will be regarded as unsatisfactory.

5.9   This is where service level agreements come in. SLAs will be discussed in Chapter 6, where we explore the use of contractual performance measures to ensure that goods and services supplied can be effectively evaluated for conformance with the specified business need.

5.10   BS 7373–3 provides comprehensive guidance for specifying a service offering including the formulation of service level agreements. The standard represents the process for delivering a service as two merging paths: Figure 4.1.

Figure 4.1 *Specifying a service*

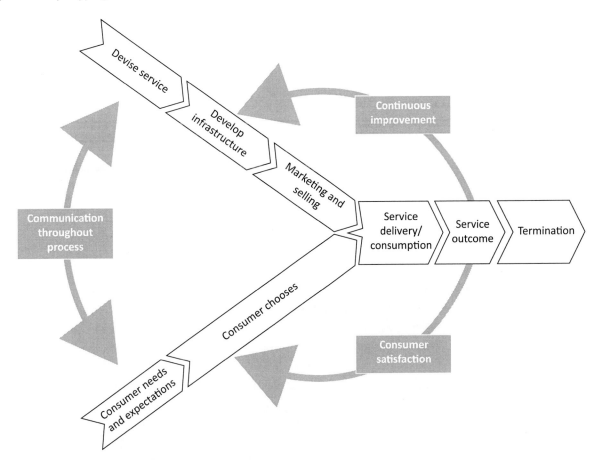

5.11   The upper path in the diagram represents the service provision and the associated infrastructure for the provider's organisation. The lower path represents features and service levels that will appeal to the consumer. These two paths come together at the point of service delivery with the objective of providing a value-added experience for both parties. The merging pathways will tend to be an iterative process of continuous improvement.

5.12   The standard argues that the process of preparing and developing a comprehensive service specification must take into account a range of considerations.

- Commercial
- Technical and infrastructure
- Consumer expectations
- Regulatory
- Ethical
- Consumer choice and experience
- Service outcome.

Outcome-based specification

5.13   The term 'outcome' specification is often used in service specification and commissioning, as the equivalent of a 'performance' or 'functional' specification for goods. In effect, the buyer specifies the outcomes to be met by the provider, perhaps with a budget within which to meet the outcomes. The provider has the responsibility of determining (in consultation with the service user) the activities that will be performed, and the standard to which they will be performed, in order to meet the outcomes. This differs from traditional service specification and commissioning, which focused on prescribing the activities to be performed, with timings and schedule attached. The approach is increasingly used in the public sector, in commissioning private or third sector organisations to deliver public services – ensuring that the public sector authority:

- Maximises the flexibility of the specification to secure the innovation and expertise available from service partners, while
- Maintaining the target outcomes of service provision.

6 Sustainable specification

6.1 As we mentioned in Chapter 1, sustainability has become an extremely important aspect of procurement policy in both the public and private sectors in recent years.

6.2 As a reminder, the 'Triple Bottom Line' concept argues that businesses should measure their performance (and develop business case justifications for projects and procurements) not just by profitability, but by how well they protect or further the interests of wider stakeholders, on three dimensions.

- **Economic sustainability (Profit)**: profitability, sustainable economic performance – and its beneficial effects on society (such as employment, access to goods and services, payment of taxes, community investment and so on)
- **Environmental sustainability (Planet):** sustainable environmental practices, which either benefit the natural environment or minimise harmful impacts upon it. This may include the reduction of pollution, wastes and emissions; repairing environmental damage and degradation; using renewable or recyclable materials and designs; reducing the use of non-renewable resources and energy; educating and managing supply chains to support environmental practices; and investing in 'green' projects such as renewable energy.
- **Social sustainability (People):** fair and beneficial business practices towards labour and the society in which the business operates. This may include: ethical treatment of employees; support for small and/ or local suppliers; support for diversity and equal opportunity in employment and supply chains; the development of skills; promoting public health; and 'giving back' to communities.

6.3 There are a number of significant sustainability issues in specification.

- The extent to which internal and external customer requirements can be steered in the direction of sustainability
- The extent to which specifications offer inclusion or exclusion of certain supplier groups (social sustainability)
- The extent to which environmental sustainability can be 'designed' in to products and services at the development and specification stage
- The extent to which the process of specification promotes efficient resource usage and adds economic value (an aspect of economic sustainability)

The sustainability of customer requirements

6.4 The primary focus of sustainable procurement activity in relation to consumer markets may be to anticipate and meet consumer demand for sustainable goods, services and processes – ideally, more swiftly, effectively and efficiently than competitors. Issues such as greenhouse gas emissions, energy consumption, animal testing and Fair Trade brands are currently front-of-awareness for many consumers, and the specification of products and services in these areas will, to a large extent, be led by market demand and risk.

6.5 The anticipation or stimulation of demand is primarily a marketing function, but procurement has a key role in the design and delivery of sustainable consumption solutions and offerings – which in turn help shift consumer norms and expectations.

6.6 For procurement, internal customer service (discussed in Chapter 1) most obviously involves fulfilling purchase requisitions and specifications drawn up by designers and users. However, a sustainable procurement orientation argues that buyers also need to partner with internal customers to support them in achieving corporate sustainability objectives. This may mean re-examining and challenging customer definitions of requirement – which may, or may not, be shaped by sustainability policies and priorities.

6.7 We will discuss the priorities of various internal stakeholders in product and service specification in Chapter 5. However, the formulation or review of purchase specifications is an ideal opportunity for demand review, asking:

- Does this item comply with or further the environmental, social and economic targets stated in the organisation's sustainable procurement policy?
- Is there a genuine operational need for this item (or this quantity of it)? Are demand forecasting methods accurate?
- Can the need be met from substitute items in stock, or by renting, leasing, sharing or refurbishing, rather than purchase?
- Could a lower specification (less resource-intensive) or a generic item be used without compromising functionality or performance?
- Could the item be used more efficiently?

Sustainable specifications

6.8 In addition to shaping the requirements of customers in the direction of sustainability, the procurement function will have to pursue sustainability in its *own* role as customer, in the specification of requirements. As a customer, the procurement function (and part-time buyers in user departments) will have to ensure that requirements are sustainable – and that they are defined and specified in a way that clearly communicates sustainability demands and expectations to suppliers.

6.9 Some of procurement's key objectives for sustainable specification may be as follows.

- To seek cost-effective (and where necessary, innovative) alternatives to environmentally or socially unsustainable materials, products and processes
- To minimise waste, including packaging, waste produced by the product (or service), and waste generated by the eventual disposal of the product
- To maximise the re-use and recycling of materials
- To ensure ethical and socially responsible trading and employment practices at all tiers of the supply chain
- To maximise access to contracts for small, diverse, local suppliers
- To maximise resource and cost efficiency in sourcing, supply and production processes.

6.10 Specification is particularly important for sustainable procurement in the public sector. EU Public Procurement Directives, for example, provide that environmental and social considerations should be built into the earliest stages of the procurement process – and opportunities to do this are limited, under competitive tendering rules, at the supplier selection and contract award stage (because of the definition of 'best value'). Design and specification thus offers the best opportunity to incorporate sustainable procurement criteria. We will suggest how this can be done in Chapter 5.

Chapter summary

- A specification describes a requirement, communicates it to a supplier, and provides a means of evaluating the supply when it is delivered. It is a core document in the contractual agreement with the supplier.
- A conformance specification details exactly what the required supply consists of. A performance specification details what the required supply must be able to do.
- Conformance specifications may be technical in nature, or may define chemical or physical properties, or may refer to a brand, a sample, a market grade or a standard.
- Preparing specifications is easier if standard templates are used.
- Services have characteristics that distinguish them from tangible goods. It is usually more difficult to specify a service than a tangible product.
- Nowadays, a specification will normally address sustainability issues (the Triple Bottom Line of profit, planet and people).

 ## Self-test questions

Numbers in brackets refer to the paragraphs where you can check your answers.

1   What are the roles of a specification? (1.4)

2   How may a buyer's work be affected in an environment of zero defects? (1.10)

3   List advantages and disadvantages of using specifications. (1.17, 1.19)

4   Distinguish between a conformance specification and a performance specification. (2.1)

5   Why are conformance specifications becoming less common? (2.2)

6   In what circumstances is it appropriate to use performance specifications? (2.5)

7   What are the advantages of technical specifications? (3.4)

8   What are the advantages of specifying by brand? (3.9)

9   List typical contents of a performance specification. (4.2)

10   List characteristics of services that distinguish them from tangible goods. (5.3)

11   What is meant by the 'Triple Bottom Line'? (6.2)

12   What are the objectives of a buyer in devising a sustainable specification? (6.9)

CHAPTER 5

Developing Effective Specifications

Assessment criteria and indicative content

 Explain the content of specifications for procurements

- Drafting specifications and developing market dialogue with suppliers
- The use of standards in specifications
- Standardisation of requirements versus increasing the range of products
- Including social and environmental criteria in specifications
- The role of information assurance in developing specifications

Section headings

1 Drafting specifications
2 Developing market dialogue
3 Information for specification development
4 Standardisation
5 Social and environmental criteria
6 Information assurance

Introduction

This chapter follows on from Chapter 4 in developing our coverage of the assessment criteria related to specifications. In Chapter 4 we covered some basic concepts and terminology in the content and use of specifications. In this chapter, we focus on the processes and decisions by which specifications are developed.

We look first at the process of specification development, and different approaches by which this can be organised, including the need for cross-functional input. We then look at the different contributions made by buyers and suppliers to the specification process – and what happens if buyers do not 'take control' of the process.

Finally, we look at a range of influences on specification development and decisions: the information required; the influence of company policy in various areas; and the need to manage risks associated with the exchange of commercial information.

1 Drafting specifications

Features of effective specifications

1.1 The process of preparing specifications is unlikely to be uniform in every case. This is true even within a single organisation, and even more so if one organisation is compared with another. We will look at some general principles in this chapter, but it is worth your looking for specific examples from your own work organisation and wider reading, to use as examples in the exam – or to help you interpret examples given in exam case study scenarios.

1.2   An effective specification, as we saw in Chapter 4, is one that is:

- Clear and unambiguous as to what is required
- Concise (not overly detailed: the shorter the specification, the less time and cost it takes to prepare)
- Comprehensive (covering all points of the requirement. As Lysons & Farrington note: 'If something is not specified, it is unlikely to be provided'. Suppliers will normally charge requirements added later as 'extras'.)
- Compliant with all relevant national or international standards, and health, safety and environmental laws and regulations
- Up-to-date (with current design solutions and supply market developments)
- Expressed in terms which can be understood by all key stakeholders (ie not too technical for suppliers or purchasers or users)
- Value-analysed: every additional requirement increases the price, so it is important to specify only requirements that positively add value.

Cross-functional contributions to specification

1.3   In most cases, the lead role in specification development is taken by users of the product (often designers or engineers) or service. After all, they may be most familiar with the requirement, and most technically 'savvy' about what is required. But this is not always the case.

- For many purchases, the process is relatively simple: the quality required is easy to define in terms of products widely available on the market. In such cases, it would be normal to leave the 'specification' (basically, ordering) to the procurement department.
- Another situation where the procurement function would usually have a free hand is in cases of purchases for internal use, rather than resale or incorporation into production. Examples cited by Baily *et al* (*Purchasing Principles and Management*) include factory seating and overalls.
- Procurement specialists may also take a lead role where they are technically expert in the product or category specified (eg knowledgeable about grades, standards and so on).

1.4   In less straightforward cases, however, the preparation of a specification may require cross-functional input, so that technical considerations are balanced with commercial ones.

1.5   **Design or engineering functions** will be well placed to contribute technical specifications. However, they may:

- Focus on features that maximise functional excellence (product orientation), or production efficiency (production orientation) – but contribute little or nothing to sales potential or customer satisfaction (marketing orientation) or sustainability (stakeholder orientation)
- Over-specify, with unnecessarily tight tolerances or non-value-adding functions, in pursuit of quality or engineering excellence – but at unnecessary cost
- Specify bespoke or custom-built items, when acceptable standard or generic items are available – again causing waste. This may arise from lack of knowledge of the supply market, or lack of attention to cost and value considerations.
- Specify for each new requirement, even where existing items could be used or adapted to the purpose – creating multiple stock items where one would do, and thus incurring unnecessary inventory, ordering costs and materials handling costs
- Write 'narrow' or 'closed' specifications, not permitting variations or alternatives, which may tie the buyer to a small supplier base, or one supplier – or which may be very difficult to source.

1.6   The **marketing function** may be able to contribute an important customer focus to the specification: seeking unique product or service features which will satisfy customer demands and gain competitive advantage for the firm, through product or service differentiation, premium pricing, reputational or brand strength and so on. However, marketing suggestions may not meet technical and cost criteria: customer-satisfying and customised features may be difficult to engineer and/or costly.

1.7 Reconciling these differences requires skilled management. Dobler and Burt (*Purchasing & Supply Management*) identify four major items that have to be brought into harmony.

- Design considerations of function
- Marketing considerations of consumer acceptance and satisfaction
- Manufacturing considerations of economical production
- Procurement considerations of markets, materials availability, supplier capability and cost.

1.8 **Procurement professionals** are in a good position to make the following contributions to the specification process.

- *Supply market awareness*: the availability of standard or generic items (for variety reduction), the availability of capable suppliers, the possibility of alternative suppliers and solutions (especially if expensive branded products are requisitioned), market prices, supply market risk factors, availability issues
- *Supplier contacts*, to discuss potential solutions in advance of specification, or to introduce pre-qualified suppliers to the design team (early supplier involvement), which may in turn improve technical specification
- Awareness of *commercial aspects* of purchases, eg the need to include requirements for just-in-time (low inventory) supply or supplier stockholding, response times, maintenance cover, spares availability, warranty periods and user training in the specification
- Awareness of *legal aspects* of purchases, eg the need to comply with national and international standards, and regulations on health and safety, environmental protection and (in the public sector) procurement methods
- Purchasing *disciplines*, for variety reduction, value analysis, cost reduction and so on. The buyer should be ready to discuss the real needs of the user, and to question desired performance levels or tolerances, to pursue gains in these areas. The greatest scope for cost reduction is at the design and specification stage.

Approaches to specification development

1.9 Dobler and Burt describe four possible approaches to organising the specification process.

- *Early buyer involvement (EBI)*. Management recognises from the outset that purchasing contacts and disciplines are important in product development. Purchasing specialists are involved in the product development team, on an advisory or full-time basis.
- *Formal committee approach*. Management recognises from the outset that preparing a specification is a matter of reconciling conflicting objectives. They appoint a committee with members representing each key stakeholder: design, engineering, production, marketing, quality management and procurement.
- *Informal approach*. Management emphasise the responsibility of all departments to consider both commercial and engineering factors. Buyers are encouraged to challenge the assumptions of users, and to suggest alternative methods and materials for consideration. Designers are encouraged to seek advice from buyers before going too far down any particular design path.
- *Purchasing co-ordinator approach*: a formalisation of the informal approach, with purchasing staff designated as 'liaison officers' to co-ordinate the required communication.

1.10 Whatever approach is used in preparing the specification, it is advisable to ensure controlled *signing off* procedures. Before a specification is released to a supplier, it must have the formal approval of the purchasing department and ideally the prior certification of the supplier. This reduces the common risk of changes being made in order to solve problems not envisaged at the time the specification was finalised. This precaution should then be followed up by ensuring that any changes which are deemed necessary are subjected to appropriate approval procedures and documented in writing.

2 Developing market dialogue

Who should drive the specification?

2.1 As we have seen, a key purpose of the specification is to describe the buyer's requirements. A specification driven by buyer-side requirements places the buyer clearly in control of the purchasing process.

- The supplier is left in no doubt as to what must be done to perform the purchase contract satisfactorily.
- Legally, goods supplied which fail to conform to the buyer's specification can be rejected and not paid for.

2.2 If the *supplier* drives the specification process, by defining what it can offer (eg in the case of specification by brand name or purchase from a product catalogue), or its solution to the requirement 'problem', the buyer takes on additional risks.

- The specification may be highly technical, based on the supplier's expertise, and may not be clearly understood by the buyer, or susceptible to meaningful measurement and evaluation.
- The requirement is defined in terms of what the supplier can offer, rather than what is actually needed (as defined by buyer-side designers, users and other stakeholders): the buyer may not get exactly what he wants or needs.
- The buyer will be unable legally to reject goods which are not suitable or relevant, but comply with specification: if he attempts to do so, he will be liable for a claim of breach of contract.

2.3 A specification should state clearly that it is a description of the buyer's requirements; what the acceptable tolerances are; and that no substitutes, alternatives or variations will be acceptable without the buyer's express agreement.

The buyer's role in specification

2.4 In general terms, the buyer's role in the specification process may include the following activities.

- *Understanding the needs of users*: ensuring that user requirements have been consulted (as the primary stakeholders in the purchase) – but also challenged, if necessary, to avoid over-specification and to promote variety and cost reduction.
- *Liaising with users*: working with users on the development of specifications (to add commercial know-how and disciplines); ensuring that users approve the final specification prior to contracting; communicating policies for user-department purchasing (eg using call-off contracts or framework agreements); working with users to monitor and measure compliance of the delivered goods or services with the specification; gathering feedback with users as to whether the specification meets the requirement or may need to be updated.
- *Minimising tolerances*: supporting quality management by ensuring that tolerances are minimised as far as possible, consistent with value added and cost incurred. For most engineering processes, the aim will now be 'zero defects' or 'get it right first time', which means negotiating and managing tight tolerances with suppliers – as well as within the production process of the buying organisation.
- *Understanding the legal implications of specification*: ensuring that the specification, and the contract upon which it is based, accurately and completely expresses users' requirements (minimising the risk of legal disputes and contract variations); and recommending performance rather than conformance specifications, where possible, in order to transfer legal liability for non-performance to the supplier.

2.5 As we saw earlier, there are significant benefits to involving purchasers at the specification stage – and potential problems if purchasing input is not taken into account. The term **early buyer involvement** (EBI) is used to describe a process whereby procurement specialists are involved in defining specifications – rather than merely turning specifications, prepared by users, into purchase orders. Where this is not the case, the procurement function may need to 'promote' its expertise and potential contribution, in order to obtain greater input.

2.6 Where EBI is implemented, procurement specialists may act in an advisory capacity to product development teams, or may be integrated into the project team on a full-time basis, or a purchasing co-ordinator may be allocated to the team to liaise with the purchasing department. Purchasing experts may provide the design and specification team with the following contributions.

- Input to make/do or buy decisions: which technologies should be kept or developed in-house and which should be outsourced
- Policy formulation for supplier involvement and internal purchasing
- Monitoring of supply markets for technological developments
- Pre-selection of suppliers for involvement in the development project
- Supplier relationship management
- Ordering and expediting of samples and prototypes from suppliers
- Information on new products and technologies already available or being developed
- Suggestion of alternative suppliers, products or technologies that could yield greater value
- Evaluation of product designs in terms of part availability, manufacturability, lead time, quality and costs
- Promotion of standardisation, variety reduction and simplification

The supplier's role in specification

2.7 The concept of **early supplier involvement** (ESI) is that organisations should involve prospective or preferred suppliers at an early stage in the product or service development and innovation process: ideally, as early as the conceptual design stage, although this is not always practical. This contrasts with the traditional approach, whereby the supplier merely provides feedback on a completed product design specification.

2.8 The main purpose of ESI is to enable a pre-qualified supplier (with proven supply and technical abilities) to contribute technical expertise which the buying organisation may lack, by making proactive suggestions to improve product or service design, or to reduce the costs of production. There are numerous ways in which suppliers can contribute to the product development process. For example, they can provide constructive criticism of designs, and suggest alternative materials or manufacturing methods at a time when engineering changes are still possible.

2.9 Dobler and Burt cite numerous areas where supplier expertise can benefit the buyer: material specifications; tolerances; standardisation or variety reduction; economic order sizes to reduce costs; packaging and transportation requirements for the product; inventory levels (taking into account lead times); potential changes required in the supplier's manufacturing and/or the buyer's assembly processes to maximise quality or achieve cost savings.

2.10 In service contracting, it is common for the potential service provider to collaboratively develop and negotiate service specifications and service level agreements as part of a cross-functional team with users and purchasers.

2.11 The benefits to be gained from ESI have mainly focused on relatively short-term organisational gains via more accurate and achievable technical specifications, improved product quality, reduction in development time, and reduction in development and product costs. However, there may also be some long-term benefits. ESI can, for example, be a catalyst for long-term partnership relationships with excellent suppliers. It can also improve the buyer's understanding about technological developments in the supply market, with potential for further exploitation.

2.12 As with most approaches, practitioners also need to be aware of potential drawbacks. The product or service may be designed around the supplier's capabilities, which (a) may be limiting, and (b) may lock the buyer into a supply relationship. This may become a problem if the supplier becomes complacent and ceases to deliver the quality or innovation he once did – or if market developments present better alternatives. In addition, ESI may pose confidentiality and security issues (eg the risk of leakage of product plans to competitors).

3 Information for specification development

3.1 If a purchaser (or cross-functional team) is asked to prepare a specification for a product or service, what information will they need to do this effectively? This is not quite the same question as 'what information will go into the specification?' (which we discussed in Chapter 4). It concerns the information that will have to be gathered to support the decisions and choices that go into drawing up the specification.

Technical requirements

3.2 The first and most basic information to be gathered is the precise technical requirements of the product or service to be purchased. As we have seen, in our discussion of technical specifications, this may include:

- Intended function or performance: what the product or service must be able to do
- Conditions under which the product or service will be required to operate, be transported, handled and stored
- Measures of quality and performance (which will be discussed further in Chapter 6 on KPIs)
- Tolerances for reliability, quality, dimension, strength and other key properties
- Features: texture, colour, aesthetics, finishing and other external properties
- Durability (the useful life of the product) and serviceability (speed, ease and cost of maintenance)
- Information provided with the product or service (eg operating, maintenance and safety instructions).

3.3 This information will come primarily from the designers, engineers and users of a product, or the users of a service, who are likely to be most expert in their own needs. Input may also be sought from other sources.

- Suppliers of goods and services, who may have additional technical expertise
- In-house providers of a service (if the service is being outsourced)
- Third party experts (eg engineering, IT, systems design, security or logistics consultants)
- Industry contacts, such as other firms using similar products or services – and even competitors (eg by 'reverse engineering' or analysing the composition and functionality of their successful products)
- Industry, national and international standards, which set out technical requirements for a range of items used for different purposes.

Availability of commercial products or services

3.4 Potential sources of supply may be useful information at this stage because:

- If there are no (or few, or inaccessible) existing sources of supply, the technical specification may need to be reviewed for feasibility
- If there is a reliable and high-quality source of supply, it may be possible to involve the supplier in the specification, to improve the quality of supply market information (early supplier involvement)
- Users may have specified items to be manufactured specially to their design ('bespoke' or 'made to order' items), while a survey of the potential supply market may identify a readily available commercial or standard item which will do the job just as well. Commercial products and services are more quickly accessed and less costly (because they do not include customisation and development costs, and because there may be more than one supplier, allowing price negotiation).

Schedules and lead times

3.5 The specification writer will need to know what the 'timeline' for the development and sourcing project is: when a potential supplier will need to be consulted; when final feedback from stakeholders will be gathered; when the specification will need to be signed off; when prototypes or samples will need to be ordered and delivered; when the requirement will be put up for quotation or tender, and the closing date for quotations or tenders to be received; when contracts or orders will need to be finalised; and – of course – when supplies will be required (in order to specify delivery dates).

3.6   The specification writers will need to gather information about the following aspects.

- The deadline for delivery of the supplies, or commencement or delivery of the services (in consultation with users and operational plans)
- The lead time for ordering, production, testing, inspection and delivery of the supplies, or development and delivery of the services (in consultation with suppliers and logistics providers) – and therefore
- The latest date at which a purchase contract or order will need to be finalised.

3.7   A range of time line, scheduling and lead time information may be included in the specification (eg turn-around and response times).

Costs and budgetary constraints

3.8   Cost pressures and expenditure budgets are key constraints on specifications. If purchasing's priority is to control or reduce costs, it may have to challenge users' tendency to customise and add variety, to over-specify features and quality, to minimise tolerances and/or to insist on swift response times, and to choose expensive branded models. All these things cost more, and in times of recession, such as the present, the priority may be to reduce costs at the expense of specified quality, speed, customisation and supplier flexibility.

Supplier processes

3.9   The processes used by potential suppliers to source, manufacture and deliver products or services also represent important information for developing a specification.

- Suppliers' process capability and expertise may suggest opportunities for quality improvements or cost savings, which can be built into the specification.
- Shortcomings in suppliers' processes may create a risk that specified quality and service levels will not be able to be met consistently. This may affect the choice of supplier, or the extent of monitoring and inspection that will be required.
- Suppliers' processes may present compliance or reputational risk, in areas such as environmental manufacturing or corporate social responsibility. The specification may need to build in controls or improvement targets in regard to pollution, energy use or waste disposal, say, or the ethical treatment of employees. Otherwise, the buyer may find its own reputation tarnished by association with the supplier.

Company policy

3.10   A range of internal company policies and external legislation, regulation and standards may impact on the development of purchasing specifications. Specification writers may have to take these factors into account – and specifications may also refer specifically to them, in order to identify minimum acceptable standards of practice or performance.

3.11   The buying organisation may have a wide range of policies embracing areas such as:

- Its intention to comply with all relevant laws, regulations, standards, codes of practice and best practice benchmarks: these may be referred to in specifications
- Its aspirations for environmental sourcing and manufacture. For example, there may be recycling policies (dictating that recyclability and reverse logistics be built into specifications); policies for the minimisation of greenhouse gas (GHG) emissions (dictating that minimal non-renewable energy use

be built into specifications); or sustainable supply policies (so that specifications require the use of sustainably managed raw materials, say).

- Its aspirations for corporate social responsibility and ethical trading. For example, specifications may require ethical sourcing of raw materials by suppliers, or ethical treatment of supplier employees (particularly in low-cost labour economies), or above-minimum standards of product health and safety.

- Sourcing policies, which may dictate that specifications are put up to tender, or are sufficiently 'open' to give opportunities to small or local suppliers, say, or whether the organisation favours early buyer involvement (EBI) and/or early supplier involvement (ESI).

- Quality, cost and pricing policies, which may dictate the relative priority given to quality, time and cost in specification decisions.

Legislation

3.12   Law and regulation places certain requirements on products and services which may need to be taken into account in developing specifications. Here are some examples.

- Quality standards and tolerances required to be *accredited* by various national and international quality standards, or to receive the European Community (CE) quality mark (discussed later in the chapter)

- Quality standards and tolerances required for *product safety*, under health and safety and consumer protection legislation and industry codes of practice (eg the strength, flexibility or weight-bearing capacity of construction materials; the chemical composition of materials to avoid health hazards; the restriction of ingredients such as additives in food products)

- Controls on the use, storage and transport of *substances and materials* which may be dangerous to health (eg chemicals, poisons, lead paint, asbestos, flammable or explosive materials, corrosive materials such as acids). Examples include the UK's COSHH (Control of Substances Hazardous to Health) and CHIPS (Chemicals: Hazard Information and Packaging for Supply) Regulations.

- *Environmental protection* law and regulation, dealing with issues such as the safe disposal or recyclability of waste and end-of-life products (including electrical and electronic waste and batteries).

3.13   Suppliers should be expected to be knowledgeable about, and compliant with, legislation relevant to their industry and products. However, the buyer is still liable in law if he incorporates outlawed materials or components in his products. One high-profile case study is the problems encountered by global toy company Mattel, which was forced to recall millions of toys, manufactured under licence in China, because the contractors had purchased paint contaminated with banned levels of lead, from unauthorised suppliers.

3.14   Buyers should therefore take proactive steps to:

- Draw the specification team's attention to known legal requirements
- Draw suppliers' attention to known legal requirements – especially if the law in the suppliers' country of operation is different from that of the buyer
- Implement their own compliance checks (audits, monitoring and inspection) on suppliers and supplies
- Use suppliers which are certified under quality and environmental standards, or encourage favoured suppliers to become so certified.

4   Standardisation

Specification by standards

4.1   Standards are documents that stipulate or recommend minimum levels of performance and quality of goods and services. Like market grades, they offer a 'short-hand' method of specifying common requirements for common products and services – and for the processes used in their production and delivery (eg environmental management and quality management).

4.2　The British Standards Institution (BSI) describes a standard as 'a published specification that establishes a common language, and contains a technical specification or other precise criteria, and is designed to be used, consistently, as a rule, a guideline, or a definition'. Standardisation is a voluntary process, based on consensus among different stakeholders such as:

- National and international standardisation organisations, led globally by the International Standards Organisation (ISO)
- National public authorities
- Industry and business associations, including representatives of SMEs
- Non-governmental organisations (NGOs)
- Scientific and academic organisations.

4.3　The buyer can simply specify that supplies be compliant with a given standard, or that the supplier's processes be accredited under a given standard scheme. We discussed this in Chapter 4.

Quality standards and processes

4.4　External quality standards may impact on specifications in various ways. The organisation may:

- Use standards as a convenient method for specifying quality, safety and performance levels, parameters and tolerances (as recognised above)
- Raise its performance to comply with quality and/or environmental management standards, both to enhance its own quality performance and to *demonstrate* capability (in order to inspire confidence in consumers) by seeking accreditation or certification under recognised quality schemes
- Require or encourage suppliers to comply with quality management standards, to support and demonstrate the quality performance of its supply chain.

4.5　If products are verified as complying with national or international quality or safety standards, they are eligible to carry various 'marks' which are a declaration of compliance (for the reassurance of consumers), and may be compulsory for goods or packaging for sale within the UK or EU in some cases.

- The British Standards Institution (BSI) 'Kitemark', for example, may be carried by products which have been produced in compliance with a particular British Standard, usually relating to health and safety.
- Particular marks may be applied for particular standards. For example, the 'Lion Mark' indicates that toys have been made to the current British and EU standards (BS EN 71), following the industry code of practice.
- The CE (European Community) mark represents a declaration *by the manufacturer* or his authorised representative that the requirements of relevant EU regulations have been complied with: ie that the products satisfy essential quality and/or safety requirements and that this has been verified by the use of competent testing and assessment procedures.

4.6　There are also various international standards for **quality management systems**, under which the organisation can seek certification. Here are some examples.

- The European Foundation for Quality Management's Excellence Model® (promoted in the UK as 'Business Excellence' by the British Quality Foundation): a total quality model, used as a world-class benchmark for quality management
- The International Standards Organisation (ISO) 9000 series of standards on establishing and maintaining quality management systems
- ISO 14001: the standard for establishing and maintaining environmental management systems – systems for assessing and minimising the impact of the organisation's operations on the environment
- Publicly Available Specification (PAS) 2050, published by the BSI, to help organisations to assess their greenhouse gas (GHG) emissions and manage their 'carbon footprint' to minimise contribution to industry-caused global warming

4.7   Organisations may use the standards frameworks as a benchmark for planning and improving their own (or their suppliers') quality management systems, or they may seek certification to demonstrate compliance to customers and clients.

Standardisation and variety reduction

4.8   The term 'standardisation' may also be used to mean variety reduction: the reduction of unnecessary variations in specified items to fulfil requirements – as opposed to increasing the range and variety of procured and stocked items.

4.9   The term 'stock proliferation' is given to the tendency for organisations to accumulate increasing numbers of similar – but slightly different – stock or production items, over time. It refers to an increase in the *range* of stock items, not the quantity of stock held. For example, a manufacturer might hold a large number of fasteners, all performing essentially the same function – but with slight differences in specification.

4.10   Unnecessary stock proliferation is highly undesirable, because the organisation ends up carrying more stock than it needs to. This leads to various adverse consequences.

- Unnecessary stockholding and handling costs, as additional variants are stocked
- Unnecessary specification costs (developing variant specifications) and transaction costs (identifying and contracting suppliers for the variant items, where a pre-qualified supplier or catalogue item would meet the need)
- Multiple small orders of variant items, with higher transaction costs, lost opportunities for bulk discounts and economies of scale
- The risk of lower quality, owing to the variability associated with small volumes and multiple variants
- The risk of waste, owing to the obsolescence, deterioration or damage of infrequently used items in storage.

4.11   Various causes of stock proliferation may be identiifed.

- One cause, as we have suggested, is user preference: technical and engineering personnel or research and development personnel might have different ideas about which item is 'right' for projects in which they are involved.
- A similar cause is staff turnover: new staff may requisition or order items according to their own preferences, even though very similar items are already in stock.
- The individuals or functions developing specifications may not make the effort to establish whether similar items are already used within the organisation, or whether the business need can be met using stocked or generic items.
- The organisation's inventory management information system may make it difficult to establish what items are already in use.

4.12   There are essentially two methods of minimising stock proliferation: standardisation and variety reduction.

- *Standardisation* involves agreeing and adopting generic specifications or descriptions of the items required.
- *Variety reduction* is a systematic rationalisation or reduction in the range of items used, stocked, bought or made.

4.13   A **proactive approach** to variety reduction means that, where possible, the organisation is committed to using standardised components and parts to make end products that are dissimilar in appearance and performance: in other words, it uses the smallest range of inputs to produce the widest range of products. Among other requirements (such as senior management commitment), this requires input from procurement and stores staff, at the specification stage, to challenge, question and justify non-standard requirements in meeting the business need.

4.14 A **reactive or remedial approach** to variety reduction is undertaken periodically by a specialist team comprising relevant stakeholders. The team examines a range of stock items to determine:

- The use for which each item is intended
- How many stock items have similar characteristics, functionality and purposes
- The extent to which similar items can be given a standard specification or description
- The extent to which similar items can be substituted for each other
- What range of variant characteristics is essential (eg in regard to different sizes of a part or component)
- How frequently each item in the range is used
- Which items may be eliminated or substituted.

4.15 Standard specifications can then be drawn up for the (smaller) list of items which remain (principally those regarded as essential or frequently used). Suppliers' standard parts and materials should be specified where possible (in preference to bespoke or customised items); and acceptable quality and safety levels should be established using published standards where possible.

4.16 In addition to challenging variant requisitions and specifications as they occur, a proactive standardisation and variety reduction project may therefore involve procurement staff working with engineers and designers to:

- Identify opportunities for using standard parts across a range of finished outputs
- Identify opportunities to reduce the number of standard parts used.

4.17 Dobler and Burt *(Purchasing and Materials Management)* cite the example of a manufacturer using 27 different types of lubricating greases in the maintenance of machinery. It turned out on review that each of these greases could be used for several different applications, which meant that the company was able to reduce the number of greases held in stock to just six.

Benefits of standardisation

4.18 The standardisation of procured items offers potential for efficiencies and cost savings in several areas.

- Specification: eg specifying generic items rather than more costly bespoke, own-design or variant items; specifying stocked or registered items rather than new buys (minimising procurement costs)
- Purchasing: eg enabling the consolidation of requirements (rather than multiple small orders of variant items), to take advantage of bulk discounts and reduced transaction and materials handling costs
- Transport: eg enabling the use of standard load and container sizes to enable inter-modal transport and efficient load planning
- Inventory: eg through reduced storage space requirements, and reduced risks of obsolescence and deterioration, for slow-moving or little-used variant items
- Quality management: eg making it easier to inspect and measure quality and conformance, since there is less variety and variation in the expectations and standards applied; and improving supplier relationship management (with a rationalised supplier base)

5   Social and environmental criteria

5.1 The importance of environmental, ethical and corporate social responsibility (CSR) criteria in defining requirements and selecting suppliers has been highlighted by a number of high-profile cases, in which a buying organisation's reputation and brand have been damaged by the exposure of poor ethical, environmental or labour practice by their first – or even lower – tier suppliers.

5.2 One example is the reputational damage suffered by social charity Oxfam, as a result of revelations that overseas producers of its 'Make Poverty History' wristbands were exploiting workers. More recently, consumer electronics icon Apple faced consumer pressure over press reports of long working hours and exploitative terms at the plants of some of its Chinese contractors, in some cases leading to worker suicides.

5.3 As we saw in Chapter 4, 'sustainability' may be used as an umbrella term for a number of criteria related to issues such as the supplier's management of environmental impacts; sustainable resource consumption; compliance with environmental protection law and regulation; ethical trading and labour and employment practices; policies for corporate social responsibility and ethical conduct; and reputation management (to avoid the buyer's reputation being put at risk by exposure of the unethical or irresponsible conduct of the supplier).

Environmental criteria

5.4 Environmental criteria inserted in specifications (and supplier pre-qualification questionnaires and appraisals) might include the following.

- Location in relation to the buyer and lower tiers of supply (which has implications for transport impacts)
- The use of less, and 'greener' (environmentally friendly), materials and packaging
- 'Green' design and innovation capability (eg design for disassembly, recycling or energy efficiency); reverse logistics and recycling capability; and so on
- The development and enforcement of strong environmental policies eg re resource efficiency (managed use of non-renewable and scarce resources), carbon footprint reduction (reduced transport miles and energy use), reduction of waste to land-fill and so on – both within the supplier and throughout its supply chain
- Robust environmental management systems – perhaps including certification under ISO 14001 environmental standards, Eco-Management and Audit Scheme (EMAS) or equivalents
- Compliance with environmental protection and emissions law and regulation in the country of operation

5.5 **ISO14000** is a series of international standards focusing on environmental management systems (EMS). An EMS gives an organisation a systematic process for assessing and managing its impact on the environment. The standard is designed to help develop such a system, as well as providing a supporting audit and review programme. The major requirements for an EMS under ISO14001 include the following.

- An environmental policy statement, including commitment to prevent pollution, improve environmental performance, and comply with all legal requirements
- Identification of all aspects of the organisation's activities that could impact on the environment
- Performance objectives and targets for environmental performance
- Implementation of an EMS to meet those objectives and targets, including employee training, instructions, procedures etc
- Periodic auditing and review, with corrective and preventive action taken where necessary

5.6 The **European Eco-Management and Audit Scheme (EMAS)** is a voluntary EMS certification process created under European Community regulations. Certification under EMAS can be obtained by an organisation or site which has an ISO 14001 certification and, in addition:

- Issues a public, externally verified report on its environmental performance
- Has a verified environmental audit programme in place
- Has no apparent failures of regulatory compliance.

5.7 **Publicly Available Specification (PAS) 2050** was launched in 2008 by the British Standards Institution (BSI). It builds on existing methods established through ISO 14040/14044, by specifying requirements for the assessment of greenhouse gas (GHG) emissions arising from products across their lifecycle, from initial sourcing of raw materials through manufacture, transport, use and ultimately recycling or waste.

5.8 The standard is designed to help organisations and consumers to understand the 'carbon footprint' of goods and services, and may also be used for a variety of processes for analysing, improving, comparing and communicating the carbon footprint performance of products and services. For organisations, PAS 2050:

- Supports internal assessment of the lifecycle GHG emissions of their goods and services
- Facilitates the evaluation of alternative product designs, sourcing and manufacturing methods, raw material choices and supplier selection, on the basis of GHG emissions
- Provides a benchmark for programmes aimed at reducing GHG emissions
- Allows for comparison of goods or services on the basis of GHG emissions
- Supports reporting (and promotion) on corporate social and environmental responsibility.

CSR and social sustainability criteria

5.9 Social responsibility, ethical criteria and labour standards might include:

- The development of robust CSR policies and ethical codes
- Location in relation to the buyer (as part of the buyer's policy of support for local suppliers and communities)
- Evidence of responsible and ethical labour policies and practices – including fair terms and conditions of work, provisions for worker health and safety, equal opportunity and diversity
- Evidence of, and commitment to, conformance to relevant legislation and regulations: eg re workplace health and safety, product safety and labelling, working hours, transport of dangerous goods, equal opportunity in employment – and so on, as relevant to the specification
- Compliance with International Labour Organisation standards (eg on supporting worker rights, upholding equality and diversity, and eradicating child and slave labour)
- Evidence of ethical trading policies and practices: supporting diverse suppliers, paying fair prices (particularly in low-cost-labour markets), and not abusing power in supply relationships
- Compliance with Fair Trade standards, or membership of the Ethical Trading Initiative
- Commitment to transparency and improvement, in collaboration with the buyer (eg willingness to undergo monitoring and evaluation of ethical and CSR policies by the buyer; willingness to identify lower-tier suppliers, so the buyer can 'drill down' through the supply chain, and so on).

Sustainable specification

5.10 Requisitions, stock replenishment orders and bills of materials will typically be formulated by user departments or inventory managers. However, as we have seen, procurement professionals may have input to requirement identification, definition and specification as part of an early buyer involvement policy, co-opting their commercial and supply market knowledge to design and development processes. They may also refer requisitions back to the originator: for clarification, or to challenge over-specification or unnecessary variation, or to suggest alternatives that will offer better sustainability benefits (including better quality or lower price) than the item requisitioned.

5.11 The need definition and specification stage of the procurement process offers the strongest opportunity to embed sustainability principles proactively throughout the sourcing process. This may be approached prescriptively by the buying organisation: eg specifying sustainability requirements for products and services. Or it may be approached more flexibly, by communicating the organisation's sustainability objectives and targets, and inviting suppliers to suggest potentially innovative solutions.

5.12 Specification or definition of requirement is an ideal opportunity to ask questions relevant to sustainability.

- Does the item further the environmental, social and economic targets stated in the organisation's sustainable procurement policy?
- Is the item really needed (or needed in this quantity)? Is a buy or re-buy needed, or are usable items in stock? The sustainable option is to use and purchase less.

- Could a lower (less resource-intensive) specification be used without compromising functionality or performance? Could a generic commercial item be used instead of a bespoke item?
- Does the item as requisitioned or specified comply with relevant environmental criteria? Is it classed as an 'environmentally preferred product': one which has a lesser or reduced effect on human health and the environment when compared with competing products or services that fulfil the same function? (Is it, for example, made of re-used, recycled or renewable materials? Does it minimise waste, pollution and GHG emissions, and/or conserve energy or water? Is it effectively but minimally packaged?)
- Can the item be sourced from local, small or diverse suppliers – or does the specification unnecessarily exclude them?
- What is the 'whole-life cost' of the item? What are its running costs, taking into account energy and resource efficiency, consumables, maintenance, spares and usable life span? What costs may be incurred in staff training, health and safety and so on?
- Will the product require special disposal arrangements, or cause environmental impacts on disposal (eg paints, solvents and oils)? Can the product be re-used or recycled once it is obsolete? Is it biodegradable in land-fill?
- If a brand or supplier is specified, how sustainable are the supplier's processes (environmental management, labour and supply chain management and so on)?

5.13 The principles of the UK waste hierarchy (Reduce; Re-use; Recycle; Rethink) may offer a useful framework for discussion with internal customers: Table 5.1.

Table 5.1 *The UK waste hierarchy*

Reduce	• Ensure products are definitely needed • Ensure products are fit for purpose to avoid wasteful mistakes • Ensure products are durable and covered by a long warranty • Ensure packaging is the minimum necessary for protection • Avoid disposable products designed for single use
Re-use	• Check for redundant equipment that could be redeployed • Specify goods that are repairable and easily upgraded • Specify goods with clear and comprehensive maintenance, repair and operating instructions, supported with guaranteed stocks of parts • Give preference to suppliers that operate take-back schemes for end of life equipment and packaging
Recycle	• Specify products made from recovered or recyclable materials • Purchase products on which the materials are identified for ease of recycling • Minimise mixed-material products which are more difficult to recycle
Rethink	• Re-evaluate precedents and assumptions • Consider and evaluate options and alternatives • Consider consortium buying, if required, to gain sufficient buying power to promote sustainable performance among suppliers.

5.14 Specifications will increasingly set performance-based standards or requirements (if not conformance-based prescriptions) for issues such as the following.

- Materials to be used in manufacture of purchased components, subassemblies or finished items: preferred sustainable materials and/or excluded unsustainable materials – or sustainability standards, attributes or functionality to be attained by materials (compliance with national and international standards, recyclability, biodegradability, renewable, sustainably managed, low-GHG emission, non-toxic)
- Processes and standards to be used in manufacture: eg ethical product testing (not tested on animals), certified environmental management systems (eg ISO 14001), quality management systems (eg ISO 9000), GHG emissions control, health and safety and labour standards
- Sourcing and supply chain management processes: eg ethically sourced materials or products, Fair Trade certification, ethical and environmental supplier monitoring and management (to avoid risks

arising from lower tiers of the supply chain)

- Logistics, transport and delivery requirements: eg transport planning and fleet management and maintenance for reduced fuel use and emissions; warehouse health and safety; location of distribution hubs to minimise community and environmental impacts and so on.

5.15 These issues may, alternatively, be set out in the broader definition of requirements (eg in tender documentation, requests for quotation, pre-qualification checklists and contract negotiations), to which product or service specifications are appended.

Sustainable specification across sectors and industries

5.16 You should be able to identify some of the key sustainable specification criteria for different types of materials and products – and therefore priority areas for different industries and organisations (which may form the context for case study questions). Here are some examples.

- Vehicles: fuel efficiency
- Paper: recycled, chlorine-free, sustainable forestry management
- Office equipment: energy efficient, clean manufacturing processes, safety, end-of-life take-back
- Energy: renewable
- Food and beverage: organic, fresh or seasonal, hygienic processes, minimised packaging, sustainable water management

Sustainable specification in public sector procurement

5.17 In the public sector, under the EU Public Procurement Directives and the Public Contracts Regulations 2015, contracts over a certain value threshold (to which the directives apply) must be awarded on the basis of competitive tender, using objective award criteria. In order to ensure fair competition, and competitive value for money, buyers are generally obliged to award contracts on the basis of:

- Lowest price *or* (more commonly)
- Most economically advantageous tender (MEAT).

5.18 In relation to non-price (eg environmental and social sustainability) criteria:

- Lowest price and MEAT criteria for contract award allow issues such as resource consumption and disposal costs, for example, to be taken into account. Social or environmental sustainability criteria used must be related directly to the subject-matter of the contract, appropriately weighted.
- Public bodies can specify sustainable award criteria. It is possible, for example, to specify recycled paper or energy-efficient IT equipment. Fair Trade options can be 'welcomed' – and an authority might require caterers to supply fair trade coffee or tea products, for example, as this would not affect competition between caterers.
- EU rules do not permit preference being given to any sector of suppliers such as local suppliers, minority-owned businesses or SMEs. The 2015 Regulations, however, remove some *obstacles* that might prevent such groups from competing for public business. This might be done by, for example, ensuring they are aware of where opportunities will be advertised and making tendering documentation and procedures as simple as possible for all suppliers.
- Authorities *must* seek explanations from suppliers which submit a tender that appears to be abnormally low and unsustainable: if the low price is the result of a breach of relevant social and environmental law the authority *must* reject the tender; if the low price is the result of state aid the authority *may* reject the tender if the supplier is unable to prove that the aid is compatible with the rules of the EU Treaty
- The best opportunity to incorporate sustainability criteria is therefore at the need definition, specification and pre-qualification stages of the procurement cycle – and through post-contract negotiated improvement agreements.

6 Information assurance

What is information assurance?

6.1 Information assurance (IA) is the practice of managing risks related to the use, processing, storage, and transmission of information or data, and the systems and processes used for those purposes. It is related to the field of 'information security' (a branch of computer science aimed at the protection of information systems and their contents, mainly by applying security controls and defences against malicious attacks). However, information assurance embraces a wider range of issues.

- Corporate governance: regulatory standards compliance, internal controls and auditing in regard to data protection, IT systems and fraud prevention
- Contingency, business continuity and disaster recovery planning in relation to key systems risks (data loss, security breaches, systems breakdown)
- Strategic development and management of IT systems to fulfil the current and future needs of the organisation (and supply chain), while minimising risk, through areas such as systems integration, compatibility, flexibility and security.

6.2 A typical IA project will involve the following steps.

- **Systematic risk assessment:** identification of information assets to be protected; identification of vulnerabilities in information assets and systems; identification of threats capable of exploiting or damaging the information assets; probability and impact analysis of identified risks.
- **Risk management planning:** proposing counter-measures to 'treat' identified risks, including prevention, detection and response to threats. These may include technical tools such as access control systems; password protection and user IDs; firewalls and anti-virus software; data encryption; data back-up protocols; the use of 'cloud' computing services; employee training in data security awareness; or the resourcing of specialist IT security departments or incident response teams. Proposed plans are tested for feasibility and cost/benefit analysed.
- **Agreement, implementation, testing and evaluation** of the risk management plan. Performance data is gathered and reviewed on an ongoing basis, so that the risk management plan can be continually revised in the light of performance gaps or emerging risks, as required.

Information-related risks in specification

6.3 As information and knowledge become increasingly systemised and transparent, so it becomes more vulnerable. A number of risks may arise from knowledge and information systems, including supplier and inventory databases; the advertisement of requirements; and the sharing of specification data, plans and intellectual property (eg designs, blueprints, samples and prototypes) with suppliers, via documentation or the corporate extranet.

6.4 Here are some of the information-related risks which might be identified by IA, in relation to specification.

- Risks to the organisation's intellectual capital from unauthorised access to specifications, designs, blueprints, samples or prototypes (eg industrial espionage, hacking and data theft); and poor implementation of confidentiality protocols, user IDs, passwords, firewalls and other protections to control access
- Risks to the organisation's intellectual capital and commercial advantage due to misuse of specification data by parties with whom it was shared (eg breach of confidentiality, sharing of specification data with competitors); and poor use of contractual protections to prevent this from happening
- Risks to the integrity and security of data, through a range of factors including software corruption; computer viruses; input or transcription errors; or deliberate fraud (eg manipulating specifications to favour a particular supplier, or to disguise fraudulent stock valuations); exacerbated by poor house-keeping and internal controls

- Risks to the integrity and value of specification data eg through poor updating and change control protocols (resulting in multiple conflicting versions), poor inventory record keeping and ineffective inventory coding systems (eg lack of significant coding, which disguises stock proliferation)
- Risks and inefficiencies in the design and implementation of management information systems, specifications databases, inventory systems, extranets and other relevant systems: eg inefficient storage and retrieval protocols; lack of integration and compatibility with supplier systems; teething problems; and systems breakdown
- Turnover of key personnel and loss of their intellectual property (where relevant) and/or knowledge of the organisation's procurement needs, supply market, stock or technical specifications
- Loss of organisational knowledge, information and capabilities through the outsourcing of functions to external suppliers.

6.5 With the increasing use of the internet, extranets and intranets in supply chain relationship management, it is ever more crucial to exert control over the corporation's information assets, knowledge and intellectual property.

6.6 A range of measures may therefore be put in place, as part of an information assurance plan, in areas such as the following.

- Ensuring that systems containing specification, contract and other potentially sensitive commercial data are subject to robust access controls (eg passwords, user IDs and firewalls) – and that 'human mediate' information exchanges (eg early supplier involvement discussions) are subject to confidentiality guarantees
- Protocols for the protection of data security in the use of information systems (eg the use of firewalls and anti-virus software, and the training of staff in security awareness)
- Protocols for the backing-up of stored data, to prevent loss due to systems failure or data corruption (eg use of 'cloud' computing, regular back-ups to external servers or hard drives and so on)
- Database management, ensuring that useful information and knowledge is captured and maintained, and obsolete information is deleted or archived.
- Protocols and controls over specification (and contract) change, variation, versions and updating (with authorised individuals having controlled rights to make amendments and administer versions)
- Internal controls, checks and balances on the use of information, to prevent misuse and fraud: examples include authorisations and sign-offs, matching of specifications against business needs, budgets and goods inwards; and separation of duties (eg the same person does not authorise specification, ordering and payment)
- Intellectual property protection, through the use of registered design rights, patents and copyrights; appropriate specification and contractual clauses to control access to intellectual property (eg via exclusive or non-exclusive licences) and to protection ownership rights (eg who will own IP generated in the course of the contract)
- Confidentiality of commercially sensitive data exchanged in the course of specification and advertisement of requirements (eg using confidentiality and non-disclosure clauses, training staff in confidentiality, and publishing and enforcing ethical codes including confidentiality)
- The use of significant coding systems to highlight stock proliferation and the opportunities for variety reduction
- Documentation of best practice, learning from projects, technical data – and other value-adding knowledge and information – to support organisational learning and prevent loss of data through personnel departure or outsourcing.

Reliability of information

6.7   It is also worth noting a more general sense of the term 'information assurance': that is, the need to 'assure' the quality, validity or reliability of information for specification and conformance or performance measurement, through robust processes for gathering, checking, verifying, analysing and interpreting supplier, supply market and performance data.

6.8   One obvious example is the need to verify supplier capability and performance data supplied by suppliers themselves in self-appraisal questionnaires (eg for pre-qualification or vendor rating).

Chapter summary

- Preparation of a specification is often a cross-functional task. Apart from user departments and purchasing there may be contributions from design and engineering, as well as marketing.
- A buyer's main contributions to the process are: understanding user needs; liaising with users; minimising tolerances, consistently with value added; understanding legal implications.
- Information required includes technical requirements, availability of products, schedules and lead times, costs and budgetary constraints, supplier processes, company policy, and legislation.
- Buyers may use standards in preparing specifications. Buyers are also concerned with 'standardisation' in another sense: variety reduction.
- Specifications may take account of social and environmental criteria.
- Information assurance is the practice of managing risks related to information. Information risks can easily arise in specification and need to be managed carefully.

 ## Self-test questions

Numbers in brackets refer to the paragraphs where you can check your answers.

1   In what circumstances might purchasing take the lead role in preparing a specification? (1.3)

2   What special attributes can buyers bring to the specification process? (1.8, 2.6)

3   What are the risks if a supplier takes the lead in the specification process? (2.2)

4   What is the main purpose of ESI? (2.8)

5   What are the sources of information relating to technical requirements for a specification? (3.3)

6   How may internal company policies impact on the preparation of specifications? (3.11)

7   How may external quality standards impact on specifications? (4.4)

8   List benefits of standardisation and variety reduction. (4.18)

9   Suggest environmental criteria that might be built into specifications. (5.4)

10 List actions for a sustainable specification that can be taken under each of the headings: reduce; re-use; recycle; rethink. (Table 5.1)

11 Define 'information assurance'. (6.1)

12 List information-related risks in relation to a specification. (6.4)

CHAPTER 6

Defining Key Performance Indicators

Assessment criteria and indicative content

1.3 Explain the criteria that can be applied in the creation of a business case

- Benchmarking requirements

2.3 Develop examples of key performance indicators (KPIs) in contractual agreements

- Defining contractual performance measures or KPIs
- The use of service level agreements
- Typical KPI measures to assess quality performance, timeliness, cost management, resources and delivery

Section headings

1. Contractual performance measures
2. Developing KPI
3. Typical KPI measures
4. Service level agreements
5. Measures of service quality

Introduction

In recent years, organisational performance measurement and the associated metrics (performance measures) have received much focus from academics and business practitioners. The role of these measures is important in supporting business management at strategic, tactical and operational levels of the business.

It is therefore not surprising that supplier performance measurement is similarly being increasingly used to assist organisations in their search for competitive advantage in today's business environments.

This chapter follows on from Chapters 4 and 5 on specification, to explore how contractual performance measures (often known as 'key performance indicators' or KPIs) can be developed and used to add 'measurability' to the definition of the business need for procurement.

We begin by looking briefly at the nature and uses of performance measurement. We then go on to define KPIs and discuss various approaches to their development or formulation. We demonstrate some typical KPI measures that might be used in supply contracts.

Finally, we explore the use of service level agreements (SLAs) to define service expectations, and the complex issues in measuring service quality.

1 Contractual performance measures

What is performance measurement?

1.1 Supplier performance measurement is the assessment and comparison of a supplier's current performance against:

- *Defined performance criteria* (such as quality standards and specific key performance indicators set out in a contract, service level agreement or continuous improvement agreement), to establish whether the aimed-for or agreed level of performance has been achieved
- *Previous performance,* to identify deterioration or improvement trends
- *The performance of other comparable organisations* (eg other suppliers) or standard *benchmarks*, to identify areas where performance falls short of best practice or the practice of competitors, and where there is therefore room for improvement.

1.2 Performance measurement is important because it supports the planning and control of operations and relationships: it is often said that 'what gets measured, gets managed'. It is intended to lead to performance improvement and supplier development, by identifying areas in which suppliers' current performance falls short of desired, competitive or best-practice levels. It is an important tool for communicating with stakeholders about their part in supply chain performance, and how they are doing: performance measures, such as KPIs, can be used to manage, motivate and reward individuals, teams and suppliers.

1.3 For the purposes of this unit, performance measures, or key performance indicators, incorporated in contracts with external suppliers also define the buying organisation's expectations in regard to performance. In other words, they define the business need in terms of measurable outputs, outcomes or behaviours which 'indicate' that the required level of performance to meet the need has been met.

1.4 Supplier performance appraisal can then be used – both for individual contracts (as part of contract management) and for the aggregate performance of multiple contracts over time (vendor rating) for the following purposes.

- To help identify the highest-quality and best-performing suppliers: assisting decision-making regarding: (a) which suppliers should get specific orders; (b) when a supplier should be retained or removed from a preferred or approved list; (c) which suppliers show potential for more strategic partnership relationships; and (d) how to distribute the spend for an item among several suppliers, to manage risk
- To suggest how relationships with suppliers can be (or need to be) enhanced to improve their performance (eg to evaluate the effectiveness of purchasing's supplier selection and contract management processes)
- To help ensure that suppliers live up to what was promised in their contracts
- To provide suppliers with an incentive to maintain and/or continuously improve performance levels
- To significantly improve supplier performance, by identifying problems which can be tracked and fixed, or areas in which support and development is needed

1.5 The process of monitoring, reviewing and appraising supplier performance, for both contract management and supplier performance management, is covered in detail in the *Managing Contracts and Relationships in Procurement and Supply* module. Our focus here is on preparing the crucial groundwork for contract and performance management, by setting up the 'yardsticks' or measures by which compliance and conformance will be evaluated.

1.6 There are a number of different approaches to setting performance targets and measures for supplier contracts, and we will examine the major ones in turn.

2   Developing KPIs

Key performance indicators (KPIs)

2.1   KPIs are clear qualitative or quantitative statements which define adequate or desired performance in key areas (or critical success factors), and against which progress and performance can be measured.

2.2   The key point about KPIs is that they state performance goals or expectations in a way that is capable of direct, detailed, consistent measurement at operational level, using available data collection systems.

2.3   Where possible, such goals will be **quantitative:** that is, 'hard', numerical, statistical or fact-based. They may, for example, be expressed in terms of cost (eg cost per service delivery, amount of cost savings), time (eg hours per service delivery), quantity of outputs (eg offices cleaned per hour, number of deliveries made on-time-in-full, number of cost reduction initiatives proposed) or other statistics (eg the proportion or ratio of deliveries made on-time-in-full, or the number of customer complaints per review period).

2.4   Some targets, however, will be more **qualitative:** that is, 'soft', subjective, pertaining to qualities or attributes that cannot readily be quantified, and drawn from less structured data (such as customer surveys). For example, you may want to evaluate customer satisfaction, the effectiveness of the supplier's account management, its flexibility and responsiveness or commitment to quality, or the professionalism of service staff.

2.5   The traditional approach to using KPIs has been based on quantitative measurement. However, with the increasing focus on non-manufacturing sectors, more qualitative measures are also required in the management of issues such as quality of service provision, innovation capability, corporate social responsibility and relationship management.

2.6   Even so, KPIs in these areas should be expressed as quantitatively as possible: the proportion of services rated satisfactory or non-satisfactory by customers; the degree of satisfaction expressed by customers (eg using rates scales or points scores); the proportion of requests and proposals responded to, and how quickly; scores on commitment to quality obtained via attitude surveys; number of 'critical incidents' illustrating professional or non-professional conduct; and so on.

2.7   Some of the key characteristics of qualitative and quantitative measures are summarised in Table 6.1.

Table 6.1 *Quantitative and qualitative measures: characteristics*

QUANTITATIVE MEASURES	QUALITATIVE MEASURES
Easier to establish KPIs	KPIs likely to be subjective
Easier to monitor over time	Monitoring over time is subjective
Focus on efficiency	Focus on effectiveness
Particularly suitable for purchase of products	Particularly suitable for purchase of services
Examples include prices, delivery performance, financial performance, reject rates	Examples include management capability, staff issues, technological development, willingness to collaborate closely

SMART performance measures

2.8   Effective performance measures (and objectives in general) are often described by the acronym 'SMART'.

- **Specific:** clear and well-defined statement of precisely what the desired outcomes or deliverables are, so that the parties to the contract know what they are committing to and accountable for.
- **Measurable:** susceptible to monitoring, review and measurement (ideally in quantitative or numerical terms) so that both parties can meaningfully assess progress and achievement.

- **Attainable:** achievable and realistic, given the time and resources available. Even if the aim is to be 'stretching' or to stimulate improvement, attainment of the required level of performance must be possible!
- **Relevant:** performance measures should be relevant to, and aligned with, the strategic objectives of the organisation; the policies and objectives of the procurement function; the critical success factors of the organisation and supply chain; and the business need.
- **Time-bounded:** given defined time-scales and deadlines for completion (or review) – ie not 'open ended'.

2.9 Some versions of the SMART model substitute, or add:

- **Stretching:** performance measures may deliberately be made challenging enough to motivate suppliers and stimulate committed performance, learning, development and improvement (eg as part of supplier development or continuous improvement agreements)
- **Sustainable** (or Responsible): KPIs should take into account potential impacts on key stakeholders, in the light of the unit's (and organisation's) ethical responsibilities towards them
- **Agreed:** incorporated in a contract, agreement or charter (formal or informal), in order to secure joint commitment and accountability.
- **Rewarded:** attainment of KPIs may be linked to positive incentives or rewards of some kind, as part of the performance management and supplier motivation process.
- **Reviewed:** KPIs should be periodically reviewed, so that they can be adjusted if circumstances or requirements have changed – or if they are designed to be 'movable' to stimulate continuous improvement

Advantages and limitations of using KPIs

2.10 Some of the benefits of using KPIs as performance measures are as follows.

- Increased and improved (results-focused) communication on performance issues
- Motivation to achieve or better the specified performance level (particularly with KPI-linked incentives, rewards or penalties). Motivation is in any case stronger where there are clear targets to aim for.
- Support for collaborative buyer-supplier relations, by enabling integrated or two-way performance measurement (with KPIs on both sides of the relationship)
- The ability directly to compare year on year performance, to identify improvement or deterioration trends
- Focus on key results areas (critical success factors) such as cost reduction and quality improvement
- Clearly defined shared goals, facilitating cross-functional and cross-organisational teamwork and relationships
- Reduced conflict arising from causes such as goal confusion and unclear expectations.

2.11 Setting KPIs for *supplier* performance, in particular, may be beneficial in the following areas.

- Setting clear performance criteria and expectations: motivating compliance and improvement
- Managing supply risk: controlling quality, delivery, value for money and so on
- Supporting contract management (to ensure that agreed benefits are obtained)
- Identifying high-performing suppliers for inclusion on approved and preferred supplier lists (which in turn supports efficient buying by user departments)
- Identifying high-performing suppliers with potential for closer partnership relations
- Providing feedback for learning and continuous improvement in the buyer-supplier relationship – both for the supplier, and for the purchasing department

2.12 It is worth noting that KPIs can have some disadvantages as well. The pursuit of individual KPIs can lead to some dysfunctional or sub-optimal behaviour: cutting corners on quality or service to achieve productivity or time targets, say, or units focusing on their own targets at the expense of cross-functional collaboration and co-ordination. Targets will have to be carefully set with these potential problems in mind.

Developing KPIs

2.13 Standard KPIs or performance metrics may be used by an organisation for certain types of routine contracts and common procurements. KPIs will not have to be systematically developed, using rigorous analysis, in all circumstances – and indeed, such a process would not be justified on cost/benefit grounds for low-value, routine purchases. However, for complex, high-value, new-buy contracts and projects, it may be necessary and justifiable to apply a systematic process to develop suitable performance metrics.

2.14 A simple process of developing KPIs can be summarised as follows: Figure 6.1.

Figure 6.1 *Developing key performance indicators*

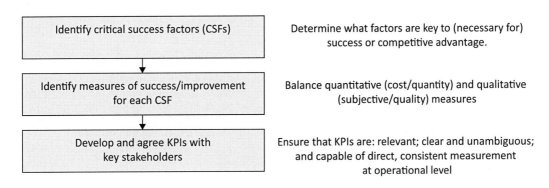

2.15 It is critical to align supplier KPIs with the business need and purchasing objectives, which in turn must be aligned with corporate goals and critical success factors for the supply chain.

2.16 You don't want to specify too many KPIs for a given contract: only those that are indicative measures of performance in areas necessary to achieve critical success factors. Otherwise, it will be too complicated and costly to monitor and measure performance – and the supplier may find the pursuit of multiple KPIs too complex and onerous. Eight to ten well-formulated KPIs may be realistic for any given planning and control period.

2.17 Effective communication is essential in KPI development. The buyer will need to be able to explain to the supplier exactly what performance standard is expected. It may issue recent history trend data (if available), with a written explanation of key issues and requirements. For complex high-value new-buy contracts, for which the effort is justified, buyers should involve suppliers in the joint development of KPIs – rather than simply negotiating their agreement with KPIs already formulated. Suppliers may be able to contribute valuable expertise and experience to the process, and consultation creates a better likelihood of 'buy in' or commitment to jointly-developed KPIs.

Benchmarking requirements

2.18 A useful definition of benchmarking is: 'Measuring your performance against that of best-in-class companies, determining how the best-in-class achieve these performance levels and using the information as a basis for your own company's targets, strategies and implementation' (Pryor). The aim is to learn both *where* performance needs to be improved and *how* it can be improved, by comparison with excellent practitioners.

2.19 A publication by the UK government has described the process of benchmarking as follows.

'Benchmarking is the practice of comparing a company's performance against others to stimulate improvements in operating practices. It can be used across almost all of the company's departments and it can also be the comparison of departments or sites within an organisation. It can be used to help clarify

where you stand, relative to others, in those practices which matter most in your area of business. The technique can also be used to help companies become as good as, or better than, the best in the world in the most important aspects of their operations.'

2.20 Benchmarking can be used to analyse any aspect of organisational performance, so it has wide application in supplier – and buyer – performance measurement. Supplier benchmarks may be selected for areas such as prices and cost management, inventory levels, delivery lead times, quality performance, staff training, innovation, use of e-procurement – and so on.

2.21 The key benefit of using benchmarked performance targets and quality standards is that they are likely to be both *realistic* (since other organisations have achieved them) and yet *challenging* (since the benchmarking organisation hasn't *yet* achieved them): the most effective combination for maintaining motivation.

2.22 At the same time, benchmarking helpfully stimulates research and communication about critical success factors, and sources of added value and competitive advantage in an industry. It can generate new ideas and insights outside the box of the organisation's accustomed ways of thinking and doing things. One of the key features of a successful 'learning organisation', according to Senge *(The Fifth Discipline)* is said to be the ability to 'SIS' or 'Steal Ideas Shamelessly' – in other words, to be willing to learn from other high-performing organisations and supply chains.

2.23 Bendell, Boulter & Kelly distinguish four types of benchmarking.

- *Internal benchmarking*: comparison with high-performing units in the same organisation. For example, the quality management function in one of the supplier's subsidiary companies might be benchmarked against a higher-performing quality management function in another division. (More likely, perhaps, the buyer's *own* performance might be benchmarked against a higher-performing procurement unit in another division.)
- *Competitor benchmarking*: comparison with high-performing competitors, in key areas which appear to give them their competitive advantage. This may be particularly valuable in business environments where whole supply chains compete with each other to meet end-customer needs more efficiently and effectively. The buyer may benchmark the performance of its supplier against the lead player in the supply market, for example, or the key supplier of its own main competitor.
- *Functional benchmarking*: comparison with the same function or process in another, high-performing organisation. For example, a company might benchmark the logistics function of its electronics supplier against that the logistics function of a construction company known for its effective logistical management.
- *Generic benchmarking*: comparison of business processes across functional and industry boundaries. The benchmark for suppliers may be set by 'excellent' companies, learning organisations, leaders in quality, ethics and innovation – or exemplars of whatever attribute the buying firm is interested in its suppliers' emulating.

2.24 The stages in the benchmarking process, as it might be applied to creating benchmarks for the performance of a key strategic supplier or supply chain, are shown in Figure 6.2.

Figure 6.2 *The benchmarking process*

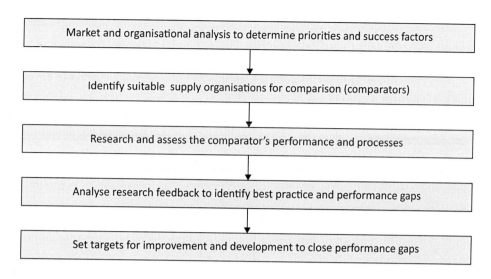

2.25 Whilst benchmarking may be useful in formulating performance measures and continuous improvement objectives for suppliers, the following points should also be considered.

- The costs associated with benchmarking projects can be significant. Typical project costs are normally associated with meetings, visits, training, possible consultancy etc and therefore projects must be carefully managed and planned.
- One of the most important requirements of a successful benchmarking project is effective communication. It is important to inform concerned parties about project progress and developments via presentations, reports, analyses, etc. This not only reduces confusion and conflicts, but may also trigger communication and ideas about how perceived best practice can be cascaded within the organisation or supply chain.

Supplier scorecards

2.26 A weighted-factor scorecard system may help to quantify performance measures, by assigning numerical values to different KPIs, and indicating to suppliers (and their subsequent performance evaluators) which performance measures are most important to fulfilling the business need and objectives, and how judgements about their performance will be 'broken down'.

2.27 This may be particularly important where performance measures are incorporated in draft contracts and specifications which are published as part of the documentation for a competitive tender. Best practice tender procedures require that clear weightings be attached to all specified criteria for supplier pre-qualification and contract award.

2.28 Scorecards recognise that some KPIs are more important in performance appraisal than others. A supplier scorecard system involves the development of KPIs (factors) and 'weights' (maximum ratings for each factor, as a proportion of the total evaluation). This is typically done by a cross-functional team, comprising relevant stakeholders in supplier performance management (eg representatives of design, operations, procurement and finance). When the time comes for contract or supplier performance appraisal, the supplier can then be assigned a numerical rating or points score on each factor, adding up to a total which reflects the 'balance' between the various performance measures.

2.29 An example of a simple scorecard for contractual performance measurement might be as follows: Figure 6.3

Figure 6.3 *Supplier scorecard*

FACTOR	WEIGHTING (%)	MAXIMUM SCORE	MEASUREMENT CRITERION
Quality	30	1.50	Quality conformance (0.7) Reject frequency (0.3)
Delivery	25	1.25	On-time-in-full delivery (1.0)
Support systems	15	0.75	Quality management systems, eg ISO 9000 (1.0)
Commercial	30	1.50	Cost savings (0.7) After-sales support (0.3)
Total	100	5.00	

2.30 Another example, suggested by Dobler *et al* (for use in the context of tender evaluation, but illustrative of the weighted points system approach) may be as follows: Figure 6.4.

Figure 6.4 *Weighted points system*

FACTORS	MAXIMUM RATING (WEIGHT)	SUPPLIER SCORE
Technical:		
Understanding of problem	10	9
Technical approach	20	19
Production facilities	5	4
Operator requirements	3	2
Maintenance requirements	2	2
Totals	40	36
Ability to meet schedule	20	20
Price	20	16
Managerial, financial and technical capability	10	10
Quality management processes	10	9
RATING TOTAL	100	91

3 Typical KPI measures

3.1 Traditionally, supplier performance measures have been based on mainly operational or contractual performance considerations relating to cost, quality, customer service levels, delivery and so on. Increasingly, however, the evaluation of suppliers is being considered more in the context of their overall supply chain contribution and capability. Considerations of work flow, relationship management, integration and compatibility, supply chain innovation and responsiveness are increasingly regarded as vital – and would almost certainly be included in KPIs for long-term partnership agreements, for example.

3.2 The 'bigger picture' is therefore that supplier KPIs may be multi-dimensional, future-oriented, developmental, relational – and applicable at all levels of business planning and management: strategic and tactical, as well as operational. In other words, they may address the long-term organisational 'business need' as well as the immediate procurement need.

3.3 Table 6.2 suggests just a small sampling of the performance measures that might be used at various levels.

Table 6.2 *Supplier performance measures at different levels*

STRATEGIC LEVEL	TACTICAL LEVEL	OPERATIONAL LEVEL
• Lead time against industry norm • Quality status and aspirations • Cost saving initiatives and potential • Supplier pricing against market prices • Risk assessment and compliance	• Efficiency of purchase order cycle times • Booking in procedures • Cashflow management • Quality assurance methodologies • Capacity flexibility • Future growth potential	• Delivery performance (OTIF – on-time-in-full) • Quality conformance: PPM (parts per million) non-conformance; service level agreements • Responsiveness: ability to react to change in planned requirements • Technical support level: customer support before and after sale

3.4 For the purposes of this syllabus, however, the focus is on *contractual* performance measures for use in assessing conformance and compliance with specification. The indicative content specifically addresses measures to assess basic operational considerations such as:

- Quality performance
- Timeliness
- Cost management
- Resources
- Delivery

3.5 There are a number of critical success factors in a supplier's performance that a buyer may want to evaluate, and a range of key performance indicators can be selected for each. In an exam, as in professional practice, you will obviously need to select or devise those most relevant to the context and (if specified by the question) the type of contract. For a general supply contract, however, performance measures may be applied to factors such as the following.

- Purchase price
- Total cost of ownership
- Quality
- Delivery performance
- Service performance
- Compliance with environmental, CSR or ethical standards
- Level of technological capability
- Level of satisfaction among other customers of the supplier

3.6 Each of these can be defined using a number of possible measures.

- A specific agreed standard or KPI, set out in the supply contract
- An established industry norm, standard or benchmark
- Past performance (eg using a year-on-year improvement percentage)
- The benchmark performance of other suppliers, including former suppliers of the same product or service (eg in measuring an outsourced service provider against the previous in-house provision of the service)

3.7 Some typical KPIs which might be incorporated in a contractual agreement (for a generic standard supply contract) are suggested in Table 6.3.

3.8 KPIs may be expressed as simple, observable or measurable statements, defining acceptable performance. A basic example, again for a generic contract, might be as follows: Table 6.3.

Table 6.3 *KPIs as statements of performance*

PERFORMANCE CRITERION	PERFORMANCE INDICATOR
Quality	Management systems and processes are clear and documented
Cost management	Consumable purchasing rates are benchmarked for value for money
Timeliness	Service is delivered within the agreed periods of availability
Quantity	Stocks are maintained to appropriate levels to ensure continuity of service
Compliance	Corporate policies and procedures are adhered to

3.9   We will discuss performance indicators and measures for services in the final sections of this chapter.

Table 6.4 *General KPIs for supplier performance*

SUCCESS FACTORS	SAMPLE KPIs
Price/cost management	• Basic purchase price or price range (and/or whole life costs or total cost of ownership • Price or whole life costs compared with other suppliers • Percentage range of acceptable price/cost variance compared with other suppliers • Value or percentage of cost reductions to be obtained during the period • Number of cost reduction initiatives proposed or implemented during the period • Percentage range of acceptable cost variance from estimated or budgeted costs (as a measure of effective cost management)
Quality performance, conformance or compliance	• Percentage or volume of rejects and returns, errors or scrapped items delivered (as a measure of the effectiveness of the supplier's quality control) • Percentage or volume of process failures (eg measured by process or output sampling) as a measure of the supplier's process capability or reliability (and quality assurance) • Number of customer complaints (eg from users or end customers) and/or returns • Adherence to benchmark quality standards (eg market grades or standards specifications) • Accreditation or certification under quality management standards (eg ISO 9000) and/or environmental management standards (eg ISO 14001)
Timeliness/delivery	• Frequency or percentage of late, incorrect or incomplete deliveries • Percentage of on time in full – OTIF – deliveries • Range of acceptable schedule variance (deadline ± x hours/days)
Service/relationship	• Competence, congeniality and co-operation of account managers • Promptness in dealing with enquiries and problems • Adherence to agreements on after-sales service
Financial stability/resources	• Ability to meet financial commitments and claims • Ability to maintain quality and delivery • Minimum number of staff or resources of specified grades to be allocated to the project (eg for service provision or outsourcing)
Innovation capability	• Number of innovations proposed or implemented • Minimum per annum investment in R&D (eg as a monetary value or percentage of turnover) • Willingness to collaborate in cross-organisational innovation teams
Technology leverage/ compatibility	• Percentage of sale or purchase transactions carried out electronically • Number and duration of technology breakdowns per period • Percentage of transactions or applications initiated by the buyer for which the supplier's systems are (or are not) compatible
Overall performance	• Benchmarking against other suppliers or supply market leaders • Commitment to continuous improvement (eg number of suggestions proposed or implemented)

Measures of quality

3.10   It is particularly important to contextualise contractual performance measures in relation to quality, because quality may 'mean' different things in different contexts. Garvin (*Competing in eight dimensions of quality*) identifies eight generic dimensions of product quality, any or all of which may be the focus of specifications and related KPIs.

- *Performance*: the operating characteristics of the product
- *Features*: value-adding characteristics and service elements (such as warranties and after-sales service)
- *Reliability*: the ability of the product to perform consistently over time
- *Durability*: the length of time a product will last (and stand up to normal usage) without deterioration or damage
- *Conformance*: whether agreed specifications and standards are met
- *Serviceability*: the ease and availability of service support
- *Aesthetics*: how appealing or pleasing the product is to the senses of the user
- *Perceived quality*: the subjective expectations and perceptions of buyers.

3.11 For a buyer looking to buy materials, components or other supplies in a commercial setting, the most important indicators of 'right quality' are likely to be fitness for purpose and conformance to specification. Note that both of these criteria are essentially focused on the supplier's ability to satisfy the needs and expectations of the buyer. Van Weele argues that: 'Quality is the degree in which customer requirements are met. We speak of a quality product or quality service when supplier and customer agree on requirements and those requirements are met.'

3.12 The British Standards definition of quality is: 'the totality of features and characteristics of a product or service that bear on its ability to satisfy a given need.'

3.13 Fitness for use or purpose was the focus of quality guru Joseph Juran, whose work you may come across in your later CIPS studies. It is also one of the key legal definitions of quality, as we will see in Chapter 7. Section 14 of the UK Sale of Goods Act 1979, for example, states that where a seller supplies goods in the course of a business, it is legally bound to provide goods:

- Of *satisfactory quality*: working and in good condition (so far as may be reasonably expected) and free from 'minor defects' (unless these are drawn to the buyer's attention or obvious to any reasonable pre-purchase inspection)
- *Fit for the purpose* for which they are commonly used, or for any specific purpose made known by the buyer to the seller.

3.14 So the basic quality KPI for an industrial grinder of the 'right quality' is one that grinds. And if the buyer specified a grinder that would tackle a particular material, and grind it to a specific degree of fineness – that is what it should do. In addition, the KPI for quality might require zero defects, or might define an acceptable tolerance for defects (eg 98% of a multi-item delivery defect free).

4 Service level agreements

What is a service level agreement?

4.1 We noted in Chapter 4 that it is harder to draft accurate specifications for services than for goods, because of their intangible nature – and yet this makes it even more important. Otherwise buyer and supplier could argue interminably as to whether the service was exactly what was asked for, or of an adequate standard.

4.2 Service level agreements (SLAs) are formal statements of performance requirements, specifying the nature and level of service to be provided by a service supplier.

4.3 The purpose of a service level specification and agreement is to define the customer's service level needs and secure the commitment of the supplier to meeting those needs: this can then be used as a yardstick against which to measure the supplier's subsequent performance, conformance (meeting standards) and compliance (fulfilling agreed terms).

Benefits and limitations of SLAs

4.4   The main benefits of effective SLAs, summarised by Lysons & Farrington, are as follows.

- The clear identification of customers and providers, in relation to specific services
- The focusing of attention on what services actually involve and achieve
- Identification of the real service requirements of the customer, and potential for costs to be reduced by cutting services or levels of service that (a) are unnecessary and (b) do not add value
- Better customer awareness of what services they receive, what they are entitled to expect, and what additional services or levels of service a provider can offer
- Better customer awareness of what a service or level of service costs, for realistic cost-benefit evaluation
- Support for the ongoing monitoring and periodic review of services and service levels
- Support for problem solving and improvement planning, by facilitating customers in reporting failure to meet service levels
- The fostering of better understanding and trust between providers and customers

4.5   SLAs are therefore a useful tool for client-supplier communication and relationship management; expectations and conflict management; cost management; and performance monitoring, review and evaluation.

4.6   Note our emphasis on ascertaining what services and levels of service are actually required, and on examining what they actually achieve and whether they add value. It is important not to over-specify requirements – for services as for goods. Specifying unnecessarily high standards or frequency of service, tight response times or grade of staff adds cost without necessarily adding value. (This is a point worth making in a time of global recession – where resource and cost efficiency is a key sustainability issue.)

4.7   Lysons & Farrington also cite the main reasons why SLAs fail to achieve their objectives.

- Lack of commitment by providers and/or customers
- Inadequate support structure (eg no SLA manager, no cross-functional project team to implement the SLA, no schedule of service level review meetings)
- Overloading of staff with extra work involved in SLAs (eg additional monitoring and reporting tasks)
- Overly detailed SLAs, which become burdensome to monitor
- Insufficiently detailed or specific SLAs, which allow problems to 'slip through the cracks'
- Inadequate staff training in the purpose and implementation of SLAs

Contents of an SLA

4.8   The basic elements of an SLA are as follows.

- What services are included (and not included, or included only on request and at additional cost)
- Standards or levels of service expected from the provider (such as response times, speed and attributes of quality service)
- Other expectations of the supplier (such as equal opportunity, environmental and employment standards)
- The allocation of responsibility for activities, risks and costs
- How services and service levels will be monitored and reviewed, what measures of evaluation will be used, and how problems (if any) will be addressed
- How complaints and disputes will be managed
- When and how the agreement will be reviewed and revised. (Service specifications may need to change as requirements, circumstances or priorities change.)

4.9   Of course, these elements will be adapted to the specific nature of the service contract – a point worth remembering if you are asked to draft an SLA for a particular type of contract in your exam. As an example, suppose a company decides to hire external contractors to provide office cleaning services. The basic service level issues for agreement will include the following.

- How often is the service to be provided?
- During what hours will the service be carried out, and will there be any disruption to office activities?
- How many staff (and, if relevant, with what skills, qualifications or experience levels) will be involved in providing the services?
- How far will the service extend (eg does it include cleaning of computer monitors and desktop areas? Does it *exclude* washing up left in the staff kitchen?)
- Does the service include special tasks caused by fault of the buyer's staff (eg wiping up spillages)? If so, how will the costs be attributed or shared?
- What speed of response is expected from the supplier when the customer makes a non-routine service request? What speed of response is expected for a request categorised as 'urgent', and what extra costs might this incur?
- What environmental guidelines and standards will the supplier be required to adopt? (Preferred or excluded chemicals, energy usage of equipment, responsibility for switching off lights and appliances, sorting of rubbish for recycling and so on.)
- What diversity, equal opportunity, health and safety and other employment policies must the supplier adhere to, in hiring, training and managing its staff? How will performance in these areas be reported or monitored?
- How will cleaners report completion of their work and any issues or problems that arose? How will customers monitor and feed back their evaluation of the work? How will customer complaints be dealt with?
- What rates will the supplier pay its staff? (If these appear to be below average, there may be an ethical issue – as well as a potential impact on the service likely to be delivered.)

Implementing SLAs

4.10   The process of developing and implementing an SLA is summarised in Figure 6.5.

4.11   This may be most effectively carried out by a cross-functional team (involving users of the service, purchasers, legal advisers, process analysts and so on), under the leadership of a project manager or SLA manager.

Figure 6.5 *Developing and implementing SLAs*

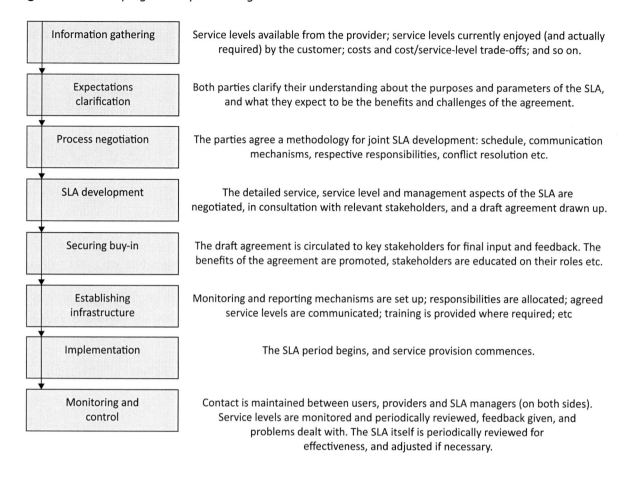

Information gathering	Service levels available from the provider; service levels currently enjoyed (and actually required) by the customer; costs and cost/service-level trade-offs; and so on.
Expectations clarification	Both parties clarify their understanding about the purposes and parameters of the SLA, and what they expect to be the benefits and challenges of the agreement.
Process negotiation	The parties agree a methodology for joint SLA development: schedule, communication mechanisms, respective responsibilities, conflict resolution etc.
SLA development	The detailed service, service level and management aspects of the SLA are negotiated, in consultation with relevant stakeholders, and a draft agreement drawn up.
Securing buy-in	The draft agreement is circulated to key stakeholders for final input and feedback. The benefits of the agreement are promoted, stakeholders are educated on their roles etc.
Establishing infrastructure	Monitoring and reporting mechanisms are set up; responsibilities are allocated; agreed service levels are communicated; training is provided where required; etc
Implementation	The SLA period begins, and service provision commences.
Monitoring and control	Contact is maintained between users, providers and SLA managers (on both sides). Service levels are monitored and periodically reviewed, feedback given, and problems dealt with. The SLA itself is periodically reviewed for effectiveness, and adjusted if necessary.

5 Measures of service quality

Specifying service levels

5.1 Lysons suggests that service levels should be:

- Reasonable (since unnecessarily high service levels may incur higher costs, and focus service providers' attention on targets to the detriment of overall service)
- Prioritised by the customer (eg as 'most important', 'important' or 'less important')
- Easily monitored (using specific, observable and quantifiable measures)
- Stated in a way that is readily understood by both customer-side and provider-side staff.

5.2 More specifically, key performance indicators (KPIs) can be drawn up to suit the needs of a particular service contract, as discussed in earlier sections of this chapter. Continuing our example of the cleaning service, for example, there might be KPIs covering the following areas.

- Time taken to complete designated cleaning tasks
- Thoroughness of cleaning (perhaps specified as amount of dust or number of stains identified in spot checks, or proportion of litter bins left un-emptied)
- Number of re-cleans (or customer complaints and requests for re-cleans)
- Customer satisfaction with overall cleaning service (eg on the basis of feedback reports, or specified as number of complaints, or proportion of complaints to approvals).

5.3 KPIs for the service levels provided by the procurement function to its own internal customers and clients will also vary according to the nature of the service: sourcing and purchasing services, consultancy, a particular purchasing or research project and so on. However, some general examples of purchasing service KPIs are given here.

- Number of complaints made to purchasing by internal customers, external customers or suppliers (and found to have merit)
- Number or proportion of supply orders delivered on-time-in-full and of specified quality (or equivalents, such as number and value of orders received incomplete, number and value of orders received over x days late, number and value of supplies rejected)
- Number of stockouts reported (or equivalents such as number and cost of production delays caused by stockouts)
- Value of cost reductions or savings achieved per period
- Number of projects completed to customer satisfaction (or equivalents, such as number of cost reduction or improvement initiatives generated)
- Lead times to fulfil the purchase cycle, from customer requisition to delivery (or equivalents, such as lead times to supply information or advice requested by internal clients, or percentage reductions in such lead times)
- Qualitative assessments of desired values such as professionalism of purchasing staff, commitment to co-operation, strategic thinking and so on

5.4 Remember that you don't want too many KPIs: only those that are indicative measures of performance in areas necessary to achieve critical success factors. Otherwise, it will be too complicated and costly to monitor and measure performance.

Service quality gaps

5.5 Supplier performance data (gathered as part of ongoing performance monitoring, audits or vendor rating exercises) will be measured against the SLA, KPIs or other benchmark targets (eg quality standards), and 'gaps' will be identified where the perceived service level falls short of the target level. Identified gaps will then be used to develop targets and actions for improvement.

5.6 It is worth remembering that 'service quality gaps' may be perceptual – as well as actual – shortfalls. There may be a gap between what is specified and what is *delivered:* that is, a shortfall which the service level agreement will entitle the customer to have addressed. However, there may also be a gap between what users or consumers expect and what service managers *think* they expect (and lay down in SLAs): the service may fall short of specification – but be quite acceptable to users, and *vice versa.*

5.7 The SERVQUAL model (developed by Zeithaml, Parasuraman and Berry) argues that the quality of a given service is the outcome of an evaluation process by which buyers compare what they *expected to receive* with what they *perceive they have actually received*: Table 6.5. Hence the importance of a robust contractual expression of expectations and of how performance will be measured.

5.8 In addition, as Lysons and Farrington point out, the services and service levels enjoyed and expected by customers do not necessarily correspond to (a) what they really need, (b) what really adds value or (c) what the service provider is capable of offering. This complicates the picture, because 'maintaining service levels' may in fact be wasteful and inefficient (if high levels of service, at high cost, do not add value), or – on the other hand – may miss opportunities for improvement (if specified services or service levels ignore value-adding capabilities of the service provider).

5.9 The service level agreement and KPIs will themselves need periodic review and adjustment, so that service quality isn't over-specified (wasting resources) or underspecified (causing user and provider dissatisfaction, or missing opportunities for improvement, innovation, added value and competitive advantage).

Table 6.5 *The SERVQUAL model of 'service gaps'*

GAP	EXPLANATION	BUYER REMEDY
Gap between buyer and supplier perceptions of quality	The supplier's definition of quality may not be the same as the buyer's: he may not know what features represent 'right quality' for the buyer, what features a service must have or what levels of performance are required.	Buyer and supplier will need to work together on developing mutual understanding of the requirement, using service specifications and service level agreements.
Gap between concept and specification	Resource constraints or poor specification skills may mean that either the buyer's needs or the supplier's concept or ideals for a service are not translated fully or accurately into buyer-side or supplier-side specifications.	Buyers will need to co-operate with users and suppliers to develop service specifications which accurately reflect their needs and expectations and the supplier's best capabilities.
Gap between specification and performance	Supplier-side specifications and service level agreements do not translate into actual service levels. Service staff may be unwilling or unable to perform to the specified standard, or work may be poorly organised, supervised or resourced.	The buyer will have to pre-evaluate the supplier's capability to deliver: checking wages paid to staff, supervision and quality management; getting references from other customers; using 'pilot' programmes prior to contract etc.
Gap between communication and performance	The supplier's communications may create inaccurate quality expectations: setting buyers and users up for disappointment (if quality is overstated) or causing them to pass over a suitable supplier (if understated).	Buyers will need to verify information provided by service providers.
Gap between buyer expectations and perceived service	What buyers or users perceive they have received may fall short of what they expected.	Buyers will need to manage user expectations and perceptions; and specify and measure service performance against objective criteria, as far as possible.

Chapter summary

- It is a buyer's task to measure the performance of his suppliers. Appropriate measures may include defined performance criteria, past performance, or performance of comparable organisations.
- Key performance indicators define desired performance in key areas (or critical success factors).
- Performance measures should be SMART: specific; measurable; attainable; relevant; and time-bounded.
- Benchmarking means measuring performance against best in class comparators.
- Supplier performance measures may be devised at strategic, tactical and operational levels.
- Service level agreements are formal statements of performance requirements, specifying the nature and level of performance required from a supplier.
- It is possible to devise KPIs for service delivery as well as for products.

 ## Self-test questions

Numbers in brackets refer to the paragraphs where you can check your answers.

1   What are the purposes of supplier performance management? (1.4)

2   List characteristics of quantitative and qualitative supplier performance measures. (Table 6.1)

3   List benefits of using KPIs. (2.10)

4   Define 'benchmarking'. (2.18)

5   List stages in the benchmarking process. (2.24, Figure 6.2)

6   List critical success factors that a buyer may wish to measure in a supplier's performance. (3.5)

7   Suggest sample KPIs for (a) price and (b) quality. (Table 6.3)

8   List benefits of effective SLAs. (4.4)

9   List basic contents of an SLA. (4.8)

10   What is meant by a 'service quality gap'? (5.5)

CHAPTER 7

Understanding Contract Terms

Assessment criteria and indicative content

3.1 Explain sources of contractual terms for contracts that are created with external organisations

- The use of express terms
- The use of standard terms of business by both purchasers and suppliers
- The use of model form contracts such as NEC, FIDIC, IMechE/IEE

3.2 Interpret examples of contractual terms typically incorporated into contracts that are created with external organisations

- Main terms in contracts for indemnities and liabilities, subcontracting, insurances, guarantees and liquidated damages
- Terms that apply to labour standards and ethical sourcing

Section headings

1. Contracts and contract terms
2. Express and implied terms
3. Standard terms of business
4. Model form contracts
5. Interpreting key terms
6. Key terms for ethical sourcing and supply

Introduction

In this chapter we move on in our discussion of the documentation included in contractual arrangements, to examine the use of the contract itself in defining procurement requirements. You will cover a range of aspects in the development and management of contracts as part of your CIPS studies. For this unit, the emphasis is on the express terms which are inserted – as standard, or by negotiation – in contracts with external suppliers.

In this chapter we begin with an overview of contracts, and then examine the sources of contract terms in supply contracts. We distinguish between express and implied terms, and outline the sources of implied terms which are relevant to defining the business need. We then go on to explore in more detail the sources of express terms which may be inserted in a contract. In the final two sections, we focus on examples of specific contractual terms that are commonly used, and how they are to be interpreted.

We leave contractual terms as to *price* for separate discussion in Chapter 8, where we address the topic of pricing arrangements in commercial agreements.

Note that, unless otherwise specified, the law discussed in this chapter is that of England and Wales, as exemplar.

1 Contracts and contract terms

What is a contract?

1.1 Contracts are a central feature of everyday life. The purchase of a study book, the boarding of a bus, the ordering of a meal in a restaurant: all constitute contracts. A contract is simply *an agreement between two (or more) parties which is intended to be enforceable by the law*. 'Agreement' means that there must be both offer and acceptance. For example, a buyer may offer to purchase certain items at a particular price, and a supplier may agree to provide them at that price.

1.2 The role of a contract is to set out the roles, rights and obligations of both parties in a transaction or relationship. A contract is basically a statement of:

- Exactly what two or more parties have agreed to do or exchange (in regard to specification or the requirement, prices, delivery and payment dates and so on)
- Conditions and contingencies which may alter the arrangement (eg circumstances under which it would not be reasonable to enforce certain terms, or agreement that if party A does x, then party B may do y)
- The rights of each party if the other fails to do what it has agreed to do ('remedies' for various forms of 'non-performance', such as breach or frustration)
- How responsibility or 'liability' will be apportioned in the event of problems (eg who pays for damage or loss of goods in transit, or losses to third parties in the course of performing the contract)
- How any disputes will be resolved (eg by arbitration or alternative dispute resolution, rather than litigation).

Contract terms

1.3 Contract terms are statements by the parties to the contract as to what they understand their rights and obligations to be under the contract. They define the content of the 'offer' which becomes binding once accepted by the other party.

1.4 Contract terms define both parties' rights and obligations, and it is important that there should be genuine and specific agreement on what these are, from the outset. After the contract has been made, it is too late for either party to alter its terms unilaterally: such a variation is effective only if it is made by mutual agreement (ie by another contract).

1.5 The contract terms that apply to a commercial agreement with an external supplier may come from various sources.

- **Express terms** are explicitly inserted into a contract by the parties to it, whether by negotiating terms specially for the particular contract; by applying the 'standard' terms of business of one of the parties; or by utilising a 'model' form contract which has been developed to represent standard terms for an industry or contract type.
- **Implied terms** are automatically assumed to be part of a contract – whether they are expressly included or not – by virtue of relevant statute (such as the UK Sale of Goods Act 1979), custom of business and other factors.

These sources of contractual terms are discussed in detail in Section 2 of this chapter.

1.6 Another important distinction between types of contract term addresses the 'importance' of the term in fulfilling the agreement between the parties.

- **Conditions** are vital terms of the contract, such that failure to perform them is effectively a 'deal breaker': in other words, breach of a condition entitles the wronged party to cancel or 'repudiate' the contract (as well as seeking damages for any losses suffered as a result of the breach).

- **Warranties** are non-vital terms of the contract, the breach of which need not cause a collapse of the contract: breach of warranty only entitles the wronged party to damages, with the mutual obligations of the contract otherwise remaining in place.

2 Express and implied terms

2.1 Terms can be expressly or explicitly inserted into a contract by either or both of the parties (*express terms*) or can be implied or assumed to be included in the contract (*implied terms*) because they are a recognised part of common or statute law.

Express terms

2.2 Express terms are clearly stated and recognised in the contract between the parties, whether they are written or oral (or a bit of both). They are often said to constitute the 'small print' of the contract (because of the literally small size of the type in which they are commonly set out).

2.3 The most common examples of express terms would be where the parties specify price, delivery dates, how carriage and insurance costs will be shared, and so on. Another example is an exclusion or exemption clause, which states that one party will not be liable (or will have only limited liability) for some specific breach of contract, or a *force majeure* clause which specifies special circumstances in which a party will not be liable for failure to fulfil its contract obligations. (We will discuss the interpretation of a number of common express terms a bit later in the chapter.)

Implied terms

2.4 Implied terms are terms which are not expressly included in the contract by either of the parties, but which are nevertheless assumed to exist (eg by virtue of common law, statute and custom), and therefore form part of the contract. In other words, in contract management, the printed terms and conditions of a contract cannot be viewed in isolation: buyers and suppliers must bear in mind that they may have responsibilities or rights not specifically dealt with in the terms of the contract.

2.5 Terms may be implied into a contract by virtue of:

- The **nature of the contract** (eg an employment contract implies certain duties of an employer and employee, such as a fair day's work for a fair day's pay).
- The **need for business efficacy** (to make the contract workable), based on the presumed intentions of the parties. In the *Moorcock case* (1889), there was an agreement by a wharf owner to permit a ship owner to unload his ship at the wharf. The ship was damaged when, at low tide, it was grounded on a hard ridge at the bottom of the river. The court held that it was an implied term of the agreement that the river bottom would be reasonably safe – otherwise the parties would not have made the agreement.
- **Statute law** (legislation). The UK Sale of Goods Act 1979, for example, implies an obligation on the part of the seller:
  — To supply goods of satisfactory quality and fitness for purpose
  — To supply goods which correspond to their description and sample (where these have been relied on by the buyer in agreeing to purchase).
  — Although not mentioned in the syllabus, these implied terms are clearly very important in relation to definition of requirement, so we will discuss them further below.
- **Custom of the trade**, such that both parties could reasonably be supposed to have had the customary term as their unstated intention. For example, in the case *Foley v Classique Coaches (1934),* in a contract to supply the petrol requirements of a bus company, no price was expressed or provided for. However, for some time before the dispute, petrol had been supplied at the supplier's standard price, to all its customers. The court held that practice indicated what was to be implied, indicating a term which the parties intended to adopt but did not express.

2.6 As a general rule, implied terms take second place to the express provisions of the contract: express terms are taken to be the most accurate reflection of the intentions of the parties to a contract, which is what contract law seeks to discover and enforce. Express terms may therefore override implied terms – except in certain circumstances, where an express term is taken to be 'unfair'. One key example (provided for in the UK Unfair Contract Terms Act 1977) is where the contract expressly attempts unreasonably to limit or exclude a party's liability for losses caused by negligence or breach of implied terms of the contract.

Implied terms relevant to the definition of requirement

2.7 The UK Sale of Goods Act 1979 draws together the legal principles relating to **contracts for the sale of goods**: that is, contracts in which a seller *transfers property* (ownership or title) in *goods* to a buyer in exchange for a *money consideration* (price). It covers both 'sales' (in which the buyer becomes the owner of the goods at the time when the contract is made) and 'agreements to sell' (when the buyer becomes the owner only at some future date, or on fulfilment of agreed conditions such as a certain number of instalment payments).

2.8 Sections 13–15 of the Act set out terms which are implied in the UK into all contracts of sale of goods, principally to protect the buyer: Table 7.1. You should be able to see the relevance of these terms for the specification and agreement of requirements.

Table 7.1 *Terms implied by the Sale of Goods Act*

S	IMPLIED TERM	EXPLANATION
13	*Sale by description*	In a sale by description, the offer includes some description (eg specification and quantity of goods, brand or model), on which the buyer relies when accepting. In such a case, the seller is deemed to undertake that the goods will correspond with the description. This may apply even if the buyer sees the goods, if the non-conformance with description is not obvious.

14	*Satisfactory quality and fitness for purpose*	Where the seller supplies goods in the course of a business, he is deemed to undertake that:
		• The goods will be of satisfactory quality:
		  — Working and in good condition (so far as may be reasonably expected, in the light of any description applied to them, the price and other relevant circumstances)
		  — Free from 'minor defects' (except defects drawn to the buyer's attention before the contract was made, or which a pre-contract inspection by the buyer revealed or ought to have revealed)
		• The goods will be fit for:
		  — The purpose for which such goods are commonly used; or
		  — Any specific unusual purpose, or any unusual circumstances in which the goods will be used, where (a) these have been notified to the seller, and (b) the buyer relies on the seller's judgment as to fitness for purpose. (The buyer is not protected if he has not told the seller of the special circumstances, or if he does not rely, or could not be expected to rely, on the skill or judgment of the seller in regard to the goods' fitness for a specific purpose.)
		at the time of sale and for a reasonable time after sale. (For example, goods are not fit for purpose if they require repair or other treatment such as washing: *Grant v Australian Knitting Mills*, 1936.)
		    Thus, a buyer cannot expect very cheap, secondhand or 'rush-order' goods to be of the same quality as expensive, new or normally-produced goods. However, goods used in the 'normal' way, which do not work properly, or fail after an unreasonably short time, or which are unsafe, are *not* of satisfactory quality.
		    Nor are goods which are originally sound but damaged in transit (being badly packed by the seller, despite knowledge of the kind of journey they would have to make).

15	*Sale by sample*	Sale by sample occurs when the contract expressly gives the buyer an opportunity to examine a small part of goods to be bought, as typical of the whole (bulk). (It is not a sale by sample merely if part of the goods was shown to the buyer during negotiations or specification: both parties must agree by express contract term that the sale is by sample.) In such cases, the seller is deemed to undertake that: • The bulk will correspond with the sample in quality • The buyer will have a reasonable opportunity to compare the bulk with the sample • The goods will be free from defects rendering them unsatisfactory, which would not be apparent from 'reasonable' examination of the sample (which does not have to be thorough examination: *Godley v Perry*, 1960).

2.9   Similar provisions, in the context of the supply of goods and services, are contained in the Supply of Goods and Services Act 1982. This Act covers situations excluded from the definition of 'contracts for the sale of goods' (and therefore not covered by SGA 1979) such as: contracts of exchange or barter; contracts for work and materials (where the substance of the contract is the buying of a skill rather than the buying of a product); contracts for hire or hire-purchase; and contracts for the supply of services.

2.10   In contracts for the supply of services, a slightly different set of terms is implied into contracts: Table 7.2.

Table 7.2 *Terms implied by the Supply of Goods and Services Act, in relation to services*

S	IMPLIED TERM	EXPLANATION
13	*Care and skill*	The supplier will carry out the service with reasonable care and skill.
14	*Time of performance*	Where the time for the service to be carried out is not fixed by contract, but is left to be fixed (in a way agreed by the parties, or by the course of dealings), the supplier will carry it out within a 'reasonable' time.
15	*Consideration*	Where consideration for the services is not fixed by contract, but is left to be determined (in a way agreed by the parties, or by the course of dealings), the buyer will pay a 'reasonable' charge.

3   Standard terms of business

3.1   Most commercial concerns do not go to the trouble of drawing up a special contract every time they purchase or sell goods or services. Instead, they rely on standard terms. Each firm will draw up its own 'standard terms of business', and will seek to ensure that these terms are accepted by other firms with whom they deal.

3.2   Lysons & Farrington suggest a general contract structure, incorporating standard terms: Table 7.3.

7

Table 7.3 *General contract structure*

The agreement	Names and signatures of the parties to the contract (usually with a statement that the parties have read and understood all terms and conditions)
Definitions	Definition of names and terms, to avoid repetition of long sentences in the body of the contract.
General terms	• *General agreements* clause • *Changes, alterations and variations* clause: eg that no variations to the contract can be made without written agreement • *Notice* clause: how and by what method any notice relating to the contract is to be sent
Commercial provisions	Rights and obligations of the supplier and of the purchaser. Standard terms of purchase, for example, might include: • *Passing of title/ownership*: at what point the goods become the property of the buyer (eg after inspection and formal acceptance) • *Time of performance*: eg a clause stating that 'time shall be of the essence', so that late delivery constitutes a breach of condition • *Inspection/testing*: the allowance of reasonable time to inspect incoming goods. • *Delivery/packing*: stipulating that this should be in accordance with instructions contained in the purchase order • *Assignment*: eg that no part of the order shall be subcontracted to a third party without the buyer's written agreement • *Liability* for damage or loss in transit (and associated insurance costs) • *Rejection*: eg a clause stating the right of the buyer to reject goods for various reasons (eg unsatisfactory quality, late delivery) • *Payment* terms
Secondary commercial provisions	• *Confidentiality and intellectual* property protection (where relevant) • *Indemnity*: eg the supplier guarantees to make good any losses suffered by the buyer as a result of product defects (eg in the form of consumer compensation claims or product recalls) • *Guarantee* clause: eg the supplier guarantees to make good any defects in the items supplied, provided that notice is received within a reasonable time. • *Termination*: eg when and how the contract will be discharged. • *Arbitration*: eg that contract disputes will go to arbitration prior to legal action being taken in the courts
Standard clauses	These may include: • *Waiver*: failure to enforce a 'right' at a given time will not prevent the exercise of that right later • *Force majeure*: exclusion of liability if a 'major force' outside the control of the parties (eg an act of God, war, flood etc) prevents or delays the performance of the contract • *Law and jurisdiction*: which nation's laws govern the contract.

Purchasers' and suppliers' terms

3.3 It may be useful to consider some of the areas where the buyer and seller have opposite interests and may therefore use conflicting clauses.

- Is it a fixed price contract or has a price escalation clause been inserted?
- If the supplier delivers late, will the buyer be entitled to end the agreement?
- Who pays the costs of carriage?
- Who bears the risk of accidental loss or damage in transit?
- When is ownership of the goods passed to the buyer?
- If the supplier delivers goods which do not match the specification, or which are not of satisfactory quality, will the buyer be able to reject them and claim damages, or has the supplier tried to exclude or limit his liability for such a breach of contract?

3.4 Legal problems may arise if one firm's terms of purchase differ from another firm's terms of sale – because of the principle of offer and acceptance discussed earlier. If in its acceptance, the offeree seeks to vary the terms in any way (eg by stipulating that the transaction will be covered by its own standard terms of business), this is interpreted as a counter-offer. This creates what is known as the **battle of the forms**.

3.5   Think of the typical procurement cycle.

- The buyer may send a written enquiry to a potential supplier on a pre-printed form stating that any purchase made pursuant to the enquiry will be governed by the buyer's standard terms (printed on the reverse of the form).
- The supplier will reply quoting details of price and availability, stating that any sale will be governed by the supplier's own standard terms (printed on the reverse of the form): a counter-offer.
- The buyer may place an order (make an offer) on a standard form repeating its own terms.
- The supplier may reply with an acknowledgement of order, repeating its terms: a counter-offer.

3.6   In such a case, the principle (known as the 'last document rule') is that the last set of terms and conditions sent constitutes the final counter-offer: the party who 'fires the last shot' wins. Usually it is the seller who is best placed to do this, by delivering the goods with a delivery note repeating its standard terms. If the buyer's goods inwards department has signed the delivery note, or simply accepted and used the goods, the courts are likely to judge that the final counter-offer was accepted and the contract was formed on the seller's terms.

3.7   It may well turn out that, because of careful counter-offers, both sides could be shown not to have accepted the other's terms. In such a case, where goods may have been transferred and used, but not paid for, the law uses the idea of **'quasi-contract'**: under the principles of equity, the buyer must pay what the goods are worth.

3.8   In order to prevent the battle of the forms, procurement staff may:

- Send acknowledgement copies of all purchase orders, which the supplier should sign and return, indicating agreement with the buyer's terms. If the seller acknowledges using its own documentation (and accompanying terms and conditions), the buyer should write back stating that delivery will be to the buyer's conditions.
- Negotiate contracts with suppliers, agreeing specific terms and conditions – which may include some of the buyer's standard terms and some of the seller's: this is likely to be a time-consuming process, only practicable for a large volume or value of business.
- Check any revised terms or conditions (counter-offers) which may be attached to supplier documentation: acknowledgement of orders, delivery notes, invoices etc.
- Stamp delivery notes 'goods received on buyer's terms and conditions' on receipt of goods.

4   Model form contracts

Standard contracts

4.1   As you may already have gathered, it would be extremely time-consuming and expensive to negotiate and formulate contract terms and clauses afresh for every new contract with a supplier. In many situations, it would also be a case of 'reinventing the wheel', since the terms would be substantially similar for most business dealings of a similar type. Buyers and sellers may therefore agree to use a *standard contract*: a contract 'template' based on generally accepted practice in an industry or supply market, or based on past negotiated agreements between the two parties concerned.

4.2   Where an organisation has recurring dealings with a supplier, or recurring requirements for a product or service, it may develop its own standard contract for use in particular types of dealings. For example, a publisher might have a standard contract for authors, another for printers, another covering sale to book distributors and another for sale to bookshops. Each standard contract would incorporate standard terms and conditions which have proved acceptable and workable in each type of contractual relationship in the past. A supplier or buyer could accept the contract as it stands, or negotiate to vary specific terms.

contracts

...model form contracts are published by third party experts (such as trade associations and professional bodies), incorporating standard practice in contracting for specific purposes within specific industries, and ensuring a fair balance of contractual rights and responsibilities for buyer and seller. They are often used in particular industries to establish conditions of contract between buyer and seller which become an acceptable and familiar commercial and legal basis upon which business is usually conducted. Model form contracts can usually be adapted to suit particular circumstances and relationships.

4.4 The most common model form contracts are used in the construction and engineering industries, but other industries – such as logistics and facilities management – are also beginning to develop them. Here are some examples.

- CIPS has published a range of model form contracts and contract clauses, which members are licensed to use in support of their employment.
- The Freight Transport Association has developed a model form of conditions of carriage, for carriage of goods by road in the UK.
- The Chartered Institute of Building has developed a model form contract for the commissioning of facilities management services.
- The Joint Contracts Tribunal (JCT) publishes a Standard Form of Building Contract (including a model form for framework or call-off contracts).
- The Institute of Civil Engineers (ICE), the Association of Consulting Engineers and the Federation of Civil Engineering Contractors issue standard forms for civil engineering.

4.5 The Institute of Civil Engineers also produced a new model form contract, standardising terms used across the construction industry. The **New Engineering Contract (NEC)** is a suite of contracts intended for use for civil, engineering, building and electrical or mechanical works (http://www.neccontract.com). The original NEC was developed in the early 1990s with the aim of introducing a non-adversarial contract strategy which would enhance the smooth management of projects. The Third Edition (NEC3) were preferred forms of contract for works relating to the 2012 Olympic and Paralympic Games in London. They encompass large and small, civil engineering and building, national and international projects. The extended NEC3 includes a professional services contract, an adjudicator's contract and a short-term contract, as well as support services including training, consultancy, software and a users group.

4.6 NEC3 is different from other Building and Civil Engineering Contracts, in that it has a core contract form (The Engineering and Construction Contract), written in simple terms, with optional 'bolt ons' for use in a range of circumstances: priced contract, target contract, cost-reimbursable contract and management contract, with various options for price adjustments, incentives, liabilities and so on.

4.7 The International Federation of Consulting Engineers (*Fédération Internationale Des Ingénieurs-Conseils* or **FIDIC**) represents the global engineering industry (http://www.fidic.org). It has developed a range of model form contracts for use by the construction industry worldwide, including:

- The Construction Contract (contract for construction for building and engineering works designed by the employer) or Red Book
- The Plant & Design-Build Contract (contract for electrical and mechanical plant and for building and engineering works designed by the contractor) or Yellow Book
- The Short Form of Contract, or Green Book
- The Design-Build-Operate (DBO) Contract
- Forms of agreement for the engagement of consultants: the Client/Consultant Model Services Agreement (or White Book); Sub-Consultancy Agreement; and Joint Venture Agreement.

4.8 The Institution of Mechanical Engineers (IMechE) and the Institution of Engineering and Technology (IET) have jointly developed a range of model form contracts for electrical and mechanical work and consultancy (including Forms of Tender, Agreements and Performance Bonds) and guides to their use. The IET has developed the **Joint IMechE/IEE Model Forms of General Conditions of Contract** (http://www.theiet.org).

Standard and model form contracts vs negotiated or bespoke contracts

4.9 A buyer may rely on its own standard terms and conditions for simple, low-value, low-risk and regular purchases, such as stock and MRO items. However, it must still be remembered that the buyer and the seller may have *different* standard terms and conditions, which are intended to protect their different interests in the transaction – leading to the 'Battle of the Forms'. It is therefore common for organisations to publish their standard terms wherever possible: on purchase order forms, order acknowledgements, invoices, receipts and so on.

4.10 The standard terms and conditions of buyers and sellers are likely to diverge in a wide range of areas, of which these are perhaps the main ones.

- Payment terms (since sellers will want quick payment and buyers will want long credit terms, to support their respective cashflow positions)
- Transfer of title (when goods purchased become the property of the buyer, and title transfers from the seller, which affects who bears the risks in the mean time)
- Time of the essence (whether the delivery date is a condition, protecting the buyer, or a warranty, protecting the seller in the event of schedule slippage)

4.11 For more complex and/or larger, more strategically critical, high-risk or non-routine purchases, standard terms are very unlikely to include the level of detail, and specific provisions, that need to be addressed in the contract. In such cases, it would be worth the time and expense of negotiation and drafting of contract-specific terms and conditions.

4.12 The *advantages and disadvantages* of using standard and model form contracts are summarised in Table 7.4.

Table 7.4 *Advantages and disadvantages of model form contracts*

ADVANTAGES	DISADVANTAGES
Helps reduce time and costs of contract development (including legal service costs)	Terms may not be as advantageous to a powerful buyer as if contract was negotiated
Avoids 'reinventing the wheel' – but can be adapted to suit particular circumstances	Terms may not include special clauses or requirements to cover the buyer's position
Industry model forms are widely accepted, reducing negotiation time and costs	Legal advice is still required if significant amendments or variations are to be made
Designed to be fair to both parties	Costs of training buyers to use model forms

5   Interpreting key terms

5.1 The assessment criterion specifically requires you to be able to 'interpret examples of contractual terms typically incorporated into contracts'. You may be asked to explain a range of key terms, and why they are important in the contractual definition of requirements. Alternatively, however, you may be given examples of express contract terms (not necessarily identified by name) as part of a case study scenario, and asked to explain:

- What type of clause they are and what they are designed to achieve
- The legal and operational effects or implications of the clause for the buyer and the supplier: what it commits – or permits – each party to do or not do, and what risks or costs are involved

- Whether the example clause, as given, expresses the buyer's requirements (and best interests) clearly, effectively and enforceably – and if not, how it could be improved.

5.2   Let's look at some of the basic contract terms you might need to interpret. Our coverage is somewhat wider than the rather limited range specified in the indicative content, to give you the best possible scope for drawing mark-earning points from a case study. We will discuss clauses related to price and payment in Chapter 8.

Time of performance

5.3   Express stipulations as to time of performance (such as dates of shipment, transfer or delivery) are normally treated as *conditions* in commercial contracts and other contracts where time lapse could materially affect the value of the goods. However, it is common to note (or 'stipulate') expressly that 'time is of the essence of the contract'. In such a case, if there is a delay in performance, the injured buyer may treat it as breach of condition and pay nothing (and also refuse to accept late performance if offered). A standard 'time of the essence' clause might be as follows:

'The time of delivery of goods, and/or completion of the work to be performed under the contract, shall be of the essence of the contract.'

5.4   When a contract does not specify any time for the performance of obligations, they must be performed within a 'reasonable' time.

Passing of title/property

5.5   The passing of property means the transfer of ownership of goods. Note that this is not the same as transfer of 'possession' (ie who physically *has* the goods). In a cash sale, for example, possession may not be obtainable until the price has been paid. In the case of goods delivered on a sale-or-return basis, however, the potential buyer is given possession – but the *ownership* does not pass until some further action has been performed in relation to the goods.

5.6   The moment when the property in the goods passes from the seller to the buyer under a contract of sale may be important in many circumstances.

- If the goods are accidentally damaged or destroyed: the allocation of risk (ie who suffers the loss) may depend on who owns the goods at the time.
- If the goods are damaged or destroyed through the negligence or other fault of a third party: an owner has stronger rights to claim for loss than a 'possessor'.
- If a buyer fails to pay in full for the goods, or becomes insolvent: an unpaid seller can sue the buyer for the price of the goods, if title in the goods has already passed to the buyer.
- A sale of goods: only a person who *owns* goods is entitled to sell them (s 12 SGA 1979).

5.7   As a general principle, property in goods passes from the seller to the buyer at whatever time the parties *intend* it to pass. If the parties do not indicate their intentions, in the UK Section 18 of the SGA 1979 lays down various rules for when property passes. However, the contract may expressly stipulate an appropriate point at which the buyer assumes title.

- A buyer may wish to stipulate that ownership passes when the goods have been delivered and formally accepted, following inspection, testing or other procedures.
- A supplier may wish to stipulate that ownership passes only when goods have been paid for in full, so that it can repossess the goods if the buyer does not pay for them (or becomes insolvent).
    This is called a **retention of title clause**, or a **Romalpa clause**, after the case of *Aluminium Industrie Vaassen v Romalpa Aluminium Limited* (1976) The claimants supplied aluminium foil to the defendants, who subsequently went into liquidation. The contract stipulated that the title to the goods did not pass to the defendants until they had paid in full. The defendants had failed to pay for a

quantity of goods (some of which they had resold) and the claimants sued to recover them. The court held that, in accordance with the conditions of the contact, the claimants were entitled to the goods belonging to them: at least, those which were still in the possession of the buyer and in their original (unmanufactured) state. A standard retention of title clause might appear as follows:

> 'All goods supplied under this contract will remain the property of the supplier until the buyer has paid for them in full.'

- A buyer may secure ownership of the goods upon inspection and payment, but may ask the supplier to retain *possession* of some or all of the goods, in order to reduce its own stockholding.
- There may be a sale 'on approval' for a defined period: ownership passes when the buyer signifies acceptance of the goods, or retains the goods without rejecting them within a stated time.

Liquidated damages and penalty clauses

5.8   A breach of contract occurs:

- When a party fails to perform an obligation under the contract: is in breach of a condition; improperly repudiates (ends) the contract; or prevents completion of the contract on his own side or by the other party, during performance. These are examples of 'actual breach'.
- When, before the time fixed to perform an obligation, a party expressly or by implication repudiates the obligations imposed on him by the contract: ie shows an intention *not* to perform. This is called 'anticipatory breach'.

5.9   In appropriate cases, the party who has suffered a breach of contract may have any of the following 'remedies' in law.

- *Damages*: financial compensation for losses suffered as a result of the breach. This is the normal remedy and by far the most common.
- *Specific performance*: an equitable remedy whereby the court orders the defendant to carry out his obligations under the contract, if damages would not be an adequate remedy (eg if the claimant wanted to buy a particular piece of land).
- *Quantum meruit*: an equitable remedy available when a contract has been partly performed, entitling a party which has provided a benefit, or performed work, to be paid a fair amount for it.

5.10   The purpose of **damages** is to put the injured party into the position it would have been in if the contract had been properly performed: they are a 'compensatory', not a 'punitive' (or punishing) remedy. So if a seller has failed to deliver goods, for example, the buyer's measure of damages will be the difference between the agreed contract price and the price the buyer needed to pay in order to get the goods elsewhere at prevailing market price.

5.11   As a proactive form of dispute and relationship management, the parties may agree a sum to be paid in the event of breach of contract – or they may not discuss this point at all.

- Where the contract does not make any provision for damages, the court will determine the damages payable. Such damages are referred to as **unliquidated damages**.
- Where the contract expressly provides for the payment of a fixed sum on breach, and if the clause is a genuine attempt at estimating the loss in advance of the breach, this is known as a **liquidated damages** clause.

5.12   There are two key points to note in using or interpreting liquidated damages clauses.

- The clause specifies the damages which will be payable for breach, at a predetermined amount (eg $x per day late) which is designed to be a *genuine estimate of the damage or loss which would be caused by the non-performance of the contract*. It will be enforceable if a breach occurs, usually without action in the courts: if both parties have agreed to the clause, the buyer can simply deduct the damages from its payment to the supplier in breach.
- Even if the actual damages suffered are greater than the liquidated damages provided for in the contract, the claimant can only claim the agreed liquidated amount.

5.13 A liquidated damages clause is used to guarantee the buyer damages against losses arising from a supplier's late or unsatisfactory completion of a contract – and to motivate the supplier to perform the contract. However, if the clause is framed purely as a disincentive or deterrent to breach of contract, it may be treated as a **penalty clause** (regardless of the name given to it in the contract!) Such clauses are not enforceable in law in the UK, and are void in the event of breach. The injured party will have to prove the actual loss suffered in court, and unliquidated damages will be assessed and awarded by the court.

5.14 So when would a court regard a liquidated damages clause as a penalty clause? Generally, a clause will be presumed to be a penalty clause if it does *not appear to be a genuine attempt to estimate the potential loss*, eg if:

- The sum stipulated appears unreasonably large. (A valid liquidated damages amount *may* be larger than the loss actually suffered, as long as it is a genuine attempt to pre-estimate the loss.)
- A single sum of damages is payable on the occurrence of one or more breaches, not distinguishing between breaches that are trivial and those that are serious
- A sum is stipulated for breach by non-payment – but is greater than the amount of the payment owed.

Force majeure clauses

5.15 The general rule is that, unless otherwise agreed, a party who fails to perform his contractual obligations is in breach of contract and liable for damages – whatever the excuse for non-performance. In the case *Cutter v Powell* (1795), Cutter was deemed to have failed to perform his complete contract (as a merchant seaman) because he *died* before arrival at the end of the voyage for which he had been contracted. You might notice that this is a little harsh.

5.16 The legal doctrine of 'frustration' in the UK was designed to reduce the severity of the general rule, by allowing for genuinely good excuses for non-performance. Here are some examples.

- Destruction of the contract subject matter. In *Taylor v Caldwell* (1863), a music hall was hired – but burnt down before the date of the concert.
- Non-occurrence of the event on which the contract was based. In *Krell v Henry* (1903), a room was hired to enable people to observe the coronation procession of Edward VII – but the procession was cancelled owing to the King's illness.
- Incapacity to provide personal performance: eg frustration of an employment contract by reason of the death of the employee.
- Extensive interruption which makes further execution of the contract impracticable or different from that originally agreed. (This does not include circumstances where a contract merely becomes more difficult or expensive to perform, or where a party has undertaken to do something which he later finds he cannot achieve…)

5.17 The purpose of *force majeure* (major force) clauses is to release the parties from liability in circumstances where their failure to perform a contract results from circumstances which were unforeseeable, for which they are not responsible, and which they could not have avoided or overcome. A simple clause might be.

'Neither party shall be regarded as being in breach of its obligations if it can show that it was prevented from performance by any circumstances of force majeure *which arose after the date of the contract. Such circumstance may include, but is not limited to, war and other hostilities, terrorist activity, revolution, riot, earthquake, flood or other natural disaster, and industrial disputes (not limited to the employees of the parties or their subcontractors).'*

5.18 A more complex *force majeure* clause should (according to the CIPS model clause):

- State the events that will constitute *force majeure*, as relevant to the industry or market
- Oblige either party to notify the other if *force majeure* events have occurred which may materially affect the performance of the contract

- State that a party will not be considered in default of its contract obligations, as long as it can show that full performance was prevented by *force majeure* events
- Provide for the contract to be suspended for up to 30 days, if performance is prevented by *force majeure* for this period
- Provide for the termination of the contract, by mutual consent, if the *force majeure* event continues to prevent performance for more than 30 days (with provisions for transfer of work done so far, in return for reasonable payment).

Guarantees

5.19 A typical contract for sale of goods or provision of services will usually contain some kind of **guarantee (or warranty) clause**. Normally, the supplier will guarantee to make good any defects in the items supplied, provided that notice is received within a reasonable time. Such clauses must always state that the protection offered does not affect any statutory rights that the buyer may be entitled to. A standard guarantee clause, designed to protect the buyer, might be as follows:

'The supplier guarantees that if the goods fail because of defective workmanship or materials, within 12 months of the date of purchase, the supplier will repair the goods, or (if repair is not possible within a reasonable time) the supplier will replace the goods. This guarantee is in addition to the buyer's statutory rights.'

5.20 Another context in which the term 'guarantee' is used is the formation of **contracts of guarantee,** in which one party agrees to guarantee (or stand surety for) the liability of another for debt, default or other problems. Such a contract must be evidenced in writing in the UK, and be signed by the guarantor or some other person authorised to sign it on his behalf. If there is no written evidence, the contract is unenforceable: no court action may be brought in relation to it.

5.21 An example with which you may be familiar is where one person agrees to be 'guarantor' for another who is seeking loan finance: if the borrower (who has primary liability) defaults on the loan, the lender is guaranteed repayment by the guarantor (who has accepted secondary liability). In commercial contracts, a contract of guarantee may arise where a contractor carries out work for a subsidiary company in a group. The contractor will often seek an assurance from the group's parent company that it will act as guarantor for the subsidiary: if the subsidiary fails to pay, the parent company will be liable for the debt.

Exclusion clauses

5.22 The term 'exclusion clause' is applied to contract clauses which:

- Totally exclude one party from the liability which would otherwise arise from some breach of contract (such as the supply of goods of inferior quality); or which
- Restrict or limit liability in some way; or which
- Seek to offer some form of 'guarantee' in place of normal liability for breach of contract.

5.23 Such clauses used to be very common in printed contracts and conditions of sale put forward by manufacturers, distributors and carriers of goods. However, the tendency of modern statutes is to limit the use of exclusion clauses – especially in dealings involving private citizens or consumers, who frequently do not read or understand the effect of the 'small print' put before them for acceptance.

5.24 To be valid, the exclusion clause must first pass a two-part 'common law' test.

- The clause must be **incorporated into the contract**.
  - If a person signs a contract document in which the clause is included, he will generally be considered to have agreed to it (even if he did not read the document: *L'Estrange v Graucob,* 1934). If the document is not signed, the person is not bound, if it can be shown that he did not know that the document contained terms of the contract, or that reasonable notice of those terms was not given to him.

- An exclusion clause cannot be introduced into a contract *after* it has been made, unless the other party agrees: *Olley v Marlborough Court,* 1949.
- The clause must be constructed in a **clear and precise** way.
  - The party relying on the clause must prove that, properly construed, it relates directly to the loss or damage suffered by the other party. In the case *Andrew Bros (Bournemouth) Ltd v Singer & Co Ltd* (1934), for example, a contract for the sale of 'new cars' contained a clause exempting the seller from liability for breach of all terms implied by law. One of the cars was not new – and the court held that the clause did not protect the seller, because there had been a breach of an *express* term, whereas the exclusion clause referred only to implied terms.
  - If there is any doubt as to the clause's meaning and scope, the clause will be interpreted against the party who is seeking to rely on it as a protection against his legal liability.

5.25 The clause must now also pass the test of compliance with the Unfair Contract Terms Act 1977, which – as mentioned earlier – restricts the extent to which a party can exclude or limit its liability for *negligence* and *breach of contract.*

5.26 In regard to **negligence**:

- A person in business cannot exclude or restrict his liability for death or personal injury resulting from negligence, and any clause purporting to do this is prohibited.
- A person in business cannot exclude or restrict liability for negligence causing loss (other than death or personal injury), unless the exclusion clause is 'reasonable'.

5.27 In regard to **breach of contract**, any term purporting to exclude or restrict liability in a standard term contract (whereby one party deals on the other party's written standard terms of business) or in a consumer contract (between a business and a consumer for the sale of goods for ordinary private use) is effective only if it is 'reasonable'.

5.28 The burden of proving **reasonableness** of the exclusion clause is on the party wishing to rely on the clause to limit its liability. The term's inclusion must be fair and reasonable, in the light of the circumstances which were, or ought reasonably to have been, known to or anticipated by the parties when the contract was made. Relevant circumstantial factors include the following.

- The strength of the bargaining positions of the parties relative to each other (eg so that the buyer accepted the exclusion clause of its own free choice)
- Whether the buyer knew (or ought to have known) of the existence and the extent of the term, on the basis of trade custom or previous dealings with the seller
- Whether it was reasonable to expect, when the contract was made, that it would be practical for the buyer to comply with any conditions attached to the term (ie where the seller's liability would be excluded or restricted if the buyer did not comply with the stated condition).

Indemnities

5.29 An indemnity clause is designed to secure an undertaking from the other party that it will accept liability for any loss arising from events in performance of the contract, and will make good the loss to the injured party or parties. This is, in a way, a similar kind of 'assurance' to a contract of guarantee – ensuring that a party injured by the default, negligence or miscarriage of another party ends up getting compensated. However, where a guarantor assumes secondary liability (if the party with primary liability *fails* to meet its obligations, the guarantor assumes them), an indemnifier assumes primary liability (committing to meet its own or a third party's obligations).

5.30 An indemnity clause might include costs or debts (eg reimbursement of rectification costs or legal claims incurred as a result of breach of contract terms); loss or damage to the buyer's property as a result of negligent or defective work; business losses incurred by a supplier's poor professional advice; or injury to the buyer's staff, customers or third parties (eg visitors) caused by the negligence of the other party's personnel – especially if they are performing work at the buyer's premises (eg in the case of a cleaning service) or at a customer's premises (eg in the case of outsourced service delivery).

5.31   A general indemnity clause, designed to protect a buyer, might be as follows.

'The supplier indemnifies the buyer against all costs and claims incurred by the buyer as a result, direct or indirect, of the supplier's breach of any obligation contained in this contract.'

Insurances

5.32   A buyer will usually wish to confirm that the supplier has the ability to pay compensation in the event of any indemnities or legal claims arising against it, and will usually make it a requirement of the contract that the supplier has the necessary insurances to cover them. The type of insurances most generally relevant to the commercial contracts are as follows.

- **Employer's liability insurance**. Every employer (and hence every supplier) transacting business in the UK for example must have employer's liability insurance. Its purpose is to protect employees who may sustain injury, illness or incapacity as a consequence of their employment. It is a legal requirement and cover normally ranges from the minimum £5 million upwards. There is no legal exemption even if the employer and employee is effectively the same person.
- **Public liability insurance**. Whilst not being a legal requirement, it is becoming increasingly common for buyers to require this cover as a condition of the contract. The insurance protects the supplier, and in turn the buyer, for claims made by third parties for personal injury or damage to or loss of property.
- **Professional indemnity insurance**. PII cover is designed to cover claims brought about where a failing by the supplier (eg poorly designed software or erroneous legal advice) has resulted in economic loss to the buyer.
- **Product liability insurance**. This covers claims made as a result of injury or damage to or loss of property from goods supplied, repaired or tested by the supplier.

5.33   The level of cover is usually assessed based on the likely risk involved in the contract, and does not usually relate to the overall contract value.

5.34   A comprehensive **indemnity and insurance** clause for use in the UK might be as follows.

'Without prejudice to any other rights or remedies available to the Buyer, the Supplier shall indemnify the Buyer against all loss of or damage to any Buyer property to the extent arising as a result of the negligence or wilful acts or omissions of the Supplier or Contract Personnel in relation to the performance of the Contract; and all claims and proceedings, damages, costs and expenses arising or incurred in respect of:

(a) *death or personal injury of any Contract Personnel in relation to the performance of the Contract, except to the extent caused by the buyer's negligence;*

(b) *death or personal injury of any other person to the extent arising as a result of the negligence or wilful acts or omissions of the Supplier or Contract Personnel in relation to the performance of the contract;*

(c) *loss of or damage to any property to the extent arising as a result of the negligence or wilful acts or omissions of the Supplier or Contract Personnel in relation to the performance of the Contract; or*

(d) *under Part 1 of the Consumer Protection Act 1987 in relation to supplies.*

'The Supplier shall at its own expense effect and maintain for the Contract Period such insurances as are required by any applicable law and as appropriate in respect of its obligations under this Contract. Such insurances shall include third party liability insurance with an indemnity of not less than [£2m] for each and every claim.

'If the Supplier cannot provide evidence of such insurance to the Buyer on request, the Buyer may arrange such insurance and recover the cost from the Supplier.

'The Supplier shall notify the Buyer as soon as it is aware of any event occurring in relation to the Contract which may give rise to an obligation to indemnify the Buyer under the Contract, or to a claim under any insurance required by the Contract.

'This Clause shall not be deemed to limit in any way the Supplier's liability under the Contract.'

Subcontracting

5.35   Since buyers have a key interest in assuring the quality of the goods produced, or the services performed, by suppliers, they will generally not want the supplier to hand over the contract to a third party – at least without the opportunity to pre-qualify and approve the subcontractor. The original supplier will remain liable for any failures on the part of the third party, but the risk may still be unacceptable to the buyer.

5.36   The general rule is that a contract can be assigned or subcontracted unless it is evident in all the circumstances that a supplier was specifically *chosen for its unique qualities* (and it would therefore not fulfil the buyer's intentions to have the work done by another party).

5.37   A subcontracting and assignment clause may be used to prevent any assignment or subcontracting without prior written consent. A typical clause might be as follows.

'The supplier shall not assign or transfer the whole or any part of this contract, or subcontract the production or supply of any goods to be supplied under this contract, without the prior written consent of the buyer.'

5.38   Of course, a supplier of manufactured goods will frequently obtain materials or components from its own supply chain. In such cases:

- The non-assignment clause can be omitted, since the buyer will obtain adequate protection by drafting clear, tightly controlled contract specifications.
- The non-assignment clause could be qualified by a rider such as the following:
  'Such consent shall not be necessary where any assignment or subcontracting is necessary for the due performance of the contract by the supplier.'

6   Key terms for ethical sourcing and supply

Ethical sourcing and supply

6.1   'Ethics' are simply a set of moral principles or values about what constitutes 'right' and 'wrong' behaviour in a given society, market or organisation.

6.2   Ethical, sustainable or responsible sourcing policies at the level of corporate ethics (or corporate social responsibility) may cover a range of matters, depending on the ethical risks and issues raised by the organisation's activities and markets. Here are some examples.

- The promotion of fair, open and transparent competition in sourcing (and the avoidance of unfair, fraudulent, manipulative or coercive sourcing practices)
- The use of sourcing policies to promote positive socio-economic goals such as equal opportunity and diversity in the supply chain; support for local and small-business suppliers; and minimisation of transport miles (to reduce environmental impacts and carbon emissions)
- The specification and sourcing of ethically produced inputs (eg certified as not tested on animals; drawn from sustainably managed or renewable sources; or manufactured under safe and unforced working conditions)
- The selection, management and development of suppliers in such a way as to promote ethical trading, environmental responsibility and labour standards at all tiers of the supply chain (eg by pre-qualifying suppliers on CSR policies, ethical codes, environmental management systems, reverse logistics and

recycling capabilities, and supply chain management; and incentivising, monitoring and developing supplier ethical performance)

- A commitment to supporting the improvement of working terms and conditions (labour standards) throughout the supply chain, and particularly in low-cost labour countries with comparatively lax regulatory regimes
- A commitment to supporting sustainable profit-taking by suppliers (eg not squeezing supplier profit margins unfairly) and to ensuring that fair prices are paid to suppliers back through the supply chain, particularly where buyers are in a dominant position (eg in developing and low-cost supply markets)
- Adherence to the ethical frameworks and codes of conduct of relevant bodies such as the International Labour Organisation (ILO), Fair Trade Association or Ethical Trading Initiative, the International Standards Organisation guidelines on Corporate Social Responsibility (ISO 26000: 2010), or the codes of ethics or conduct of relevant professional bodies (such as CIPS)
- A commitment to compliance with all relevant laws and regulations for consumer, supplier and worker protection.

6.3 The contract – or associated documentation (such as specifications or service level agreements) may make explicit:

- The buyer's commitment to adhere to specified ethical principles, standards or codes of conduct (and/ or to uphold and promote them through its supplier management and development policies)
- The buyer's requirement and expectation that the supplier will adhere to specified ethical principles, standards or codes of conduct (and will uphold and promote them through its own supply chain management)
- The seller's agreement to indemnify the buyer for any losses, claims or costs arising from breach of ethical principles, standards or codes of conduct during performance of the contract.

6.4 Contract terms and/or KPIs relating to ethical and labour standards might refer to:

- Compliance with the buyer's CSR policies, labour standards and ethical codes of conduct (supplied as part of the contract documentation, or by reference to the buyer's website or extranet)
- Specific KPIs in relation to responsible and ethical labour policies and practices – including fair terms and conditions of work, provisions for worker health and safety, equal opportunity and diversity
- Compliance with International Labour Organisation (ILO) standards (eg on supporting worker rights, upholding equality and diversity, and eradicating child and forced labour) or membership of the Ethical Trading Initiative (whose base code covers similar issues)
- Compliance with Fair Trade standards (supporting diverse suppliers, not abusing power in supply relationships, and paying fair prices, particularly in low-cost-labour markets)
- Commitment to transparency and improvement in ethical and labour performance, in collaboration with the buyer (eg willingness to undergo monitoring and evaluation of ethical and CSR policies by the buyer, on agreed terms of access; willingness to identify lower-tier suppliers, so the buyer can 'drill down' through the supply chain, and so on).

Health and safety

6.5 In addition to the insurance and indemnity provisions discussed in the last section, there is additionally a statutory requirement in the UK for both buyers and suppliers to observe the Health and Safety at Work Act 1974 and related regulations.

6.6 It is common for buyers to use contract terms to remind suppliers of the statutory requirements imposed on the parties by the Health and Safety at Work Act 1974; of the supplier's responsibility for compliance; and of the supplier's duty to ensure that staff working at the premises of the buyer (or the buyer's customers) comply with the health and safety requirements of those premises. The buyer may also require the supplier to indemnify it against any liability, costs, losses or expenses sustained by the buyer if the supplier fails to comply with the legislation.

6.7 A simple clause of this type may be formulated as follows.

'All goods shall have all necessary safety devices fitted. You are responsible for compliance with the Health and Safety at Work Act 1974 in relation to Goods and Services and will indemnify us against any liability, costs, losses or expenses we may sustain if you fail to do so.

'When you are working at our premises or the premises of our customer in the performance of any services or installation of the goods you shall ensure that your staff comply with our or our customer's requirements at the premises.'

Chapter summary

- A contract is a legally enforceable agreement between two parties, typically a buyer and a seller. The agreement may include both express and implied terms.
- Implied terms may arise from the nature of the contract, the need for business efficacy, the provisions of statute law, or the custom of the trade. The implied terms contained in SGA 1979 are particularly relevant to buyers.
- Most buyers and sellers have standard terms of business. This can give rise to a 'battle of the forms'.
- Model form contracts are published by third party experts such as trade associations and professional bodies, reflecting standard practice in particular industry sectors.
- Specific terms commonly found in buyer/seller contracts cover time of performance and payment, passing of title, liquidated damages, force majeure, guarantees, exclusion clauses, indemnities, insurances and subcontracting.
- Increasingly, buyer/seller contracts incorporate terms relating to ethical conduct.

Self-test questions

Numbers in brackets refer to the paragraphs where you can check your answers.

1   Define a contract. (1.1)

2   Distinguish between a condition and a warranty. (1.6)

3   List sources of implied terms in contracts. (2.5)

4   Explain the term implied by the UK SGA 1979 in relation to satisfactory quality and fitness for purpose. (Table 7.1)

5   Describe the documents that may give rise to a 'battle of the forms'. (3.5)

6   How can buyers overcome the problem of 'battle of the forms'? (3.8)

7   Give examples of published model form contracts. (4.4)

8   List areas where the terms and conditions of a buyer are likely to differ from those of a seller. (4.10)

9   What is meant by 'time is of the essence'? (5.3)

10   What is a Romalpa clause? (5.7)

11   Distinguish between liquidated and unliquidated damages. (5.11)

12   What are the tests for validity of an exclusion clause? (5.24, 5.25)

13   List ethical and CSR issues that might be included in a supply contract. (6.4)

CHAPTER 8

Assessing Pricing Arrangements

Assessment criteria and indicative content

 Assess the main types of pricing arrangements in commercial agreements

- The use of pricing schedules
- The use of fixed pricing arrangements
- Cost plus and cost reimbursable pricing arrangements
- The use of indexation and price adjustment formulae
- The use of incentivised/gainshare pricing arrangements
- Payment terms

Section headings

1 What is the 'right price'?
2 Pricing schedules
3 Fixed pricing arrangements
4 Cost-based pricing arrangements
5 Payment terms

Introduction

In Chapters 4–6 we looked at various documentary elements that may define the procurement need, as part of a commercial arrangement with external suppliers: product and service specifications, service level agreements and key performance indicators. In Chapter 7, we focused on the sources and interpretation of a range of express contract terms or clauses that may be included in the formal supply contract itself.

One element of the definition and contractual agreement of the business need that we have left largely out of the picture so far is *price*. The syllabus tackles the development of pricing arrangements in commercial contracts as a distinct discipline, so we cover it on its own here. However, you should bear in mind that price is closely interwoven with definition of the business need, and justification of the business case for a procurement. Price is central to a contract, because it represents the 'consideration' (payment or exchange of value) that is essential for a valid contract to be formed. Price (and cost) may act as a constraint on the level of specification and tolerances that is possible – and if the buyer wants to gain 'extra' timeliness, service or quality from a supplier, there will be price consequences.

In this chapter we explore a range of issues around price, and various contractual arrangements by which pricing may be structured and agreed.

1 What is the 'right price'?

1.1 Price may be defined as 'the value of a commodity or service measured in terms of the standard monetary unit' (Lysons & Farrington). In other words, price is what a supplier charges for goods or services – and if two suppliers quote different prices, a purchaser can readily compare the relative value offered by each.

1.2 The 'right price' for the supplier or seller to charge (the sales price) will be:

- A price which 'the market will bear': that is, a price that the market or a particular buyer will be willing to pay
- A price which allows the seller to win business, in competition with other suppliers (according to how badly it needs the business, and the prices being charged by its competitors)
- A price which allows the seller at least to cover its costs, and ideally to make a healthy profit which will allow it to survive in business and to invest in growth.

1.3 The 'right price' for the buyer to pay (the purchasing price) will be:

- A price which the purchaser can afford: allowing it to control its costs of production and make a profit on sale of its own goods or services
- A price which appears fair and reasonable, or represents value for money, for the total package of benefits being purchased
- A price which gives the purchaser a cost or quality advantage over its competitors, enabling it to compete more effectively in its own market
- A price which reflects sound purchasing practices: requiring suppliers to price competitively; negotiating skilfully; recognising the difference between strategic (critical) and non-critical (routine) purchases; and so on.

1.4 We discussed the methods by which suppliers determine their prices in Chapter 2, together with price and cost analysis, by which buyers can assess the reasonableness of supplier pricing: recap that material if it doesn't 'ring a bell'.

Contract provisions on price

1.5 Negotiation and agreement on 'price' may include a range of matters.

- The type of **pricing arrangement**: determining whether and how the supplier will be able to increase the price through the life of the contract, or add 'extras' (eg consumables, overtime payments or insurance costs) not included in the original quotation or tender
- The **price or fee schedules** (if any) on which the supplier will calculate the amounts charged
- Costs and charges incurred by the supplier in the course of the contract which are to be **reimbursed** by the buyer
- Methods by which **new prices or price changes** will be determined and jointly agreed (contract price adjustment)
- Available **discounts**, and the conditions under which they will be applied (eg for orders over a certain amount, or for early payment)
- **Terms of payment and credit** (timescales and methods of payment)

Pricing arrangements

1.6 Price arrangements or agreements in contracts are basically of two types: firm (or fixed) price, and flexible (generally, cost-based) price. However, these two options cover a range of possibilities, on a continuum from:

- Fixed price agreements, in which a schedule of fixed fees or payments is agreed in advance (and the supplier therefore bears all the risk of cost variances) to
- Cost-plus agreements, in which a fixed percentage is added to the supplier's cost of production or delivery (and the buyer therefore bears all the risk of cost variances).

1.7   Lysons and Farrington depict the various options (adapting the work of Behan, *Purchasing in Government,* 1994) as follows: Figure 8.1.

Figure 8.1 *Pricing arrangements (showing risks to the buyer)*

1.8   We will now go on to look at a range of these pricing arrangements. If you are asked in an exam for three types of arrangement, you might take the line of Burt, Dobler & Starling (*World Class Supply Management)* and cite the three broad categories of: (a) fixed price agreements, (b) incentive contracts and (c) cost-plus or cost reimbursement contracts.

2   Pricing schedules

2.1   Lysons and Farrington use the term **firm price agreements** to describe 'contracts that are negotiated with fixed payment schedules, payment based on milestones, or payment based on fixed fees for a service'. Examples include prices set per volume delivery, or fees per person per hour (eg for cleaning services). Under such a contract, if the supplier finds that performing the contract is more difficult or costly than anticipated, it is still obligated under the contract to deliver the product – and to receive no more than the contracted price.

2.2   An agreement based on a pre-negotiated firm pricing schedule might be appropriate for procurements for which:

- A reasonably comprehensive and accurate specification is available
- Fair prices can be estimated and established more or less accurately, based on more or less predictable costs
- There is relatively little risk of cost variation, or the supplier is willing to *bear* any risks of cost variation in order to win the contract
- Electronic purchase to pay systems are utilised, enabling automatic payments, at fixed prices, to be triggered by verified deliveries or milestone attainment.

2.3   The key point about firm price agreements and payment schedules is that these are advantageous to the buyer, in terms of:

- Financial risk, since its total price commitment is known in advance, and the supplier bears all the risk of cost fluctuations.
- Cashflow management, since the timing of payments (related to milestones or instalment deliveries) will be pre-planned
- Supplier motivation: a fixed price schedule gives the supplier a strong incentive to complete the work efficiently and on time, since any cost savings (below the agreed price) are kept by the supplier – and

it is also liable for any cost blowouts. In other words, the amount of the supplier's profit depends on the actual cost outcome – without a minimum or maximum profit limitation.

- Administrative simplicity and contract management costs, since the buyer will not be concerned with monitoring or auditing cost performance.

Pricing schedules for major projects

2.4 For major projects, such as construction or systems development, a firm price arrangement may be expressed in a **lump sum contract.** The principal and contractor agree a fixed sum for completing a specified programme of work by a given date. This type of contract will usually include an element of flexibility: it may include a contract price adjustment clause (discussed further below), usually based on agreed cost indices to take account of price fluctuations, outside an agreed limit, arising from contingency factors such as exchange rate movements, fluctuations in commodity prices or high levels of inflation over the life of the contract.

2.5 The role and accuracy of the specification is paramount in awarding lump sum contracts, as it forms the basis for the contract. As with other forms of firm price agreements, a lump sum approach ensures a high degree of contractor motivation – and it can also lead to quality or performance concerns, if the supplier is forced to cut corners, to reduce its exposure to cost blowouts, towards the end of the contract. The project manager needs to monitor progress carefully (particularly on quality issues).

2.6 If the buyer is unable to draw up a detailed enough specification to base the contract and pricing schedule on, it may agree a **schedule of rates or charges** (eg per hours worked, or per volume of materials used) associated with aspects of the anticipated work. (This is sometimes known as a 'measured form contract'.) Payment is then made against actual quantities, applying the agreed rates.

3 Fixed pricing arrangements

Reasons for cost/price variations

3.1 In practice, the supplier's costs in performing a contract may fluctuate, or be higher than forecast at the time of contract, for a wide range of reasons.

- Under-estimation of costs at the forecasting stage (eg owing to the difficulties of measuring or specifying the scale of production or amount of work required)
- Price inflation, escalating materials costs
- Wage inflation, escalating labour costs
- Commodity and energy price fluctuations
- Exchange rate fluctuations (affecting international supply costs)
- Overtime or incentive payments required to 'crash' the schedule (reduce lead times or meet urgent requirements)
- Failure costs incurred by unforeseen quality problems (scrap, re-work, damages and so on)
- Changes in the scope of the contract: additional requirements or changes
- Unforeseen contingencies (eg additional transport costs due to carrier failure).

3.2 In order to maintain the security of supply and a sustainable and equitable supply relationship, it is often seen as desirable to reduce the financial risks to both buyer (on the basis of a cost-plus agreement) and supplier (on the basis of a firm price agreement). This can be done by incorporating variations – allowing flexibility – into a firm pricing arrangement.

Firm fixed price (FFP) agreements

3.3 A fixed price agreement is basically a firm agreement to pay a specified price when the items (services) specified by the contract have been delivered and accepted. Once agreed (on the basis of negotiation or competitive bidding), the price remains fixed for the duration of the contract. However, some flexibility may expressly be permitted for adjustments to the price arising from changes in the scope of the contract: for example, if additional requirements are added (adding cost) or a project component is removed (subtracting cost). There may also be flexibility for the supplier to request some relief for losses arising from escalating costs, if the customer has contributed to those costs (eg by changing designs) – especially if the supplier is in a strong position (eg because no alternative suppliers are available at the right time or price to meet the need).

3.4   A simple contract clause, specifying a firm price for the duration of the contract, with flexibility for variation, may be as follows.

'The price of the goods and/or services shall be as stated in the purchase order [or pricing and payment schedule]. No increase will be accepted by the buyer unless agreed by him in writing in advance of delivery or performance.'

3.5   Such an arrangement would be suitable where standard items are purchased from stock, or for short-term production requirements, for which the risk of significant cost variation will be minimal.

Fixed price with contract price adjustment (FPCPA) agreements

3.6   A fixed price may be set, but with **provision for upward or downward revision** on the occurrence (or non-occurrence) of specified contingencies, through the insertion of a contract price adjustment (CPA) clause. Such arrangements are used to recognise volatile labour or supply market conditions which make firm fixed pricing difficult – and would otherwise necessitate large 'contingency allowances' in the contract price (which may disadvantage the supplier if forecast price rises are greater than expected, or the buyer if they are less than expected).

3.7   The contract may stipulate that negotiated price adjustments are allowable, based on:

- **Actual increases or decreases** in material, labour, commodity or energy and fuel costs (depending on the cost vulnerabilities of the supply market) within the life of the contract, beyond the control of the supplier, and beyond a specified range of variation. Eligible costs and contingency events (eg exchange rate fluctuations outside an agreed range, or a rise in air freight costs due to new taxes, rising oil prices or carbon offset requirements) will have to be identified and closely defined, or subject to negotiation. The supplier's cost schedules and breakdowns will have to be monitored and verified to justify price adjustments.
- **Links to specified indices** relevant to supply market costs.

3.8   In economics, an 'index' (plural: 'indices') is a statistical measure of average changes in a group of data over time. The term 'price indexation' is used for the linking of prices to rises or falls in specified indices, such as:

- Commodities indices, or commodity price indices, which track the weighted average of selected commodity prices, and are designed to be representative of a broad commodity asset class or a subset of commodities (such as energy, metals or agriculture). Examples include the World Bank Commodity Price Index, the Goldman Sachs Commodity Index, the Thomson Reuters/Jefferies CRB Index, the S&P Commodity Index; and the Merrill Lynch Commodity Index eXtra (MLCX).
- The Labour Market Index (LMI), which tracks the weighted average of wages and salaries, according to labour type and location, as a guide to labour costs

3.9   Fixed price arrangements with contract price adjustment or indexation clauses may be suitable where the supply market costs are likely to be volatile within the contract period. They are commonly used in the procurements of commodities and construction services, for example.

The use of indexation and price adjustment formulae

3.10   In addition to the linking of contract price adjustments to published indices, there are a number of other uses of index calculations (the mathematics of which is beyond the scope of this syllabus).

3.11   The calculation of average changes in the price or cost of an item or group of items over a period of time can be used to:

- Estimate the current average prices or costs of a product, by using price/cost data for similar items at a previous 'base' date
- Eliminate the effects of inflation or deflation when analysing price and cost trends
- Allow for currency fluctuations when estimating or negotiating future prices or costs
- Compare the cost performance of different suppliers, or a particular supplier over time
- Identify and define average price/cost changes, as the basis for contract cost or price adjustment calculations (which in turn will be the basis for price adjustment clauses).

3.12   Various formulae for **contract price adjustment (CPA)** have been developed to suit the needs of different industries. An important example, used as the prototype for similar formulae used by other industries and public sector bodies, is the British Electrotechical and Allied Manufacturers Association (BEAMA) formula.

3.13   In essence, the BEAMA formula calculates the likely variation of labour and materials costs, based on industry average data, throughout the contract period, as a percentage of the total agreed contract price. The resulting industry-average cost variations can then be justified, as the basis of a claim for contract price adjustment.

3.14   The process (for electrical machinery, using the BEAMA formula) may be described as follows.

- The total negotiated contract price is divided into standard proportions of 5% fixed costs; 47.5% labour; and 47.5% materials.
- Materials cost variations are calculated using cost indices (in this case, provided by the Office for National Statistics) at two data points: (i) the date of tender (or 'cost basis date'), and (ii) the average of the indices between the dates identified at two-fifths of the contract period and four-fifths of the contract period.
- Labour cost variations are calculated by using a labour index (in this case, developed by the BEAMA itself, based on adjusted Department of Employment average earnings statistics) at two data points: (i) the date of tender, and (ii) the average of the indices published for the last two-thirds of the contract period (ie after the date identified as one-third of the contract period).
- The bases for price adjustment are calculated by inserting these average cost variation figures into a complex mathematical formula, giving a percentage adjustment figure for labour costs; a percentage adjustment figure for materials costs; a total percentage adjustment for labour and materials combined; and a monetary amount based on that percentage of the total contract price.
- If the *actual* cost to the contractor of performing the contract is increased (or decreased) owing to a rise (or fall) in labour costs or materials, these amounts are simply added to (or deducted from) the contract price. However, any costs incurred by the contractor's error or negligence are *not* taken into account.

3.15   Lysons and Farrington recommend the following procedures for dealing with post-contract price adjustments or increases.

- Adjustments should be authorised by a single responsible official, where possible, to maintain control over total budget variance.
- Adjustments should be confirmed in writing, as part of contract version control.
- All relevant contract stakeholders (eg design, estimating, project management) should be notified of agreed adjustments.
- Where standard costing is in operation (as discussed in Chapter 3), there should be a procedure for monitoring price adjustments and variances against standard material uses.

- Where adjustments are calculated in accordance with an agreed contract price adjustment formula, records should clearly identify the cost base date(s) of the original contract, and the circumstances giving rise to the adjustment.
- Suppliers should be asked to provide data to justify any price increase claimed.
- If a buyer and vendor cannot come to agreement on a proposed price increase, the buyer may need to consider alternative suppliers or materials, or the use of longer-term contracts (requiring longer notification of increases and adjustments).

Fixed price incentive (or incentivised/gainshare) contracts

3.16 A fixed price arrangement may provide for **adjustment of the final price to include various supplier incentives**: additional 'bonus' payments, profit allowances or value gain sharing, as an incentive for the supplier to shorten lead times or deliver on time, improve quality or technical performance, or achieve cost savings. The final price will usually be subject to a pre-negotiated maximum or 'cap', to avoid open-ended liability.

3.17 Here are some options for incentive or incentivised contracts, of different types.

- The establishment of a negotiated **target cost** for supply, on which a fixed maximum price (including a 'target profit' for the supplier) is based. The target cost will be an agreed amount that represents the most likely result under 'normal' business conditions. If the supplier achieves cost savings – ie comes in under the target cost – the amount of the savings will be shared with the buyer, on an agreed percentage or proportion basis. (A numerical example is given in Figure 8.2 later in this chapter.)
- Staged payments (so that the supplier only gets paid in full on completion of the project) or contingency payments (eg part of the payment is linked to KPI performance or cost savings) or faster payment for early delivery (eg pay-on-receipt arrangements)
- Specified bonus payments (or incentive fees) added to the fixed price, linked to attainment of specific key performance indicators (KPIs), cost savings or improvement targets (eg for extra units of productivity, or each day or week ahead of schedule): various options are discussed under the heading of 'cost-plus' arrangements later in this chapter.
- Revenue, profit or gain sharing (eg allocating the supplier an agreed percentage or flat fee bonus for cost savings). Where supplier improvements create added value, revenue or profit for the buyer, the 'gain' is shared: a 'win-win' outcome.
- A fixed price for the product or service that *decreases* year on year through the contract, motivating the supplier progressively to improve efficiency in order to preserve its profit margins
- Price penalties for performance failure: ie a liquidated damages clause (based on a genuine attempt to estimate losses to the buyer incurred by supplier failure or breach of contract).

3.18 In an incentive contract based on cost targets or reductions, the cost responsibility is shared by the buyer and supplier. As well as motivating the supplier to control costs, this may prevent the supplier from inflating or 'padding' the contract price to minimise the risks of cost uncertainty.

3.19 Incentivised contracts are suitable where it is regarded as desirable to motivate the supplier or contractor to cut costs and improve performance: either as part of a long-term, continuous improvement and gain-sharing agreement (as in a supplier partnership) or where supplier performance management is critical.

Fixed price with review or re-determination clauses

3.20 Fixed price arrangements may also allow for the agreed price schedule to apply for an initial, specified duration, which may be shorter than the duration of the contract. The contract price adjustment clause will provide that at the end of the specified period, or at specified intervals, the price will be amended or opened to review and re-negotiation, in the light of cost fluctuations, supplier performance and contingency factors.

3.21 This may be suitable where the parties are unable to agree on an accurate and fair fixed price for the whole duration of a long-term contract.

- Supply market costs and conditions may only be forecastable for a short period ahead owing to uncertainty or volatility
- The nature of the work on a project may be less accurately specifiable after the initial stages
- Costs on an innovative project with a new supplier may fall over time as suppliers gain experience, the 'learning curve' becomes less steep, and the costs of labour, managerial time, learning and error rectification grow less.

'Level of effort' term contracts

3.22 For some contracts, it may be impossible accurately to specify outcomes or outputs, or to estimate costs. Examples might include research and development or software development contracts, for which:

- The expenditure of effort, time and expertise may not relate directly to measurable results or deliverables achieved (because outcomes are uncertain)
- Costs are difficult to estimate, as parameters and process requirements may not be known in advance of learning and experimentation.

3.23 In such cases, the contract may require the supplier or contractor to provide a specified level of effort (eg hours per week or 'best effort' standards) over an agreed period (eg the term of the contract) in return for a fixed amount. The work itself can only be specified in general terms.

4 Cost-based pricing arrangements

4.1 At the other end of the spectrum from firm price agreements, or pricing schedules, **cost price or cost-reimbursable arrangements** are based on guaranteeing that the supplier covers its costs incurred in performing the contract, in addition to earning an agreed profit percentage. Most cost-type arrangements include a cost limitation clause or 'cap', which sets a limitation on the reimbursement of costs.

Cost-plus pricing

4.2 Under a cost-plus arrangement, the buyer agrees to reimburse the supplier for all allowable, allocable (ie directly attributable to the work undertaken for the buyer) and reasonable costs incurred in performing the contract *plus* a fixed fee or percentage representing the supplier's profit.

- A **cost plus fixed fee (CPFF)** contract includes payment of allowed costs *plus* a pre-determined fixed amount, as the fee for doing the work. The terms will specify a best-estimate and/or capped cost and the amount of the fixed fee, which will change only if the scope of the contract changes (ie regardless of the cost outcome). The buyer should calculate the effect on total price of higher than estimated costs (ie costs + fixed fee for a range of final cost totals), in order to anticipate total liability. This type of arrangement contains no incentive for the supplier to manage costs, so is used chiefly for highly uncertain contracts with few options (such as R & D contracts).
- A **cost plus incentive fee (CPIF)** contract includes payment of allowed costs *plus* a higher fee for meeting or exceeding performance or cost targets or KPIs. This may be used where the cost risk suggest the need for a cost-type arrangement, but an incentive can be established to motivate the supplier to reduce costs: eg for initial production runs of a new product.
- A **cost plus award fee (CPAF)** contract includes payment of allowed costs *plus* a fee (bonus) based on the contractor's performance. This was pioneered by NASA for the procurement of highly complex hardware and professional services. It is a preferred option for services (such as cleaning, design or software development) 'where the ability to reward the supplier for non-quantitative aspects of its performance, on a subjective basis, makes good business sense' (Burt *et al*). An award sum is set aside for the periodic payment of the supplier for 'the application of effort in meeting the buyer's stated needs': in other words, on the basis of the buyer's subjective evaluation of the supplier's effort and customer service.

4.3 Alternative arrangements include:

- **Cost without fee**, for non-profit-making providers. Universities, for example, frequently do research work for government and industry on this basis, and seek to recover all overhead costs (including facilities costs and remuneration for personnel involved in the contracted work).
- **Cost sharing**, where the supplier stands to benefit from its own work (eg if its research or development work will benefit its own product portfolio, as in the electronics industry). In such cases, the buyer and supplier may agree on a fair basis for sharing the costs (often 50: 50).
- **Time and materials,** for contracts (such as repair services) where the precise work to be done cannot be predicted in advance. Instead, the parties agree on a fixed rate per labour hour (including overhead and profit), *plus* materials supplied at cost.

4.4 From what we have already noted about the risks of cost fluctuations, you should be able to appreciate that such an arrangement is basically disadvantageous to the buyer, in terms of:

- Financial risk, since its total price commitment is *not* known in advance, and it bears all the risk of cost blow-outs, exchange rate fluctuations and other factors
- Supplier motivation, since there is little motivation for suppliers to monitor or manage cost-related risks which will be borne by the buyer
- Administration and contract management costs: suppliers' cost schedules will have to be carefully scrutinised by cross functional teams (including financial and management accountants, and relevant specialists such as engineers and project planners) and monitored throughout the life of the project to ensure accurate accounting and reimbursement.

4.5 There are advantages, however, in that the final cost may be less than a fixed price contract, because the supplier does not have to quote or negotiate an inflated price in order to cover its cost-related risks. Cost-plus contracts are often used when long-term quality is a more significant business need than cost minimisation.

4.6 In practice, however, it will be preferable to acknowledge cost-related risks (due to factors such as underestimation of costs, wage and price inflation, fluctuating commodity prices, schedule blow-outs and incentive rates, exchange rate fluctuations and so on) by building protections for the buyer into cost-based agreements. One key technique for doing this is target costing.

Target costing

4.7 Target costing is an approach pioneered by Japanese firms which differs considerably from the cost-plus approach.

- The cost-plus approach builds up the cost of a product by analysing its components step by step. A profit margin is then added and the result is the selling price of the product. With luck (from the supplier's point of view) this will be a price that the market can stand. And with luck (from the buyer's point of view) it will also be an accurate enough forecast of the actual cost to minimise financial risk in a cost-plus pricing arrangement.
- A target costing approach starts at the other end of the equation. The supplier estimates the maximum selling price that the market will be willing to pay for a product with specific features, or negotiates a maximum price (including an agreed profit) with a particular buyer. It then works backwards to calculate the production cost that must be achieved in order to provide a reasonable profit, and attacks costs to reduce them to the required level.

4.8 Target costing requires close cooperation between members of the supply chain. Each member must work closely with the others to identify opportunities for cost reductions, progressively seeking to drive costs and prices downwards.

4.9 Lysons & Farrington envisage two types of flexible pricing arrangements based on target cost.

- Target cost with maximum price
- Target cost without maximum price

Target cost with maximum price

4.10 In a target cost with maximum price (or target price) arrangement, the contract stipulates a **target price** (based on target cost, including an agreed profit margin) *and* a **maximum or ceiling price** for the contract. Any excess costs, over and above the maximum price, are borne by the supplier. Any cost savings, below the target cost, are shared on an agreed percentage basis, between the supplier and the buyer.

4.11 Such an approach is the same as a fixed price incentive contract, discussed earlier. It may be suitable where:

- Target cost can be determined with a reasonable degree of accuracy and certainty *but*
- Exact total costs cannot be accurately forecast at the time of the contract *and*
- The buyer has the power to negotiate a position in which it does not have to bear the risk of extra costs, or indeed can share in any gains made by the supplier in the form of reduced costs.

4.12 A better way to look at this is as a situation where there is a price agreed on the contract, but the supplier and buyer agree that any savings experienced by the supplier on the costs it has estimated on the contract will be shared between the supplier and the buyer.

Example

B agrees to buy goods that the supplier, S, estimates will cost $100,000 to make. The price is agreed at $120,000 (so S will make a margin of $20,000 or 16.67%), but B and S agree that any saving in actual against estimated costs will be shared between them in the ratio 40: 60 (so 60% of the cost saving will be kept by S, but 40% will be handed over to B).

In the end S's costs are $10,000 less than estimated, at $90,000. Of the $10,000 saving, $6,000 is retained by S but $4,000 is deducted from the final price paid by B:

	$
Agreed price	120,000
Less: 40% of cost saving	(4,000)
Final price paid by B	116,000

Another way of looking at this calculation is from the point of view of S:

	$
Costs incurred	90,000
Margin on agreed price	20,000
60% of cost saving	6,000
Final price received by S	116,000

In the end, S's total margin is $26,000, or 22.4% of the final price, while B has paid 3.3% less than it expected.

Target cost without maximum price

4.13 In an arrangement for target cost without a maximum price, there is no price 'ceiling' to protect the buyer. A target price is determined, on the basis of target cost. Any excess costs, over and above the target price, are shared between the supplier and purchaser on an agreed percentage basis. Any cost savings below the target cost are similarly shared in agreed proportions.

4.14 Such an approach may be suitable for longer-term contracts, especially in volatile supply markets: over the life of the contract, it may be anticipated that suppliers' costs will fluctuate above or below the target cost. In order for the contract to be fair and sustainable, therefore, the supplier may require to be partially compensated or reimbursed for costs incurred over the forecast target. By the same token, it will expect to be fairly reimbursed for cost savings or reductions, compared to the forecast target: this element creates an incentive for cost management.

4.15 Lysons and Farrington offer a numerical example, to illustrate the point: Figure 8.3.

Figure 8.2 *Target cost without maximum price*

Target cost per item: $10 (plus $1 profit)
Cost variations above or below this target cost to be shared in the ratio 50: 50 (supplier: purchaser)

Cost ($)	Profit ($)	Price ($)
10.00 (target)	1.00	11.00
11.00	1.00	11.50
9.50	1.50	10.75

Cost reimbursable pricing arrangements

4.16 The terms 'cost reimbursement contract' or 'cost reimbursable contract' is generally used inter-changeably with the term 'cost-plus contract', where a contract is paid for all of its allowed and allocable costs to a set limit, plus an additional payment to allow for profit and incentive payments.

4.17 An alternative use of the term may be where the contract provides for a fixed price for performance of the contract, but adds a guarantee that the buyer will reimburse the supplier for specified allocable costs incurred in performance of the contract, up to a specified maximum. This is basically a cost plus fixed fee (CPFF) contract – but with the fee comprising the main price, and contingency 'expenses' reimbursable as an 'add on'.

4.18 This is a common arrangement in contracts for professional services (such as legal, accountancy or consultancy services) where a fee schedule will be based on the billable hours of the professional's time, and a separate provision will be made for the reimbursement of specified costs (such as communication, transport, materials and consumables used in performance of the contract) to be itemised for the buyer by the supplier. In a contract for cleaning services, ancillary costs are likely to be factored into the price schedule (eg cost per hour of the service, inclusive of materials, labour, transport, insurances etc). In a contract for professional services, however, the nature of costs may not be amenable to accurate estimation in advance.

5   Payment terms

5.1 Unless the seller agrees, there is a principle that payment and delivery are concurrent obligations: the seller must be ready and willing to give possession of the goods to the buyer in exchange for the price, and the buyer must be ready and willing to pay the price in exchange for the possession of the goods (Section 28 of the Sale of Goods Act 1979). A contract may expressly stipulate 'payment on delivery'. Frequently, however, the seller allows the buyer to have possession before any payment is required, the sale then being called a 'credit sale'.

Payment methods

5.2 Some approaches to payment are favourable to the buyer and some to the seller, and this will be the focus of pre-contract negotiation.

- **Payment in advance** (or payment with order) might be requested by some suppliers in high-risk supply contexts (eg an unknown customer in an international market, or a known payment risk because of a history of late payments). The buyer usually has to pay on signing of the contract or placing of the purchase order. This will be very beneficial for the supplier's cashflow and risk management – but not for the buyer's.
- **Payment on delivery** is similar in effect to payment with order, except that the buyer commits to payment on verified receipt and acceptance of the goods or service.
- **Open account or credit:** the buyer has a credit account with a supplier, allowing it to pay the supplier within an agreed period after delivery of the items or receipt of the supplier's invoice (typically 30 or 60 days).

Credit terms

5.3   The negotiation of credit terms is the standard payment approach for commercial purchasing. Businesses which sell goods on credit terms generally specify a standard credit period: usually, 30 days (with 60 or 90 days representing 'extended credit terms'). In general, a supplier will try to ensure that buyers accept as few days credit as possible – while a buyer will try to extend credit terms as far as possible (especially if it will be holding procured items in stock for a long time before realising their value through re-sale or use). A discount may be available for agreement to shorter credit terms, or the supplier might charge at a premium rate for extended payment terms.

5.4   The contract may incorporate express terms to vary standard payment terms.

- The contract may stipulate exactly how the credit terms are to be interpreted. For example, it may stipulate that payment will fall due 30 days after the end of the month in which the supplier's invoice is received. This would mean, for example, that an invoice received on 2 April would not be paid until the end of May.
- A prompt or early payment discount may be offered or negotiated for the payment of invoices earlier than the agreed credit terms, or for the agreement of shorter credit terms. For example, a supplier might give a discount of 2% if the invoice is paid within 10 days. This might be worth pursuing by the buyer, provided that the cashflow implications are taken into account – and that the buyer's payment protocols are flexible enough to allow early payment.

Credit limits

5.5   Suppliers face the risk that the buyer will be unable or unwilling to pay when the debt falls due. In order to minimise this risk, suppliers will generally screen potential customers before granting them credit. It should be standard practice to seek references from the potential customer's bank and from other trade creditors. In some cases, it may be appropriate to get a full-scale credit reference from a specialist credit agency (such as Dun & Bradstreet). An appropriate credit limit should then be set.

5.6   Once trading begins, the supplier's order processing system should automatically flag any occasion when an order would push the customer over his agreed limit for a given period. This can then be assessed by credit control staff and a decision taken as to whether the sale should proceed.

5.7   Where orders have been fulfilled, credit control staff should also have procedures for chasing payment from the buyer in timely fashion, to avoid debts becoming old. Failure to send out invoices on time or to follow up late payers will have an adverse effect on the cashflow of the business.

Stage or progress payments

5.8 Stage payments (sometimes known as 'progress payments') are usually used for capital projects although they might also be used for material that would be held in stock by the purchaser. Here, an initial payment (for example 10% of the total cost) would be made at the time the purchase order is placed. This is then followed with agreed percentage payments at agreed 'stages' of project completion.

5.9 For large capital procurements and complex projects, the terms of payment will usually be based on instalments. An initial payment (a negotiated percentage of the total cost) might be made on contract, or initial delivery. The supplier then invoices agreed percentage amounts at agreed dates or stages of project completion, and the buyer makes payment in accordance with agreed credit terms.

- The supplier will want as much payment as possible up front: to minimise the risk of non-payment by covering its costs, as well as to manage its cashflow.
- The buyer will want to defer payment for as long as possible: to minimise delivery risk by ensuring that it has secured as much as possible of the value it is paying for, as well as to manage its cashflow.

5.10 This provides good scope for negotiation. Whatever is agreed at the contracting stage, however, the buyer should certainly insist on a reasonable **retention**. For example, it might insist that 10% of the contract price will become due for payment only after certain agreed performance criteria have been met during operation of the procured asset, or only after a programme of work has been satisfactorily completed to a required progress milestone or project stage.

Commercial and legal considerations in regard to payment terms

5.11 There are many commercial and relationship considerations in regard to payment terms. The length of credit periods, for example, is important:

- In securing cashflow (eg by getting money in from debtors more quickly than you pay money out to creditors)
- As a bargaining tool (eg a supplier offering extended credit in return for other benefits)
- As a source of short-term finance (eg by delaying payments to suppliers).

5.12 Paying bills late can be regarded as a source of short-time finance and positive cashflow. The supplier has in effect – probably unwillingly – 'loaned' goods to the business. It might agree to do so, temporarily or occasionally, in order to reap benefits of goodwill and extra business. However, repeated late payment is likely to have a negative effect on supplier relationships, customer status (supplier preferencing) and supply security in the long term. Ultimately, a supplier may refuse to supply goods on credit.

5.13 Under the UK Sale of Goods Act, any time stated for payment is *not* 'of the essence' (ie a vital condition of contract), unless the contract states otherwise. In the absence of an express term to this effect, therefore, the seller is *not* entitled to refuse to supply goods on the grounds of late payment in the UK.

5.14 However, in the UK:

- Under the Late Payment of Commercial Debts (Interest) Act 1998, statutory interest of 8% above base rate is automatically payable by the buyer if payment is late.
- The Sale of Goods Act 1979 provides for a number of remedies for an 'unpaid seller': a seller who has not been paid the whole agreed price at the time when it falls due, where property/title in the goods has already passed to the buyer. In such a case the seller has remedies against the goods (to retain possession of the goods until he is paid) and against the buyer (to sue for payment). These are discussed below.

5.15 It should also be noted that there is potential for ambiguity, misunderstanding and contractual dispute around the definition of 'standard' credit or payment terms. As an example, payment terms of '60 days credit' may be agreed. The supplier interprets this as meaning payment within 60 days of goods being delivered; the buyer believes it means two months after the end of the month in which goods were delivered – or two months after the end of the month in which the *invoice* for the goods was received.

5.16 **Express payment terms** may therefore be inserted in the contract to specify:

- *When goods will be paid for* (eg at the end of the month following the month in which the goods are received, or in which the invoice for the goods is received, whichever is the later)
- What *interest,* if any, the buyer will be liable for in the event of late payment (eg a rate which compensates the seller for losses directly caused by the late payment, so long as this does not exceed the rate of statutory interest)
- Whether time for payment shall be *'of the essence'* of the agreement, giving the supplier the right to repudiate the contract if the buyer fails to pay on time (From a buyer's point of view, the contract will ideally state that time of payment is *not* off the essence of the contract.)

Statutory remedies for an unpaid seller in the UK

5.17 An unpaid seller's remedies against the goods in the UK include:

- The right of **seller's lien** (ss 41–43 SGA 1979): the right of an unpaid seller still in *possession* of goods in respect of which the price is owing, to *retain* them until the price has been paid, or his debt secured or satisfied
- The right of **stoppage in transit** (ss 45–46): the right of an unpaid seller to require a carrier in possession of the goods *not* to deliver to the buyer, by giving notice of his claim to the carrier in possession before transit is completed – or by taking actual possession of the goods.
- The right of **resale** (s 48): the right of a seller to resell the goods, if the buyer expressly or by his conduct repudiates the contract (and therefore relinquishes his rights to the goods).

5.18 Note that these remedies apply where property/title in the goods has passed to the buyer, though the seller has not yet been paid. Where the seller retains the property in the goods, such remedies do not apply, because the seller has the right to retain or recover the goods by right of ownership (eg in the case of the use of a retention or Romalpa clause, discussed in Chapter 7).

5.19 Remedies against the buyer in the UK include:

- **Action for the price** (s 49 SGA 1979). The seller may sue the buyer for the price where the property in the goods has already passed to the buyer and the buyer fails to pay the price in accordance with the contract. He may also sue for the price if the price is due but unpaid on a date specified in the contract – regardless of whether the goods have been delivered, or property in the goods has not yet passed to the buyer.
- **Action for damages for non-acceptance** (s 50). If the buyer wrongfully neglects or refuses to accept or pay for the goods, and the property has not passed, the seller can sue for damages for loss resulting from the breach of contract.

Chapter summary

- The pricing arrangements agreed will typically subject the buyer to a mix of financial risk and performance risk. There is a trade-off between the two.
- Firm price agreements are advantageous to the buyer, but may expose the supplier to risk.
- There are many reasons why a supplier's costs may fluctuate from the level contemplated in the supply contract. Contract price adjustment agreements are a method of protecting both buyer and supplier.
- It is possible, and often advisable, to incorporate supplier incentives in pricing agreements.
- Cost-based pricing agreements are intended to ensure that the supplier at least covers his costs. However, unless carefully drafted, they can expose the buyer to unacceptable levels of risk.
- Target costing is based on first agreeing an acceptable price, and then attacking costs so that the supplier is left with an acceptable profit.
- It is normal practice for a supplier to allow credit terms to the buyer. If the buyer fails to pay, or fails to pay on time, the seller has statutory remedies.

 ## Self-test questions

Numbers in brackets refer to the paragraphs where you can check your answers.

1. What is meant by the 'right price' from the perspective of a buyer? (1.3)

2. Explain the trade-off between a buyer's financial risk and his performance risk depending on the type of pricing agreement. (1.7, Figure 8.1)

3. In what circumstances might a firm pricing schedule be appropriate? (2.2)

4. List reasons why a supplier's costs may fluctuate from the level contemplated in the contract. (3.1)

5. How does a CPA clause work? (3.6, 3.7)

6. List possible supplier incentives that might be included in a pricing arrangement. (3.17)

7. List possible variations of cost-plus pricing agreements. (4.2)

8. Explain how target costing differs from traditional cost-plus pricing. (4.7)

9. In what circumstances are stage payments normally used? (5.8)

10. What statutory remedies are available to a supplier if the buyer fails to pay or pays late? (5.14, 5.17)

CHAPTER 9

Outsourcing

Assessment criteria and indicative content

4.1 Differentiate outsourcing from other types of procurement

- Make or buy decisions
- Defining outsourcing
- Outsourcing non-core and core work or services

4.2 Assess how outsourcing can impact on procurement

- Costs and benefits of outsourcing
- Risks in outsourcing
- The market development and growth of outsourcing

4.3 Develop a plan for procuring outsourced work or services

- Determining core competencies and outsourcing opportunities

Section headings

1 Make/do or buy decisions
2 What is outsourcing?
3 The growth of outsourcing
4 Risks, costs and benefits of outsourcing
5 What should be outsourced?

Introduction

In this chapter we turn our attention to a major area of procurement study: the practice of outsourcing activities, previously carried out within an organisation, to external contractors.

At a strategic level, this raises important 'boundary of the firm' or 'make/do or buy?' decisions. Should the firm make products or perform activities itself, or devolve these tasks to external suppliers? What kinds of competencies and resources should be retained in-house, and which might be devolved to the 'extended enterprise'? What risks and opportunities are involved?

At a tactical and operational level, outsourcing raises a wide range of issues around: planning, business case development and exit strategy; risk management; contracting; the protection of employees' rights in transfer and/or redundancy; and supplier relationship management.

In this chapter we will explore the primarily *strategic* issues: defining outsourcing and assessing its effect on procurement. In Chapter 10 we will go on to explore the tactical and operational issues in procuring outsourced work or services.

1 Make/do or buy decisions

1.1 The nature of the make/do or buy decision can be stated in fairly simple terms. At one extreme, a firm could make its products (or develop its services) entirely in-house, buying in perhaps nothing but raw materials. The value of the final product will have been created almost entirely from the work done by the firm. At the other extreme, a firm could minimise its own activities, buying in almost everything from outside suppliers (who would therefore be adding almost all the value in the finished product).

1.2 In most cases, of course, firms will occupy a middle position somewhere between these two extremes. This is the nature of the make/do or buy decision: where exactly should the firm position itself along this spectrum of possibilities? Where is the 'boundary of the firm'? Do we make in-house? Do we invest in machinery and/or technology and/or labour? Do we need to control the operation internally as core to our business? Have we the skills to manufacture goods or deliver services in-house? Or do we buy in materials, resources, skills and expertise from outside?

1.3 Make-or-buy decisions face all organisations, at three levels of planning.

- **Strategic make/do or buy decisions** determine the long-term activities, capabilities, resources and 'boundaries' of the firm, by influencing: what products the organisation makes (or what services it performs); what resources it invests in; what capabilities and knowledge it retains in-house for future business development; and how it structures its supply chain
- **Tactical make-do or buy decisions** reflect the organisation's response to short-term or cyclical changes in demand for its products or services, in order to utilise available productive capacity efficiently. If demand exceeds the organisation's capacity to make/do using internal resources, it may need to 'buy in'. If demand falls, and internal capacity is being underutilised, the organisation may need to bring in-house work previously bought from external suppliers.
- **Operational or 'component' make-or-buy decisions** are basically product design and manufacturing decisions, determining whether a particular component of a product should be manufactured in-house or bought in from the external supply chain.

Factors in make/do or buy decisions

1.4 Make/do or buy decisions depend on a range of strategic and operational factors.

- Whether the item or activity is strategically important or 'core' to the business
- The effects on total costs of production of buying in or incurring costs in-house – and whether in-house provision is competitive with external provision
- The availability of in-house competencies and production capacity; how readily they can be acquired or expanded; and whether they will be consistently available in future. (Lack of adequate competency or capacity will push the firm towards the 'buy' end of the spectrum.) Note that if a firm lacks design or manufacturing capability, it may choose to 'buy in' *either* components and assemblies (designed/manufactured by external suppliers) *or* design/manufacturing capability (eg by outsourcing design and manufacture to an external contractor).
- The availability of suitable external suppliers and positive supplier relationships. (A lack of suitable suppliers would push the firm towards the 'make/do' end of the spectrum.)
- The assessed risks of devolving activities to the external supply chain (eg in terms of loss of control, loss of in-house knowledge and skill, risks to confidential data and intellectual property, and so on)
- Human resource impacts. Will a decision to buy-in lead to redundancies? Will a decision to make/do in-house lead to a need for training and/or recruitment?

1.5 Make/do or buy decisions will primarily be based on **economic criteria**: whether the organisation can viably deploy or develop resources to produce the item or deliver the service in-house, or whether it would be more economically advantageous to outsource production or provision and buy-in goods and services. We will look at some of the cost and profitability considerations in Chapter 10, where we discuss the business case for outsourcing, but they include:

- Comparison of the cost of buying in (the vendor's price and total costs of acquisition) with the marginal cost of making/doing in-house
- The opportunity cost of using in-house productive capacity to make/do one item or activity rather than another (potentially more profitable) item or activity.

1.6   Other considerations in make/do or buy decisions, highlighted by the procurement literature, include the following: Table 9.1.

Table 9.1 *Factors in make/do or buy decisions*

FACTORS SUPPORTING MAKING/DOING	FACTORS SUPPORTING BUYING IN
Opportunity to extract value from otherwise idle capacity and resources	Quantities required are too small for economic production
Potential for lead time reduction	Avoid costs of specialist machinery and labour
Cost of work is known in advance	Reduced inventory costs
Desire to exert direct control over production and/or quality	Financial risk shared with supply chain
Protection of confidentiality and intellectual property (requirement for design secrecy)	Access to supplier's specialist research, expertise, technology, patents, designs and so on
Less supply risk and supplier risk (if suppliers are unreliable)	Augmented production capacity, if production facilities are limited
Desire to maintain a stable workforce (in periods of declining sales)	Desire to maintain a stable workforce (in periods of rising sales)

1.7   Such decisions also relate to the **core competencies** of the organisation. Does it have the capabilities (capacity, resources, processes, knowledge and skill base) to produce the item competitively in-house, or can greater value be added by harnessing the extra capacity, technology, resources and competencies of external suppliers?

1.8   Focus on 'core competencies' (or what Peters & Waterman called 'sticking to the knitting': focusing on what you are good or competitive at) has led many companies to buy in products, components or assemblies previously produced in-house, and to outsource a range of support functions (such as maintenance, catering, warehousing and transport, and staff recruitment and training) and even core functions such as sales and customer service (eg in call centres).

1.9   We will discuss this important question of core and non-core competencies later in the chapter.

The contribution of procurement to make/do or buy decisions

1.10   Make/do or buy decisions require the input of many different functions *and* supply chain collaborators. The procurement or supply chain management function may be particularly well placed to assess the implications of the 'buy' option, because it is familiar with: the supply market; supplier capabilities, capacity and compatibility; and likely comparative costs.

1.11   It will also have a key role in the successful implementation and control of any outsourcing (buy) strategy, through supplier evaluation and selection, price negotiation, quality and service level specification, contracting, and ongoing contract and relationship management – as discussed in Chapter 10.

1.12   In a more technical sense, the term **supply chain management** (or SCM) has been given to a particular strategic approach which recognises the interdependent nature of supply issues, and what Saunders *(Strategic Purchasing and Supply Chain Management)* calls 'the systemic nature of supply activities, as captured by such phrases as "supply chains", "value systems", "networks" and "extended enterprises".'

1.13 Supply chain management has been defined as:

- 'The management of upstream and downstream relationships with suppliers and customers to deliver superior customer value at less cost to the supply chain as a whole' (Christopher)
- 'The integration and management of supply chain organisations and activities through co-operative organisational relationships, effective business processes, and high levels of information sharing to create high-performing value systems that provide member organisations a sustainable competitive advantage' (Handfield & Nichols)

1.14 SCM consists primarily of building collaborative relationships across the supply chain, so that the whole chain works together to add value for the end customer in a profitable way. In Chapter 1 we saw the view of Martin Christopher:

'The real competitive struggle is not between individual companies, but between their supply chains or networks... What makes a supply chain or network unique is the way the *relationships and interfaces in the chain or network are managed*. In this sense, a major source of differentiation comes from *the quality of relationships that one business enjoys, compared to its competitors.*'

1.15 Supply chain management, in this sense, also contributes to make/do or buy decision-making.

- It encourages decision-making at a strategic (rather than purely operational) level, considering long-term objectives and impacts across the supply chain.
- It supports the use of the value stream or value system as a strategic framework, challenging each stage in the process from extraction of raw materials to purchase of the finished product by consumers to play its part in adding value.
- Managers are forced to take a broad view of the entire supply chain as a repository of skills and expertise. If a supplier has a greater ability to add value at low cost than in-house units, the buy option should be considered. Monczka argues that outsourcing is best regarded as a supply chain question ('Looking at the entire supply chain, who should be doing what?') rather than a piecemeal outsource question ('Should we outsource this activity?').
- Established supply chain relationships support decision-making: suppliers' capabilities will be known; a level of trust may have developed; information-sharing and relationship management systems may already be in place; and suppliers may be more likely to understand and support the firm's strategic goals.

2   What is outsourcing?

2.1 Although there is nothing inherent in the term 'outsourcing' that confines its meaning to the purchase of *services*, it is normally used in the service context, as the 'buy' option of a '*do or buy*' decision. This is sometimes called **business process outsourcing:** 'the transfer of responsibility to a third party of activities which used to be performed internally' (Ellram & Maltz, *Outsourcing Supply Management*).

2.2 Outsourcing may be defined as the process whereby the outsourcing organisation delegates major non-core activities or functions, under contract, to specialist external suppliers, potentially on a long-term relational basis. Outsourcing may be undertaken:

- On a project basis eg for the duration of an IT systems development, R & D, management consultancy, relocation or construction project. (The project management itself might also be outsourced, as in the case of the London Olympic Authority's procurement for the London 2012 Olympic and Paralympic Games.)
- On a long-term ongoing basis: where the outsource supplier is given full responsibility for a selected function, such as cleaning or security.

2.3   Organisations now routinely contract with specialist suppliers to provide services such as cleaning, catering, security, facilities management, IT management, recruitment and training, accounting, legal, transport and distribution – and procurement.

2.4   In many cases, the same personnel may carry out the outsourced tasks, but instead of being employed by the outsourcing organisation they work for the supplier. There are instances where the original staff remain *in situ*, and even work on the same equipment: the only difference is in the status of the staff (working for the contractor) and the ownership of the equipment (transferred from outsourcing firm to supplier).

2.5   Outsourcing is thus the ultimate expression of a firm's attitude to the supply chain as an extension of in-house resources, as seen in the concept of supply chain management. Functions performed in-house are delegated to external suppliers, typically working very closely with the outsourcing organisation.

Terminology

2.6   You might be wondering what the difference is between: a company hiring a cleaner to clean its offices under a service contract; a company subcontracting its cleaning services to a subcontractor; and a company outsourcing its cleaning services – for example. Let's clarify the terminology: Table 9.2.

Table 9.2 *Terminology relating to the sourcing and outsourcing of services*

DEFINITION	EXPLANATION
A **service contract** is a supply contract concerned with sourcing a service rather than a tangible product.	Company A wishes to purchase a service, eg consultancy or cleaning, and enters into a contract with a selected supplier (Company B) to have the service performed on agreed terms.
Subcontracting is the use of a supplier by a buying organisation to do work that the latter cannot do itself, because of a temporary shortage of resources or lack of capacity.	Company A contracts Company B, as the main contractor, to perform certain work, such as cleaning services. Company B lacks capacity to perform all the work itself (because the contract is too big, or because it is a busy period, say). In order to meet Company A's requirements, B as buying organisation subcontracts some of the work to another supplier, Company C (the subcontractor), if permitted to do so by its contract with Company A.
Outsourcing is the strategic contracting out of major work, previously carried out in-house by the organisation, to an external supplier.	The outsourcing organisation (Company A) will draw up a long-term contract specifying the work to be performed and the service levels to be achieved by a supplier (Company B). The outsourcing organisation retains responsibility for satisfactory completion of the work (requiring close contract, performance and relationship management), but delegates all day-to-day operations to the supplier.
Insourcing is the opposite of outsourcing.	The organisation previously outsourced the work, but now decides to bring it back in-house.

Outsourcing and subcontracting

2.7   Perhaps the most subtle distinction is between outsourcing and subcontracting: Lysons and Farrington (*Purchasing and Supply Chain Management*) explain the difference between them as a long-term strategic versus a short-term tactical approach: 'If you want a beautiful lawn in the neighbourhood and you hire someone to take responsibility for every aspect of lawn care, it's strategic outsourcing. But hiring someone to cut your lawn is subcontracting.'

2.8   Organisations of all kinds subcontract aspects of their activities as main contractors, and subcontracting is often viewed as a means of supplementing the main contractor's limited resources and skills while enabling the subcontractor to concentrate on their main area of expertise. In construction, for example, the ultimate buying organisation often entrusts work to a main contractor (or lead provider), which manages the project and subcontracts the various specialist tasks involved in the project. The subcontractors will usually remain legally responsible to the main contractor, rather than directly to the buying organisation. This may be the case even in those situations where the latter has stipulated which subcontractor is to be used.

2.9 In other contexts, the main objective of subcontracting is to overcome shortage of capacity by a main contractor to meet orders. In manufacturing, such as batch production, the term 'subcontracting' is used to denote work which *could* have been undertaken by the buying organisation, but is farmed out because of its lack of capacity or resources:

- Where the level of orders exceeds the productive capacity of machinery or labour
- Where extra capacity is required to meet delivery deadlines or urgent orders
- Where specialist technology or expertise is required on a job
- Where uncertain future demand does not justify investment in permanent extra capacity
- Where it is more cost-effective to buy in than to make/do in-house.

2.10 What is purchased by the buying organisation or main contractor is, in effect, the ability to undertake a job, be it in respect of capacity, expertise and/or time.

Outsourcing and 'managed services'

2.11 The term 'managed services' is increasingly used instead of 'outsourcing' to refer to the practice of delegating a task to an outside supplier rather than performing it in-house. 'Outsourcing' usually refers to the delegation of a service (though it could equally refer to farming out a part of the production process); 'managed services', of course, *always* refers to delegation of a service.

2.12 Although rhe term 'managed services' has recently come into common use, it describes a situation that has prevailed for many years. In the construction industry, for example, it is common for a single main contractor to be appointed by the ultimate buying organisation, whose task is to identify, commission and manage the services of appropriate subcontractors (or lower tiers of the supply chain).

2.13 Such a situation radically simplifies supply chain, supplier and contract management from the ultimate buying organisation's perspective: Figure 9.1. The client deals with just one organisation, the main contractor – which has responsibility for dealing with all the subcontractors.

Figure 9.1 *Managed services in the construction industry*

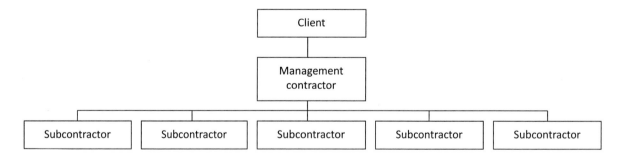

2.14 This has plenty of parallels in other sectors. For example, an organisation may hire an agency to look after all of its marketing, promotional or advertising activities. The agency will deal with numerous suppliers: designers, media, printers etc. Another example would be the outsourcing of facilities management.

3   The growth of outsourcing

Reaction against over-diversification

3.1   Outsourcing has developed in part as reaction to the over-diversification strategies of the 1970s and early 1980s. Companies then looked to spread their business risk by diversifying into a number of different business areas through mergers and acquisitions. For example, British American Tobacco (BAT) diversified into paper manufacture, US retailing and insurance as well as remaining in cigarettes. (They have since divested, and remain operational only in cigarettes.)

3.2   In the majority of cases, the diversifying strategies were not successful, as the acquiring organisations basically lacked the skills and knowledge to be effective in new business areas.

3.3   Many organisations reviewed their activities and decided to concentrate on core activities. The influential book *In Search of Excellence* (1982)*, by Tom Peters & Robert Waterman, identified 'sticking to the knitting' (focusing resources on doing what you do well and competitively) as one of the key characteristics of 'excellent' companies, which consistently produce commercially viable new products and respond effectively to change.

3.4   The strategic view, subsequently discussed by Hamel and Prahalad in their work *Competing for the Future* (1994), encouraged organisations to identify their core business – the parts of their business that are at the heart of their operation and where they excel – and build on this. Areas outside this should be considered for outsourcing to suppliers who consider the outsourced area *their* core competency.

3.5   Outsourcing has increasingly been used in respect of many different functions. Organisations have contracted with external suppliers to provide cleaning or catering services previously performed by internal staff; banks have outsourced their information systems development to specialist external consultancies; major international businesses have outsourced their accounting and tax planning functions to firms of chartered accountants.

3.6   Burt *et al* note that: 'Companies that formerly only outsourced IT now outsource many business processes that are not core competencies. Advertising, maintenance, auditing, travel and human resources are all types of functional services commonly outsourced. In addition, companies are beginning to outsource major business systems including logistic, real estate, and software systems development... The success experienced by outsourcing business processes has encouraged many firms to outsource entire operational functions.'

The influence of globalisation

3.7   Globalisation is 'the increasing integration of internationally dispersed economic activities' *(Boddy)*.

3.8   This integration may involve the globalisation of **markets**. In the early 1980s, *Theodore Leavitt* argued that with worldwide access to media, travel and communications, there was a convergence of consumer needs and wants: major brands (such as Coca Cola and McDonald's) could be sold worldwide, essentially without modification for particular geographic markets. Instead of firms being 'multinational', they could be 'global': standardising the distribution and marketing of their products worldwide, and allowing efficiency and economies of scale as a source of competitive advantage. This approach lost ground in the 1990s, however, as global brands lost market share against locally-adapted brands which catered to specific national and regional cultures, tastes and conditions.

3.9   A parallel development, however, has been the globalisation of **production**. Since the 1960s, firms in developed countries have faced the problem of high domestic labour costs for labour-intensive operations, enabling intense competition from cheaper imports originating in countries with lower-cost labour. (Think about industries such as electronic goods, clothing, footwear and toy manufacture, for example.)

3.10 This has stimulated the growth of outsourcing, as developed countries outsourced the production of finished goods and components (and the delivery of services) to countries such as Taiwan, China, South Korea and India. The media is full of examples of companies 'offshoring' administrative work and telephone enquiries (eg major banks) and product assembly (eg Dyson, Hitachi, HP).

3.11 As infrastructure and educational development keeps pace with these demands, some regions develop particular fields of expertise, and become a focus for them. For example, some cities in India are focal points for call centres and software development.

Outsourced service delivery in the public sector

3.12 A parallel development has been the growing emphasis on outsourcing public service delivery in the public sector: the 'commissioning' or 'externalisation' by local authorities of services previously provided to the public by local authorities themselves (such as housing and roads construction, garbage removal, leisure and arts services, children's and youth services, health and aged care services, and so on), where external partners – especially in the private and third sectors – have better resources or capabilities to meet community needs.

3.13 In the absence of the profit motive, the main driver for public sector strategy and policy is the need to develop and maintain the quality of services delivered to the public, while simultaneously ensuring best-value use of public funds. The practice of outsourcing or commissioning services in the public sector in the UK has been promoted by pressures for improved efficiency and value for money (and cost reductions), arising from the 2004 Gershon Efficiency Review and similar expressions of government policy.

3.14 The National Procurement Strategy for Local Government (2003), for example, included 'delivery partnerships' as one of its key visions for the future. It advocates that authorities increasingly move away from the business of 'service delivery' to a 'commissioning' role, involving sourcing, developing and managing external service providers and partners. 'This requires a broader understanding of the full range of delivery options, providers and partners through contracting, grants, shaping markets and partnerships.'

3.15 Another key public sector trend, in pursuit of procurement efficiencies, has been the development and use of regional or national buying agencies and e-procurement platforms – essentially outsourcing non-core procurement operations.

Drivers for outsourcing

3.16 A number of factors may be seen as contributing to the growth of outsourcing. Fill & Visser (*The Outsourcing Dilemma*) cite the following key drivers.

- Quality drivers: increased quality demands, lack of capability to secure quality in the short term, and the potential for outsourcing to 'bridge the gap' by providing transitional resources and capacity to meet demand
- Cost drivers: the potential of outsourcing to control or decrease costs, supporting competitive advantage (eg on the basis of cost leadership)
- Business focus drivers: the use of outsourcing to enable the organisation to focus its effort and resources on primary value-adding and revenue-generating activities (in Porter's 'value chain' model), rather than secondary or support activities
- Financial drivers: the need to free up (limited) capital funds for investment in competitive, value-adding business activities
- Relationship drivers: the need to minimise supply chain conflict and divergence of interest, by clarifying responsibility for shared activities, through outsourcing

- Human resource drivers: the need to acquire skills, expertise and experience relatively swiftly, compared to in-house recruitment and development; and possibly also (Lysons & Farrington) to by-pass internal resistance to necessary changes in work processes and structures.

4　Risks, costs and benefits of outsourcing

4.1 In the exam, you might be asked about the benefits of outsourcing, or the drawbacks. If a question asks you to 'evaluate', 'assess' or 'discuss' outsourcing, you need to present *both* viewpoints – ideally with your own examples of successful and unsuccessful outsourcing.

Benefits of outsourcing

4.2 Outsourcing allows the buying organisation:

- To focus its managerial, staff and other resources (including capital funds) on its core, distinctive, competitive competencies
- To leverage the specialist expertise, technologies, resources and economies of scale of suppliers, with potential to add more value at less cost than the buying organisation could achieve itself, for *non*-core activities
- To increase the flexibility of productive capacity in response to fluctuations in demand
- To benefit from cost certainty in the performance of activities (through a negotiated contract price for outsourced provision, transferring cost-related risks to the supplier).

4.3 The benefits, however, can only be secured by excellent supplier relationship management, because of the risks of: selecting the wrong supplier; failing to control service standards; and potential reputational damage if service or ethical issues arise. High-profile case studies (such as British Airways' problems arising from poor employee relations at Gate Gourmet, to whom it had outsourced all its catering services) show that careful management is required to control the relationship, output and service quality, ethical and employment standards – and their consequences for the outsourcing organisation and its brand.

Overview of benefits and risks

4.4 Broadly speaking, some of the potential advantages and disadvantages of strategic outsourcing can be summarised as follows: Table 9.3. (You should be able to convert this data into the corresponding arguments for and against *internal* service provision or 'insourcing'.)

Table 9.3 *Advantages and disadvantages of outsourcing*

ADVANTAGES/BENEFITS	DISADVANTAGES/RISKS
Supports organisational rationalisation and downsizing: reduction in the costs of staffing, space and facilities	Potentially higher cost of services (including supplier profit margin), contracting and management: need to compare with costs of in-house provision, and consider potential loss of cost control
Allows focused investment of managerial, staff and other resources on the buying organisation's core activities and competencies (those which are distinctive, value-adding and hard to imitate, and thus give competitive advantage)	Difficulty of ensuring service quality and consistency and corporate social responsibility (environmental and employment practices): difficulties and costs of monitoring (especially when supplier is offshore)
Accesses and leverages the specialist expertise, technology and resources of suppliers: adding more value than the buying organisation could achieve itself, for non-core activities	Potential loss of in-house expertise, knowledge, contacts or technologies in the service area, which may be required in future (eg if the service is insourced again).
Access to economies of scale (and smoothing of demand fluctuations) since suppliers may serve many buyers	Potential loss of control over key areas of performance and risk (eg to reputation, if service or ethical issues arise): over-dependence on suppliers
Adds competitive performance incentives, where internal service providers may be complacent	Added distance from the customer or end-user, by having an intermediary service provider: may weaken external or internal customer communication and relationships, and weaken market knowledge
Leverages collaborative supply relationships, and can support synergies (2 + 2 = 5) from collaboration and partnership	Risks of 'lock in' to an incompatible or under-performing relationship: cultural or ethical incompatibility; relationship management difficulties; supplier inflexibility, conflict of interest, complacency or loss of focus.
Cost certainty (negotiated contract price) for activities where demand and costs are uncertain or fluctuating: shared financial risks	Risks of loss of control over confidential data and intellectual property
	Ethical and employee relations issues of transfer or cessation of activities
	Potential risks, costs and difficulties of insourcing if the outsource arrangement fails

Costs involved in outsourcing

4.5   In the previous chapter we examined some of the benefits that a buyer will be looking to achieve by outsourcing. However, the buying organisation must also reckon on significant costs attached to the exercise. These are summarised in Table 9.4.

Table 9.4 *The costs involved in outsourcing*

COST	EXPLANATION
Planning and sourcing costs	• Costs of preparing and analysing the business case • Costs of identifying potential suppliers • Costs of the supplier selection process • Costs of negotiation and contracting
Contractual price	The actual sums payable to the supplier under the terms of the contract – although these should represent a reduction compared with in-house cost, if the business case is strong
Failure costs	Costs arising if the supplier fails to perform: lost customer goodwill and sales; rework, returns and compensation; lost reputational and brand equity and so on
Performance costs	Cost of all activities designed to ensure successful completion of the contract: • Changes to systems and processes (eg integration, performance monitoring) • Transitional and learning curve issues • Contract, performance and relationship management costs • Communication costs and so on.
Hidden costs	• Costs of procurement staff helping to implement the contract • Costs arising from vagueness or ambiguity in the specification (leading to unexpected difficulties) • Costs of over-specifying service levels • Opportunity cost of lost skills, experience and knowledge in-house (loss of future competitive resources)

Why does it go wrong?

4.6　Numerous surveys, together with anecdotal evidence, suggest that outsourcing projects often fail to deliver the expected benefits to the buying organisation. Some of the possible reasons for this are listed below.

- The organisation fails to distinguish correctly between core and non-core activities.
- The organisation fails to identify and select a suitable supplier, leading to poor performance of the outsourced activity, or in the worst cases to supplier failure.
- The organisation has unrealistic expectations of the outsource provider, owing to exaggerated promises and claims in negotiation, or underestimation of the risks or costs (and potential for cost escalation).
- The outsourcing contract contains inadequate or inappropriate terms and conditions.
- The contract does not contain well-defined key performance indicators or service levels, which means that it is difficult to establish where things are going wrong.
- The organisation lacks management skills to control supplier performance and relationships.
- The organisation gradually surrenders control of performance to the supplier, which is then able opportunistically to take advantage of the organisation's dependency.

Much of this can be avoided if the outsourcing exercise is carefully planned within a defined strategic framework.

4.7　Figures indicate that up to 50% of outsourcing arrangements break down in the first three years. This clearly is a concern for buying organisations as the impact of outsourcing risk is both internal and external.

4.8　Effective contract negotiation and management is an essential part of ensuring outsourcing success. Measurement against key performance indicators, regular meetings and defined contracts are vital. From a risk perspective, outsource deals require careful and ongoing monitoring with concerns logged in a risk register.

9

Key sourcing issues

4.9   Here are some key sourcing issues in outsourcing (and subcontracting).

- The need for the outsource decision to be based on clear objectives and measurable benefits, with a rigorous cost-benefit analysis
- The need for rigorous supplier selection, given the long-term partnership nature of the outsource relationship to which the organisation will be 'locked in'. In such circumstances, selection should not only involve cost comparisons but considerations such as quality, reliability, willingness to collaborate, and ethics and corporate social responsibility (since the performance of the supplier reflects on the reputation of the buying organisation).
- Rigorous supplier contracting, so that risks, costs and liabilities are equitably and clearly allocated, and expected service levels clearly defined
- Clear and agreed service levels, standards and key performance indicators, with appropriate incentives and penalties to motivate compliance and conformance
- Consistent and rigorous monitoring of service delivery and quality, against service level agreements and key performance indicators
- Ongoing contract and supplier management, to ensure contract compliance, the development of the relationship (with the aim of continuous collaborative cost and performance improvement), and the constructive handling of disputes. This is essential if the buying organisation is not to gradually surrender control of performance (and therefore reputation) to the supplier.
- Contract review, deriving lessons from the performance of the contract, in order to evaluate whether the contract should be renewed, amended (to incorporate improvements) or terminated in favour of another supplier (or bringing the service provision back in-house).

Case study: British Airways and Gate Gourmet

4.10   At its height, Gate Gourmet operated in 30 countries and employed 22,000 people. Most of its workers in the UK were employed at London's Heathrow Airport. British Airways (BA) sold its catering operations to Gate Gourmet in 1997, and GG become BA's sole catering supplier, normally packing 88,000 in-flight meals per day. The company was bought by American venture capitalists in 2003.

4.11   GG's Heathrow division had been losing money steadily since 2000; it lost its catering contract with Virgin Atlantic; and in 2005, it stopped making interest payments on its £332 million debt. In August 2005, GG sacked 670 workers after they refused to work in protest over the company's decision to employ 120 casual workers while sacking permanent staff. The following day, 1,000 baggage handlers at Heathrow walked out in sympathy, forcing British Airways to cancel 700 flights – affecting more than 100,000 passengers.

4.12   An editorial article in *Supply Management* (Rebecca Ellinor, 25 August 2005) analysed the situation as follows.

'It remains unclear the extent to which BA's contract with Gate Gourmet led to the catering company's financial problems, which prompted the original sackings and subsequent first round of industrial action. Did the personnel issues at Gate Gourmet take BA by surprise? And, given that Gate Gourmet is its only in-flight meal provider at Heathrow, how could this happen? Without provisions for alternative suppliers, the effect of a disruption was likely to have a far-reaching impact on the airline.

Also the geography may not have helped. In many cases, a contractor will be based a long way from its client – increasingly it may be on the other side of the world. But Gate Gourmet and BA are in close proximity at Heathrow: so much so that some local families had members working at both firms. Given this, together with the strength of local union representation, grievances of one set of employees could always spread to the other.

It also raises the question of whether something as critical to customer service should be outsourced… European companies haven't lost their appetite for outsourcing, but maybe this episode will make them think more carefully about the terms of new deals and the extent to which they are sustainable for suppliers.'

4.13   Libby Purves, in *The Times,* raised another set of risks and issues.

'Companies and public services gaily cast off everything beyond the 'core': not only frills such as hospitality, but security, IT, accounting, answering the phone.

Once 'peripheral' divisions are off the books, managers rejoice: life is lean and mean with less personnel management, pensions and welfare. Never mind that there is also less loyalty: who cares, when you can trim the margins because the service company needs you? Gate Gourmet claims it was so squeezed. Who, in British Airways head office eight years ago, put his hand up and said: 'Er, suppose the buyers sell it on to American venture capitalists who sack people by megaphone? They might not know that the food workers are related to our baggage handlers… Guys, this could ground us…' They'd have laughed.

A few voices dare dissent. An American study of outsourcing recently observed: "Providers automatically use the least qualified and cheapest staff they can get away with." Another peril, noted in The Banker *magazine, is that the centre itself gets deskilled: 20 years on we may have "a generation of banks with no technology or resources internally… dependent on the outsource provider for everything." We are a long way from the days when companies felt safer being self-sufficient. Now, they gladly risk losing not only control but comprehension of mission-critical parts of the operation….'*

4.14   The BA/Gate Gourmet example highlights the need for risk management measures such as:

- Multi-sourcing, rather than putting all strategic eggs in one basket
- Careful supplier appraisal, including criteria related to human resource management, ethical standards and employee relations
- Robust contract development and management processes to protect the buying organisation against supplier non-performance or failure
- Careful risk assessment, contingency planning and business continuity planning
- Ongoing monitoring of the supplier's financial health and stability, and ensuring that the contract terms are sustainable for the supplier as well as the buying organisation
- Ongoing monitoring of outsource activities and standards, employee relations and other risk factors in maintaining performance and reputation
- Ongoing management of the relationship with the supplier
- Exit planning, to ensure that unacceptable risk factors can be responded to by early termination of contract, transfer of service provision, or other contingency plans.

Case study: BT

4.15   As a counter-example of **successful outsourcing** and its **benefits**, an article entitled 'It's good to outsource' (*Supply Management,* 4 August 2005), described the BT group's 20-year record of successful sourcing from low-cost countries on a large scale: a strategy of 'ensuring value for money and getting the right skills and the right economies'.

4.16   The article describes BT's effective managerial focus on:

- Corporate social responsibility and ethical sourcing from low-cost economies
- Risk management: physical audits of suppliers and their supply chains, to ensure that environmental, human and financial aspects conform to BT's standards
- Managing cultural differences: eg cultural sensitivity training for BT managers
- Planning the physical logistics of the supply chain and undertaking thorough cost-benefit analysis.

Offshoring

4.17   The term 'offshoring' refers to the relocation of the buying organisation's business processes to a supplier in a lower-cost location, usually overseas. This practice is in essence a form of outsourcing, but the overseas element gives rise to additional considerations, such as: patent protection (in countries where intellectual property law is weak); additional transport and logistics risk from long supply chains to domestic markets; and cultural, legal and linguistic differences.

4.18   Clearly a major attraction for companies in developed nations is the cost advantage that offshoring makes possible. It is easy to exaggerate this. During 2005, an outsourcing consultancy (Ventoro LLC) carried out a major survey of organisations who have adopted offshoring, and found that cost savings actually achieved (approximately 19% on average) fell far short of what had been expected (40% or more). Even so, this is a significant saving.

4.19   Apart from the possible cost savings, supporters of offshoring point to the benefits of free trade, providing jobs to the less-developed country and lower costs to the origin country. Although jobs may be lost in the origin country, the workers are (in principle) able to move to higher-value jobs in which their country has a comparative advantage. Naturally, this last point is disputed by those workers in developed countries who have lost their jobs.

4.20   From the buyer's point of view, there may be concerns that the quality of the service provided may decline. Many large companies have met with hostility from customers who have received poor customer service and technical support from offshore centres. Often the complaints have focused on an inadequate level of skill in spoken English, together with the resentment that some people feel at the general principle of 'exporting jobs overseas'.

4.21   A further criticism of offshoring is that workers in less developed countries are subject to exploitation. Some critics even go so far as to say that the very reason why companies are adopting this approach is so that they can avoid the higher standards of employment and health and safety protection that prevail in developed countries.

4.22   Offshoring also, arguably, increases the level of risk in the supply chain, since it is more difficult for a buyer to exercise control over a supplier who is geographically distant (eg in terms of quality, environmental and ethical monitoring). Recent reputational problems have been faced by Apple, for example, owing to the exposure of poor employment conditions at several of the companies in China to which assembly of its products has been outsourced, allegedly resulting in the suicide of several workers.

In-sourcing or the internal supply option

4.23   So far we have looked at the outsourcing of services to an external supplier. However, an alternative is to set up an internal function to provide services previously performed by external suppliers. 'Insourcing' is the opposite of outsourcing, and involves an organisation bringing work in-house.

4.24   One obvious reason why organisations might do this is that an outsource supplier might not be doing a very good job. There may be problems with service quality, or the supplier may not be delivering the expected cost savings. In this case it will be appropriate to terminate the contract.

4.25   Even here, though, one might expect the buying organisation to find an alternative external supplier: work will generally be insourced only if the organisation believes that no external organisation is able to perform satisfactorily or offer competitive value for money. However, there are other possibilities. For example, the organisation may have re-thought its conclusions on what activities are core and non-core. If it now believes that the activity is core (or the activity has *become* core because of market changes), it may bring it under its own internal control for strategic reasons.

4.26 These advantages of internal supply may be summarised as follows.

- The transaction costs are low, because there is no process of supplier identification, supplier evaluation, tendering etc to go through.
- The relationship between 'customer' and 'supplier' is likely to be long-term and stable, enabling the supplier to refine the service in line with customer requirements.
- There is (usually) no profit motive within the internal supplier, which means that they can concentrate instead on the quality of service offered.
- Buyer and supplier are part of the same organisation, meaning that they should share the same culture and values.

4.27 However, there will also be disadvantages (corresponding to the *advantages* of *outsourcing*, covered in Table 9.3).

5 What should be outsourced?

5.1 In the exam, you might be asked to analyse *which activities* should or should not be outsourced in a given scenario, or to present a business case for outsourcing a given activity. Or you may be able to identify and recommend an opportunity for outsourcing (or insourcing) as the solution to the resource, capacity or capability problems of a case study business. Any such question will raise a range of issues of core competency, vulnerability and contractor competency.

Competitive resources and competencies

5.2 A systematic process of strategy formulation generally includes an analysis of the internal and external environment of the organisation, to determine the (internal) strengths and weaknesses and (external) opportunities and threats they present to the competitive position of the organisation. However, there are two views as to which of these sets of variables has a greater or more lasting impact on competitive advantage.

- A **positioning-based approach** to strategy suggests that the source of an organisation's competitive advantage is mainly in how it achieves strategic 'fit' with its external environment, exploiting opportunities and minimising threats. In other words, you set your strategic objectives by identifying product/market opportunities within a given environment, and then develop and deploy the organisational resources required to get you to where you want to be. In this 'outside-in' approach, you start with environment conditions, and adapt the organisation to exploit them.
- The **resource-based approach** suggests that the source of an organisation's competitive advantage lies mainly in how it exploits its distinctive (unique and hard to imitate) internal resources and competencies, setting strategic objectives based on what they enable it to do. In this 'inside-out' approach, you start with the organisation's strengths, and seek an environment that will enable you to exploit them: the organisation will change environments to suit what it does best – rather than changing what it does best to fit the environment.

5.3 Traditional approaches to strategic management have mainly been based on a positioning approach. A number of writers, however, have argued that competitive advantage based on positioning is not sustainable in the long term, because:

- The speed and unpredictability of change in the business environment undermines the assumptions behind positioning. Product and market changes constantly overtake long-range strategies. A more effective source of lasting competitive advantage is the ability to adapt flexibly and swiftly to such changes.
- Positioning is based on generic sources of advantage (such as differentiation and cost reduction) which can eventually be duplicated by competitors. A more effective source of lasting competitive advantage is some resource or capability that competitors do not possess and cannot easily imitate.

5.4 One of the key insights of the resource-based view is that not all organisational resources are a potential source of competitive advantage. In order to be advantage-creating, resources must be:

- Valuable: capable of creating customer (and shareholder) value, by allowing the firm to implement strategies that will enable it to meet customers' needs more efficiently and effectively than competitors. Stalk *et al* ('Competing on capabilities': *Harvard Business Review)* suggest that organisational competencies can be used to outperform rivals on five dimensions: speed, consistency, acuity (environmental sensitivity), agility (flexibility) and innovation.
- Rare and in high demand (eg retail locations, natural resource deposits or scarce skills)
- Inimitable or difficult for competitors to imitate (eg protected by patents, trademarks or operating licences, or intangible resources such as relationships, goodwill, skills and knowledge, and brand identity)
- Difficult to substitute.

5.5 'Resources' are closely bound up with 'competencies': the activities or processes through which the organisation deploys or utilises its resources – or what the organisation does with what it has. A unique, value-adding resource will often create a distinctive competency.

Core and non-core competencies

5.6 **Competencies** are 'the activities or processes through which the organisation deploys its resources effectively' *(Johnson, Scholes and Whittington)*.

- **Threshold** competencies are the basic capabilities necessary to support a particular strategy or to enable the organisation to compete in a given market. (The effective use of IT systems would now be considered a threshold competency in most markets.)
- **Core** competencies are distinctive value-creating skills, capabilities and resources which *(*Hamel and Prahalad: *Competing for the Future,* 1994*)*:
  — Add value in the eyes of the customer
  — Are scarce and difficult for competitors to imitate
  — Are flexible for future needs
  — Offer sustainable competitive advantage: for example by enabling differentiation or cost leadership, or putting up barriers to competitor entry into an industry.

5.7 Hamel and Prahalad argue that 'senior managers must conceive of their companies as a portfolio of core competencies, rather than just a portfolio of businesses and products'.

5.8 The concept of core competency suggests that any given organisation will want to 'stick to the knitting' to some extent: in other words, to leverage its resources by doing what it is best at – and outsourcing to others what *they* are best at and can perform more efficiently on its behalf.

Identifying outsourcing opportunities

5.9 So what activities should – and should not – be outsourced? Drawing a range of arguments together, we can argue that strategic outsourcing should only be applied to:

(a) **Non-core competencies** which, if outsourced:
  - Will benefit from expertise, cost efficiency and synergy of specialist suppliers
  - Will enable the organisation to leverage its own core competencies
  - Will not disadvantage the organisation with loss of in-house capability or vulnerability to market risks
  - Will enable the organisation to exploit technology or other operational capabilities which it lacks (and would find too costly to develop) in-house.

Activities such as strategic planning, finance, quality management and legal compliance, for e may be regarded as too strategically sensitive and central to the business to be outsourced w very strong justification.

(b) Activities for which **external suppliers have the required competency or capability**. Various options can be summarised in a simple matrix originally devised by Ray Carter: Figure 9.2.

Figure 9.2 *Competencies and supplier competence*

		Competence of contractors	
		High	Low
Core importance	Low	Outsource/buy in	Develop contracting
	High	Collaboration	In-house

(c) Activities for which **value for money** is offered by outsourcing (owing to the supplier's cost/profit structure, economies of scale, or potential for the buying organisation to divest itself of assets), in relation to the service levels that can be obtained. We will discuss the issue of value for money in detail in Chapter 10, where we look at the business case for outsourcing.

(d) Activities which:

- Are **resource-intensive** (especially in terms of high labour or capital costs, which can be borne by the supplier)
- Are **relatively discrete** (so that they can be separated out from the buying organisation without undue trauma or complexity: eg catering, cleaning, security, IT, HR, transport or procurement)
- Are characterised by **fluctuating demand and work patterns** (leaving internal capacity sometimes over-utilised and sometimes under-utilised), which outsourcing absorbs efficiently and flexibility (being resourced as required by the supplier)
- Depend on **specialist competencies** (which would be costly for the buying organisation to develop and retain in-house) but *not* on a specific or unique knowledge of the business (which only in-house resources can really develop)
- Are performed in dynamic, fast-changing markets (so that it would be costly for the buying organisation to recruit, train and retain specialist staff, or invest in fast-developing technology, itself).

5.10 Lysons and Farrington identify potential for outsourcing services as diverse as: car park management, cleaning, building maintenance, catering, security, reception, library, travel administration, IT, research and development, recruitment, training, legal services, payroll administration, records management, information assurance, telemarketing, customs brokerage, and fleet management and maintenance.

5.11 Johnson, Scholes and Whittington *(Exploring Corporate Strategy)* identify the following key issues that need to be addressed in relation to the wider value system or network.

- Where cost and value are created
- Which activities are centrally important to the buying organisation's own strategic capability, and which are less central. This will influence its decisions about which activities it needs to retain direct control over, and which can be outsourced to lower cost suppliers.
- Where the 'profit pools' are: the potential profits at different parts of the value network. Strategy can then focus on areas of greatest profit potential.
- Make/do or buy (outsourcing) decisions. ('Of course, the more an organisation outsources, the more its ability to influence the performance of other organisations in the value network may become a critically important competency in itself, and even a source of competitive advantage.')
- Who might be the best partners in the various parts of the value network, and what kinds of relationships will best leverage their potential?

Outsourcing logistics and distribution services

5.12 Most manufacturers regard logistics as a support function rather than as a core activity. Even those who still maintain an 'own-account' operation are willing to make use of logistics and distribution suppliers to a greater or lesser extent.

5.13 The potential benefits that may be realised by manufacturers include the following.

- Outsourcing frees up resources – above all, financial capital and management time – which can more profitably be devoted to core activities.
- Logistics specialists are well placed to recognise and respond to rising customer expectations. This would be a serious management burden if distribution remained in-house.
- Outsourcing gives greater flexibility in times of difficulty. Firms with their own operation may suffer if employees go on strike, or if demand is very variable during the year. Access to outside specialists enables these risks to be spread.
- Buying firms gain access to specialist expertise which may enable them to develop improved distribution systems, offering better service than their customers would otherwise have received.

5.14 Despite the benefits outlined above, not all manufacturers are willing to outsource the logistics function. Several reasons may be suggested for this.

- Most fundamentally, a firm may be concerned that suppliers will not give the required level of service. There has been some justification for such a view in the historical development of specialist logistics suppliers. Nowadays, however, the range of services offered has increased, standards are high, and advances in information technology have enabled buying firms to monitor the service provided very closely.
- A firm may fear that a large number of separate logistics suppliers – for storage, materials handling, haulage etc – would complicate matters. This too has been a justified worry in the past, but can now be overcome by making use of one of the various suppliers that offer an integrated service covering all logistics areas.
- Finally, reluctance may stem from a general policy of wishing to retain control. Handing over major functional areas lock, stock and barrel to external suppliers runs counter to this natural instinct. Again, the solution lies within the varied offerings available from logistics suppliers. These range from management-only contracts (in which the buyer retains ownership of logistics assets, but outsource their management), through various forms of joint venture, to full system takeover by the outside supplier.

Outsourcing ICT

5.15 An area where outsourcing has become particularly prevalent in recent years is that of information communications technology (ICT) development and support. Many organisations have handed over their data processing functions, and in some cases their systems development functions as well, to external specialist suppliers.

5.16 The technical complexity of this area makes it an attractive candidate for outsourcing. The cost of maintaining ICT expertise inhouse is high. But in some cases the move to outsourcing has been made for the wrong reasons.

5.17 As with all outsourcing, the objective should be to draw on specialist expertise, not to abandon all responsibility for the outsourced activity. A consultant quoted in *Supply Management* summed it up as follows: 'The management that wants to outsource problems in order to get rid of them is a disaster waiting to happen. You've got to solve the problems first before you outsource'.

5.18 Even assuming that management are outsourcing for the right reasons, it remains difficult to measure the success of the project. The main problem is in defining the level of service. It is highly unlikely that one supplier will offer exactly the same level of service as another, which means that the costs they quote are not strictly comparable. At the level of detail, what one supplier is offering to do will differ from the other's offering.

5.19 In practice this will lead to serious problems of evaluation, but it is clear that a proactive procurement function has an important role to play. Essentially, the problem is one of specification: the buyer must know in advance, and in detail, exactly what he requires the supplier to provide. In the light of a detailed specification it will be much easier to monitor performance and to assess value for money.

Outsourcing facilities management

5.20 We have looked above at some specific services that may be outsourced, such as logistics services or ICT services. A more radical approach to this general issue goes by the name of facilities management. Under this kind of agreement a specialist facilities management company is contracted to run services such as buildings maintenance, catering, heating and lighting, security and waste disposal.

5.21 At its extreme this approach is summed up in the words of a car manufacturer wishing to open an overseas manufacturing facility. 'Provide everything I need in support services: that's what I pay you for. All I want to do is make cars.' In a case like this the facilities management company will take on a very wide range of responsibilities, and the manufacturer must be certain that service provision will be up to the appropriate standard and at the right cost.

5.22 Experts in the field believe that the impulse towards outsourcing comes not from cost considerations (though of course value for money is important), but from a wish for greater efficiency. Buyers want to tap in to specialist expertise so as to increase the quality of service.

5.23 Another stimulus to this kind of agreement has undoubtedly been a desire to share risks. Buyers have sometimes welcomed the idea that if things go wrong it is an outside supplier that is to blame. While this may be regarded as a somewhat negative attitude – it would be better to concentrate on ensuring that things don't go wrong – it does highlight the fact that there are indeed serious risks in the services underpinning a company's operations.

5.24 Some of these risks were amusingly summarised in a 'nightmare' facilities management contract devised by a firm of solicitors specialising in the field. In their fictional example a company suffered the following series of disasters.

- Staff walked out after failing to receive their wages because of a technical problem with the payroll.
- Other staff left when the heating failed on an unexpectedly cold Autumn day.
- A subcontractor wiped out all the information on a customer database.
- Staff suffered food poisoning because of hygiene failures in the canteen.

5.25 The scale of these problems underlines the importance of quality assurance in all cases where services are outsourced.

Outsourcing procurement

5.26 Like any other activity, procurement and supply chain management can be considered as a candidate for outsourcing. More and more firms are following a strategy of focusing on their core competencies, while outsourcing more peripheral functions.

5.27 Lysons and Farrington identify a number of situations in which outsourcing of the procurement function should be considered: see Table 9.5.

Table 9.5 *When procurement should be outsourced*

CIRCUMSTANCES	WHAT ACTIVITIES TO OUTSOURCE
Procurement is a peripheral rather than a core activity (low or generalised skill requirements, internally focused responsibilities, well-defined or limited tasks, jobs that are easily separated from other tasks)	• Purchase orders • Locally and nationally procured needs • Low-value acquisitions • Brand name requirements • Call-offs against framework agreements • Administration and paperwork associated with purchasing needs
The supply base is small and based on proven cooperation, and there are no supply restrictions	• Well-defined or limited tasks • Jobs that are easily separated from other tasks • Jobs that have no supply restrictions
The supplier base is small, providing non-strategic, non-critical, low-risk items	• Outsource purchasing to specialist purchasing and supplier organisations, or to buying consortia

5.28 There has been much debate in the professional media about the benefits and costs of procurement outsourcing: that is, the transfer of some, or all, of an organisation's procurement activity to a third party supplier. Here are some of the benefits of outsourcing procurement.

- The freeing up of resources (eg management time, office space and equipment) which may be deployed for greater added value elsewhere
- The ability to draw on procurement (or particular category) knowledge, experience, expertise, contacts, systems and technology (eg e-auction software) which may not be available in the in-house procurement function, and may be costly to develop. This may enable the implementation of best-practice procurement processes and practices.
- The potential for suppliers of procurement services to aggregate buying organisations' demand and consolidate orders for different clients, resulting in cost savings through economies of scale, bulk discounts and so on. Conversely, suppliers of procurement services may be able to break bulk for buying organisations, getting around the constraints of minimum order quantities.
- The re-focusing of remaining internal procurement staff on strategic issues such as input to make/do or buy decisions, sustainable procurement policy, setting of KPIs for the outsourced service, and so on.
- Greater flexibility to adjust to peaks and troughs of demand for procurement activity. The buying organisation no longer has to cope with excess payroll in slack periods or overtime in peak periods.

5.29 As with any outsource strategy, however, there are also risks and costs associated with outsourcing procurement functions.

- The organisation loses a critical commercial skill and knowledge base.
- The organisation may lose control over vital data and intellectual property (as a result of sharing plans and specifications with a third party).
- An additional management layer is needed to manage the outsource provider.

5.30 A case study in this area was provided by RoadChef Motorway Services. RoadChef Motorway Services has 20 sites and multiple franchised brands (such as Wimpy, Pizza Hut Express and Premier Travel Inn). Because of its multi-faceted requirements, it had outsourced both direct and indirect (telecom, utilities and washroom services) procurement to third-party supplier 'Buying Team', which also managed the supply chain routes into each site and franchised brand.

5.31   According to an article in *Supply Management* ('To outsource or not to outsource', Anna Cooper, 10 May 2007):

'The decision to outsource … was initially based on the realisation that a shortage of internal category knowledge and experience prevented RoadChef from fully realising its purchasing potential…

RoadChef says the service is flexible and delivers significant cash savings while maintaining the highest standards of the end product. It also continually meets KPIs set by the board.

In addition, the outsourcing arrangement delivers non-cash benefits through best-practice procurement processes set as standard at head office and site level. These include proven product recall systems, supplier disaster recovery plans and a central product and supplier database which incorporates all product information and a supplier confirmation process for product changes.'

5.32   Another fruitful case study is the outsource plan for the 2012 Olympic Games in London. The Olympic Delivery Authority (ODA) outsourced the bulk of its project management, including utilities and venue construction.

'We will have the capacity to drill into specifications and design briefs and really understand them and value manage. But having done that, we intend a project management organisation to deliver it for us… The outsourced body would carry out the procurement of designers and contractors and be responsible for the management of them… Lifecycle costing, sustainability, training, health and safety, supplier diversity, fair employment and ethical sourcing were among the key considerations for procurement.' (Supply Management, 2 February 2006).

Chapter summary

- Every firm must decide the extent to which it is desirable to produce in-house or to source from outside. This is the make/do or buy decision.
- A key factor in this decision is the core competencies of the firm. A firm will wish to keep core competencies, at least, in house; non-core activities are candidates for outsourcing.
- Outsourcing means the delegation of the buying oganisation's major activities to an outside supplier. It is a strategic decision (whereas subcontracting is a short-term tactical decision).
- Outsourcing has become more common in recent decades, partly as a philosophy of 'stick to the knitting', and partly as a result of increasing globalisation.
- The outsourcing decision has often led to expensive failures and needs to be considered very carefully in strategic terms.
- Various structured models have been devised to help in deciding which activities to outsource. The matrix developed by Ray Carter is particularly helpful.

Self-test questions

Numbers in brackets refer to the paragraphs where you can check your answers.

1   List factors to be considered in the make/do or buy decision. (1.4, 1.6)

2   How can the procurement function contribute to the make/do or buy decision? (1.10–1.12)

3   Distinguish between outsourcing and subcontracting. (2.6, 2.7)

4   What is meant by 'managed services'? (2.11ff)

5   How has globalisation contributed to the increase in outsourcing in recent years? (3.7ff)

6   List other drivers for the increase in outsourcing. (3.16)

7   List some of the costs involved in outsourcing. (Table 9.4)

8   What are the benefits of offshoring? (4.17–4.19)

9   Explain the positioning-based approach and the resource-based approach to achieving competitive advantage. (5.2)

10 Distinguish between threshold competencies and core competencies. (5.6)

11 In what circumstances might it be appropriate to outsource procurement? (Table 9.5)

CHAPTER 10

Planning Outsourced Procurements

Assessment criteria and indicative content

4.2 Assess how outsourcing can impact on procurement

- Regulations affecting employees' terms of employment

4.3 Develop a plan for procuring outsourced work or services

- The procurement process for outsourcing
- Developing a business case for outsourcing
- Express contract provisions for outsourcing
- Establishing exit plans for outsourcing

Section headings

1 The business case for outsourcing
2 The procurement process for outsourcing
3 Contract provisions for outsourcing
4 Regulations affecting terms of employment
5 Establishing exit plans

Introduction

In this chapter we follow on from Chapter 9 by looking at the tactical and operational aspects of outsourcing, including the areas in which procurement staff are most likely to be involved. Obviously, much of our coverage here will be generic – whereas in practice (as in the exams), the planning and management of an outsource contract will be highly contextual: taking into account the detailed circumstances, requirements, costs and risk factors of a particular organisation (or case study organisation).

Nevertheless, this chapter should give you a basic framework for considering the practicalities of: presenting a business case for a particular outsource contract; implementing a systematic and risk-managed procurement process for outsourcing; assessing express contract terms for outsourcing; appreciating the legal aspects of outsourcing relating to the employment rights of staff; and planning for termination and transfer of outsource contracts.

1 The business case for outsourcing

1.1 As we saw in Chapter 2, the main criteria for making a business case for any procurement proposal are:

- Costs and benefits
- Evaluation of options
- Alignment with organisational needs and timescales

1.2 We have already discussed, in Chapter 9, many of the arguments that can be used to justify (a) outsourcing in general, and (b) the outsourcing of a particular activity. We will not repeat that material here. However, we will draw together some comments under the headings of the business case criteria, and focus more particularly on 'hard' calculations of cost and value for money.

1.3 Remember that in an exam, you may be asked to develop a business case for a particular outsourcing proposal or scenario. If so, you will need to demonstrate that you have *contextualised* your answer by referring to *particular* costs, benefits, problems to which outsourcing is a viable solution, strategies and policies with which outsourcing is aligned, core activities which could benefit from increased investment as a result of outsourcing – and so on. Use the material in this section as a general framework for your thinking…

Cost/benefit analysis

1.4 We have discussed the general **benefits and costs** of outsourcing in Chapter 9, Section 3: recap those points, for inclusion in a business case proposal, if you need to.

1.5 Clearly a major reason for outsourcing is the possibility that it will be more cost effective – or represent better value – to buy in services than to develop and perform them in-house. A key component in a business case for outsourcing will therefore include a **comparison of the costs of internal and external provision.** This is not necessarily an easy matter to establish.

1.6 The first step is to learn as much as the supplier is willing to disclose of its cost and profit structure. This will facilitate comparison with alternatives. The total cost of the service should be compared with prices offered by alternative suppliers, and with the costs of in-house operation if these are known (they may not be, if it is a new type of service that is being developed).

1.7 In a make/do or buy decision, the supplier's price (the cost of buying in) will be compared with:

- The marginal cost of in-house production or provision *plus*
- Lost contribution to profit arising from the fact that, if the product or service is brought in, some of the organisation's productive capacity will be idle (not generating revenue), while some of the related fixed overhead costs will still be incurred (and will not be absorbed into production).

1.8 Marginal cost is the cost of one unit of product or service which would be *avoided* if that unit were not produced or provided in-house. Variable costs are included in the unit cost, but fixed costs are treated as a deduction from total contribution to profit for the period.

1.9 The mathematics of marginal costing are beyond the scope of the syllabus. However, it may help to consider a simple numerical example, using a straightforward make or buy scenario. (Recap our coverage of fixed and variable costs in Chapter 3 if you need to.)

Example

A company manufactures an assembly used in the production of one of its product lines. The current annual requirement (usage rate) is for 10,000 assemblies per year.

The department in which the assembly is produced incurs fixed costs of $24,000 per year (or $2.40 per unit). If in-house production ceases, 50% of these costs will still be incurred.

The variable costs of production (materials and labour) are $14.00 per unit.

The assembly could be bought from external suppliers at a cost of $15.50 per unit.

Should the company continue to manufacture the assembly, or should it be purchased from the outside suppliers?

At first glance it might seem that buying-in is less expensive than making in-house: $15.50 per unit compared to $16.40 per unit (fixed plus variable cost per unit). That's $0.90 less per unit, which for 10,000 assemblies would amount to a saving of $5,000 per year.

However, when we take account of the fixed costs, the picture is very different. Remember that 50% of these costs will still be incurred even if we outsource.

	Make	Buy
Variable costs × 10,000 units	$140,000	$155,000
Fixed costs	$24,000	$12,000
	$164,000	$167,000

From this, it is clear that it is more profitable to make than to buy: by buying in, total costs actually increase by $3,000.

However, management might look further at its current fixed costs: if a greater proportion of these could be saved by ceasing in-house production, the calculation might change.

1.10 Why might the supplier be able to carry out the same service more cheaply (lower cost) or cost-effectively (better quality or productivity for the same cost) than can be achieved in-house? The supplier may benefit from:

- Economies of scale (eg because it delivers services on behalf of multiple buyers, and hence justifies a much larger operation than any individual buyer)
- Greater productivity and efficiency arising from the volume of transactions they handle, and the specialist expertise, resources or technology they possess.

1.11 In the consideration of better value – as opposed to simply cheaper cost – the effectiveness of the supplier must also be evaluated by a comparison of outputs achieved against specified objectives, targets and service levels. Definition of the business need (in the form of specifications, service level agreements, KPIs and contract terms) will be a crucial foundation for pre-qualifying and managing supplier performance.

1.12 Apart from cost savings (arising from cheaper external provision than internal provision), the organisation may be able to **divest itself of assets** (office and factory space, vehicles, machinery and equipment) that would otherwise be required to provide the service in-house. This can have a favourable impact on the financial stability of the company, and in particular on its return on assets ratio, and may (if the assets have residual re-sale value) liberate capital for re-investment in core activities.

Operational arguments for outsourcing

1.13 Costs are always an important issue but, as we have seen, there are other justifications for outsourcing.

- The buying organisation may be unable to keep up with the pace of technological change in a particular activity, while attempting to do so would divert its management's attention from more directly value-adding tasks. This is a reason why many companies have outsourced their IT applications, for example.
- The buying organisation may simply lack capability or capacity to perform the activity competitively. Rather than devoting resources to improving its performance in a non-core area, it may be preferable to access the resources and expertise of a supplier which specialises in that activity.
- The buying organisation may be able to transfer the resources used to make/do to another activity which will save cost or increase revenue.

1.14 As we saw in Chapter 9, however, there will be a number of counter-arguments and qualifications to be considered, and management will need to ensure that, for example:

- The activity is suitable for outsourcing, minimising related risks

- The potential supplier can be relied upon to meet requirements in terms of quantity or capacity, quality and service level, delivery timescales, price stability and so on.

Consideration of options

1.15 Any business case for outsourcing will have to acknowledge and evaluate alternative options. Lysons & Farrington cite a number of options which should be considered before making an outsource decision, based on the work of Batram *(The Competitive Network)*.

- Produce the goods or services in-house (if this can be done competitively)
- License the technology or designs to external producers, to make or deliver under licence or franchise
- Buy from a qualified external supplier
- Establish a joint development project with another organisation
- Enter a long-term development or supply partnership
- Acquire a world-class supplier (backward integration)

If these options are unavailable, unsuitable or uneconomic for the business need – and if the organisation has the capability to establish cost-effective management of outsource supply – the decision to outsource should be made.

Alignment with business need

1.16 At a strategic level, alignment with the organisation's objectives and requirements will involve **explaining the strategic reasons for outsourcing.** The proposal will need to demonstrate that:

- The activity to be outsourced is suitable for outsourcing (using the criteria discussed in Section 5 of Chapter 9)
- The outsourcing proposal has the potential to contribute to the strategic objectives of the organisation and/or procurement function: added value, competitive advantage, cost reduction, technology leverage, the solution of strategic problems (eg fluctuating demand) and so on (as discussed in Chapter 2)
- The strategic risks of outsourcing can be effectively managed.

1.17 At the tactical level, alignment with a specific business need for procurement will involve demonstrating that the outsourcing proposal is the **most effective and cost-effective solution** to the procurement need or problem.

- That it offers value for money, operational and other value-adding advantages over alternative sourcing solutions (including internal provision, and 'standard' multi-sourced procurement using service contracts)
- That the supply market (or pre-identified suppliers) are capable of consistently providing the quantity, quality and service levels, availability and lead times, price stability, risk management, and collaboration and compatibility to meet the source requirement, as expressed in a draft service specification and draft service level agreement
- That the organisation has the capability to manage the risks, performance and relationship of the outsource contract effectively
- That the outsource arrangement can be in place in time to meet any deadlines or timescales for the requirement (eg in the case of an IT or construction project)
- That possible *negative* impacts on staff, employee relations, intellectual and reputational capital and competitiveness have been taken into account, and associated risks can be managed and mitigated.

2   The procurement process for outsourcing

2.1   In general terms, the procurement process for outsourcing will follow the generic procurement cycle – only 'more so': as for major capital procurements, and other strategic or critical procurements, robust and systematic attention will have to be given to key points of the process to manage the organisation's risk in committing to an outsource contract.

2.2   An outline outsource procurement process is illustrated in Figure 10.1. We will look at some of the key stages of the process in more detail, especially where they differ from 'standard' procurements. (The operation of tendering, for example, is covered extensively in other units, and will not be discussed in detail here.)

Feasibility study and business case development

2.3   These issues have been considered in detail in Chapter 9, and in Section 1 of this chapter.

Defining the requirement

2.4   These issues have been considered in detail in Chapters 4–6 of this Course Book. Essentially, the outsourcing of services raises the full range of challenges in specifying services and service levels, and establishing clear measures of service quality.

2.5   As we saw in Chapter 4, the more work that can be done at the pre-contract stage the better. This means agreeing service levels, schedules, and the basis for charges in as much detail as possible before the final agreement is signed. Often, the difficulties which arise subsequently turn out to stem from different expectations held by the buying organisation and the supplier.

2.6   This point is particularly vital if the decision relates to outsourcing a function currently performed by in-house staff. Once the decision to outsource is taken, the buying organisation will typically close down its own internal service provision: disposing of equipment, making staff redundant, using office space for alternative purposes and so on. Once this has been done, the supplier of the outsourced function is in an extremely strong bargaining position, and should not be given the leeway opportunistically to renegotiate the terms of the contract, on the basis that the original specification was ambiguous, unclear or incomplete.

2.7   One possible precaution is to include the requirement that:

- Shortlisted external suppliers 'audit' the service currently being carried out in-house (or by another present supplier)
- Outsource quotations or tender bids be on the basis of providing at least an equal level of service to that provided in-house.

In the event of dispute as to scope, it should then be easy for the buying organisation to demonstrate that a given task was carried out by the audited supplier and is therefore part of the service specification.

2.8   In addition to the standard documents discussed in earlier chapters (specifications, and draft service level agreements, KPIs and contracts), which may form the basis of invitation to tender documentation, Lysons & Farrington highlight the use of a **statement of source requirements** (SRR), describing the scope and parameters of the outsource requirement, for use in market testing. In other words, this document does *not* constitute a specification or invitation to tender: it is merely a description of requirement to enable potential suppliers to self-screen for suitability and to develop solutions in advance of tender; and to act as a basis for competitive dialogue or collaborative solution development.

10

Figure 10.1 *The outsource procurement process*

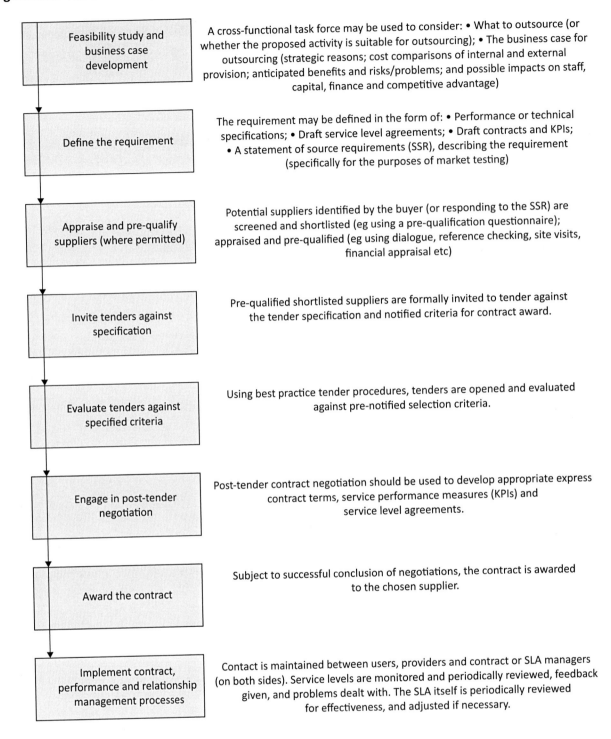

| Feasibility study and business case development | A cross-functional task force may be used to consider: • What to outsource (or whether the proposed activity is suitable for outsourcing); • The business case for outsourcing (strategic reasons; cost comparisons of internal and external provision; anticipated benefits and risks/problems; and possible impacts on staff, capital, finance and competitive advantage) |

Define the requirement — The requirement may be defined in the form of: • Performance or technical specifications; • Draft service level agreements; • Draft contracts and KPIs; • A statement of source requirements (SSR), describing the requirement (specifically for the purposes of market testing)

Appraise and pre-qualify suppliers (where permitted) — Potential suppliers identified by the buyer (or responding to the SSR) are screened and shortlisted (eg using a pre-qualification questionnaire); appraised and pre-qualified (eg using dialogue, reference checking, site visits, financial appraisal etc)

Invite tenders against specification — Pre-qualified shortlisted suppliers are formally invited to tender against the tender specification and notified criteria for contract award.

Evaluate tenders against specified criteria — Using best practice tender procedures, tenders are opened and evaluated against pre-notified selection criteria.

Engage in post-tender negotiation — Post-tender contract negotiation should be used to develop appropriate express contract terms, service performance measures (KPIs) and service level agreements.

Award the contract — Subject to successful conclusion of negotiations, the contract is awarded to the chosen supplier.

Implement contract, performance and relationship management processes — Contact is maintained between users, providers and contract or SLA managers (on both sides). Service levels are monitored and periodically reviewed, feedback given, and problems dealt with. The SLA itself is periodically reviewed for effectiveness, and adjusted if necessary.

2.9 Generic content for a statement of source requirements (SSR) might include the following.

Introduction

Description of the business

Market testing objectives

Scope

Services included in the description

Services *not* included in the description

Relationships with other providers (eg existing contractual commitments)

Service requirement

> Service-specific requirements: functionality, outcomes or outputs
> Service level requirements (frequency, capacity, response times, staffing – based on the draft SLA)
> Performance monitoring and measurement methods KPIs (including quality, security, sustainability and other relevant standards)
> Transitional arrangements (eg for testing, start-up, probationary periods, handover)

Service management

> Standards, methods and best practice expectations
> Contractual matters (eg liability and dispute resolution)
> Service constraints (eg current service provision, technical environment, cost constraints)

Instructions

> Procurement or tender process and timetable
> Criteria used for supplier pre-qualification and selection (essential and desirable requirements)
> Potential for post-tender negotiation
> Format, terms and conditions for submission of proposals or expressions of interest

2.10 You might give some thought to how our 'generic' service performance measures and service level agreement contents could be adapted for the service-specific requirements of commonly outsourced activities such as cleaning, IT or procurement. A contract or SLA for the outsourcing of IT functions, for example, might include KPIs such as: response times for maintenance or emergency call-outs and problem-handling; maximum downtimes for systems in a given period; average turnaround times for services (or a specified schedule for routine services such as maintenance).

Appraising and pre-qualifying suppliers

2.11 As we have seen, an outsource arrangement represents a significant commitment on the part of the buying organisation, because it involves a potentially radical restructuring of the firm's activities and resources – and a high level of dependency on the supplier(s) to maintain service quality and value, and to protect the organisation's reputation (especially where the outsourcing concerns the delivery of services to external customers). The *capability and capacity* of the supplier to deliver the requirement reliably is therefore a crucial factor in (a) the decision to outsource and (b) the selection of supplier.

2.12 The purpose of supplier appraisal or pre-qualification is to ensure that a potential supplier of outsourced services will be able to perform the contract to the required standard. Such a process avoids the risk – wasted cost, time and effort – of awarding an outsource contract (on the basis of lowest price or best value) to a supplier which, post-tender, *subsequently* turns out to lack capacity or technical capability to handle the work, or turns out to have systems and values that are incompatible with the buying organisation, or turns out to be financially unstable and unable to complete the work because of cashflow problems or business failure.

2.13 Note that a pre-tender screening or pre-qualification process may not be permissible in public sector procurements above a certain threshold, for which open competitive tendering is generally required (under the EU Public Procurement Directives and related UK regulations such as the Public Contracts Regulations 2015). However, the 2015 Regulations encourage pre-market engagement with suppliers, to improve the quality of the tendering procedure. In such circumstances, providers will be qualified purely by their bids' conformance to the procurement specification and invitation to tender, plus some general criteria for disqualification (such as technical capacity).

2.14 Where permitted, a supplier appraisal should cover a wide and complex variety of factors that a buyer may consider essential or desirable in its suppliers of outsourced services. Pre-qualification criteria should be related to the requirements of the particular buying organisation and the service being outsourced,

10

but one model frequently referred to in the procurement literature is the '**10 Cs**', which we have adapted (from Ray Carter's original framework) as follows.

- *Competence* (or *capability)* of the supplier to fulfil the outsource contract: whether it can produce the kinds of items, or deliver the kinds of services, required; what management, innovation, design or other relevant capabilities it has – and what value these add, compared to the buying organisation's internal resources
- *Capacity* of the supplier to meet current and anticipated future requirements: eg how much volume the supplier will be able to handle; and how effectively it manages its own supply chain and suppliers
- *Commitment* of the supplier to key values sought by the buying organisation, such as quality, service, sustainability, ethical management or cost management – and to a longer-term relationship with the buying organisation (if desired)
- *Control* systems in place for monitoring and managing performance, service levels, resources and risks; eg willingness to comply with procedures, rules or systems required by the buying organisation; quality or environmental management systems; financial controls; risk and reputation management systems; information assurance systems (for IT services); and so on
- *Cash* resources to ensure the ongoing financial stability of the supplier: its profitability, cashflow management (whether it reliably has working funds to pay its bills, buy materials and pay workers), the assets it owns, the debts it owes, how its costs are structured and managed, and so on. These factors will reflect on the ability of the supplier to fulfil the contract over time, as well as its cost/price stability.
- *Consistency* in delivering and improving levels of quality and service: eg a 'track record' of reliability, or 'process capability' (robust processes, quality assurance and controls)
- *Cost*: price, price stability, whole life contract costs and value for money offered by the supplier
- *Compatibility* of the supplier with the buying organisation: both cultural (in terms of values, ethics, work approach, management style and so on) and technological (in terms of processes, organisation and IT systems)
- *Compliance* with environmental, corporate social responsibility or sustainability standards, legislation and regulation
- *Communication* efficiency (and supporting technology) to support co-ordination and performance management.

Supplier selection

2.15 There are various approaches to supplier selection and contract award, depending on the circumstances.

2.16 There may be only one available supplier, or the buying organisation may already have a preferred supplier or sole supplier agreement with a dependable supply partner. In such a case, the buyer may simply negotiate an outsource contract for the requirement with the available, preferred or designated supplier.

2.17 The organisation may send a request for quotation (RFQ), request for proposal (RFP) or statement of source requirements (SSR) to one or more short-listed suppliers. Proposals or quotations received in response may be evaluated:

- On a competitive basis: eg the best value proposal or quotation 'wins' the contract (as in competitive bidding or tendering)
- As a basis for negotiation or dialogue with potential suppliers to develop and refine solutions
- On the basis of 'competitive dialogue', whereby the buying organisation engages potential suppliers in dialogue to develop solutions – and *then* invites submission of 'best and final' proposals or bids, to be evaluated on a competitive (best value or lowest price) basis. This is an approved procedure for complex contracts in public sector procurement, for example.

2.18 For large-value, high-risk outsourcing contracts, the buying organisation may prefer to use a formal competitive bidding or tendering procedure, in which pre-qualified suppliers are issued with an invitation to tender or bid for a contract, with the buyer intending to choose the supplier submitting the best value or lowest price bid.

2.19   The general principle is that the successful tender will be the one with the lowest price or the 'most economically advantageous tender' (on whatever value criteria have been specified). However, there is more to it than this.

- The evaluation team may need to analyse whether and how effectively each bid meets the requirements of a performance specification or SSR.
- There may be considerable variety in the total solution 'package' being offered by bids: one may be more attractive (innovative, environmentally friendly, risk-reducing, value-adding) than another – even if price tells against it.

2.20   It will be important, therefore, for any invitation to tender to state clearly that the buyer will *not* be bound to accept the lowest price quoted, and that *post-tender negotiation* may be entered into, if necessary to qualify or clarify tenders, or to discuss potential improvements or adjustments to suppliers' offers.

Contract negotiation

2.21   Negotiation may be the main approach by which contract terms are arrived at, or may be used in support of tendering (eg to improve aspects of the preferred tender, or to ensure that all aspects of the requirement, bid and contract are understood).

2.22   Outsource contract negotiations may offer an opportunity to:

- Clarify and fine-tune aspects of the supplier's proposal, or secure additional value, including the total cost of providing outsourcing
- Involve specialist outsourcing expertise (in-house or external consultants) in contract development
- Agree service performance and quality measures and KPIs, and procedures and timescales for monitoring, audit and review of performance
- Finalise and agree the terms of a Service Level Agreement
- Develop express contract terms for issues such as: dispute escalation and resolution procedures; incentives for performance and improvement; penalties for non-performance; price adjustment (eg if business volume or input costs change over the life of the contract); contract variation protocols; the valuation of assets transferred to the supplier; the protection of confidential data and intellectual property; the hiring of existing in-house personnel on equivalent terms and conditions; and arrangements for contract termination and transition. We will discuss a range of these matters in the remaining sections of this chapter.
- Nominate account, vendor or contract managers and executive sponsors to manage the ongoing contract and relationship.

2.23   CIPS defines **post-tender negotiation** as: 'negotiation after the receipt of formal tenders and before the letting of contract(s) with the supplier(s) submitting the lowest acceptable tender(s), with a view to obtaining an improvement in price, delivery or content in circumstances which do not put other tenderers at a disadvantage or affect their confidence or trust in the competitive tendering system.'

2.24   Post-tender negotiations are restricted for tenders let under EU Public Procurement Directives in the public sector: however, this does not prevent clarification and fine-tuning of tenders.

2.25   If post-tender negotiation proves unsuccessful on important terms of the tender, it may be necessary to abandon the first choice supplier and move on to the second choice. The first supplier must have irreversibly been eliminated from the process before any negotiations can commence with the second supplier: the purpose is *not* to permit a drawn-out post-tender bidding war, or unethical leverage and manipulation of suppliers.

10

Awarding the contract

2.26   The contract should now be formally recognised by issuing the relevant contract documentation. Typically, the components for the actual outsource contract will be the specification and/or invitation to tender, the supplier's written proposal, plus any terms or modifications which may have been agreed in negotiation, and the joint service level agreement. The contract should be issued in duplicate and signed by both parties, with each party retaining an original copy.

2.27   Where practical, all contract papers should be bound together in date order, and a duplicate copy issued for the supplier's retention, so that both parties can be satisfied as to the completeness of contract documentation. Any subsequent contract variations should be attached to all the copies as and when they are issued.

Post-contract management

2.28   As you may have gathered, post-contract supplier management is crucial to the success of an outsource contract. This arguably lies outside the scope of the syllabus (which deals with definition of requirement rather than management of performance), but it is worth noting that there is a wide range of ways in which a supplier under an outsource contract may struggle or fail to perform its obligations under the contract or service level agreement, owing to misunderstandings or disputes, performance problems, intervening risk factors or *force majeure* events.

- There will be obligations and actions to be followed up on either side (for example, instalment payments made for stages of project completion, or shared responsibility for risk and quality management activities).
- If risk events or contingencies arise, the contract may (or may not) lay down how they should be handled.
- If the supplier shows signs of struggling to conform with contract requirements, agreed standards or service levels (falling behind schedule, say, or receiving higher than acceptable complaints from users, or seeking price variations), remedial or corrective action may have to be taken: monitoring and controlling processes more closely, for example.
- If performance fails to conform to agreed terms and standards, there will be a variety of options for pursuing and escalating the dispute, enforcing the terms of the contract or gaining remedies (such as reducing payment, suing for damages, or in the last resort 'stepping in' to replace the supplier).
- Circumstances and requirements will often change over the life of a long-term outsource contract, and terms may have to be re-negotiated, agreed and amended accordingly.

Handling all these issues is an ongoing process through the life or duration of the outsource contract: basically, to 'stay on top of' contract performance and compliance.

2.29   The key elements and processes involved in post-contract management of outsourcing are summarised in Table 10.1.

Table 10.1 *Key elements of contract management*

ELEMENT	COMMENTS
Contract development	The formulation of a legally binding agreement, setting out detailed terms and conditions of business, and the specification of requirement.
Contract communication	Copies of the contract documentation, service level agreements and delivery plans (and notification of any changes, as they are incorporated) should be distributed to those involved with managing them on a day-to-day basis.
Contract administration	The implementation of procedures, by buyer and supplier, to ensure that contract obligations are fulfilled. This may include procedures for: • Contract maintenance, updating and change control: ensuring that changes to the contract are agreed, authorised, accurately documented and implemented by both parties, and ensuring that all versions and related documents (such as budgets and service level agreements) are consistent • Budgeting and monitoring of costs and charges • Payment procedures • Management reporting
Managing contract performance	• *Risk management*: collaborating with users and suppliers to identify potential risks or barriers to performance, so that they can be managed or mitigated • *Performance monitoring and measurement*. Service level agreements (SLAs) and KPIs may be used to express the desired outputs from the contract. These documents will form an operational tool (usually more flexible than the contract itself) with which buyer-side and supplier-side outsource managers can monitor performance on a day-to-day basis. • *Continuous improvement planning*. Buyer and supplier may work collaboratively over the life of the contract to set periodic improvement targets, solve performance issues and so on. The contract may need to be revised to reflect new targets and agreements – or may make a general provision for improvement. • *Supplier motivation*: incentives and rewards for performance, or sanctions and penalties for non-compliance. • *Performance management*: problem-solving and corrective action in the event of shortfalls in progress or performance; pursuing dispute resolution procedures (as set out in the contract); pursuing remedies to mitigate loss or damage as a result of breach of contract or non-compliance.
Relationship management	Developing the working relationship between the buying organisastion and supplier, through regular contacts, communication and information-sharing; developing and applying supplier incentives; managing and resolving conflicts; developing approaches to collaboration and mutual support; and so on. This activity may be carried out by dedicated outsource or account managers within the contract management team.

Contract renewal or termination	Towards the end of the contract period, the contract manager(s) should review both (a) the success of the outsource contract or relationship and (b) the status of the supply need.
	     If an ongoing need remains, the contract has been satisfactorily fulfilled by the current provider, and there is no immediate value to be added by supplier switching (eg to take advantage of a more innovative supply solution) or being re-opened to competition (eg to take advantage of competitive pricing), the contract may be renewed.
	     If the need has been met, or has changed, or if the current supplier's performance has been unsatisfactory, the contract may be terminated: exit planning is discussed later in the chapter.

Implications of outsourcing for commercial relationships

2.30   Outsourcing has some implications for the buying organisation's commercial relationships.

- The organisation now has a greater dependence on an external supplier than before.
- The organisation needs to consider what type of relationship it should be developing with the supplier: dependence and risk management suggest a close collaborative relationship – although not all outsourcing relationships are strategic enough to justify partnership relations (eg outsourced cleaning or catering).
- Many individuals within the organisation may be slow to recognise the implications of the change, and may continue to treat the outsourced service as something that 'belongs' to the organisation – particularly if it involves the same staff, working in the same premises (but now employed by the supplier).

10

- The relationship needs to be performance- or value-driven, rather than a 'cosy' relationship: the supplier must be encouraged to seek excellence and continuous improvement in performance, rather than rely on its strong position and grow complacent.

2.31   The typical situation is that an internal department – for example, the IT department – previously carried out work which has now been outsourced to an external supplier. User departments are likely to experience a different relationship with the external supplier. This is the case even when the supplier has taken over the staff and assets that previously used to belong internally. The very fact that the personnel are now 'outsiders' inevitably affects the relationship.

2.32   The main difference will be an increase in formality. Naturally, user departments should always behave with complete professionalism in their dealings with the IT department, but there is likely to be a degree of informality if the IT staff are 'internal'. Once the IT function is carried out by an external supplier, the need for formality increases, even with no change in actual personnel.

2.33   This has an obvious effect on prioritising of tasks. If the IT staff are internal, senior managers can simply instruct them to drop Task A and move on immediately to Task B, if Task B happens to have become important. Once the activity is outsourced, this is no longer an option. Managers must go through agreed processes and this forces an increased degree of forward planning (which of course is always desirable in any case).

2.34   Another consequence is an increase in the requirement to report. As an external supplier, the department will have to account closely for the time it has spent (and charged for). This may lead user departments to scrutinise the IT department's work more closely. There may be a feeling that trust has declined. This may equally lead to a reduction in the amount of information exchanged informally – while formal reports may have to include defined items of information, there will be less informal 'grapevine' exchanges. To avoid the adverse consequences of these changes it is important for client and supplier to communicate closely in a spirit of cooperation.

3   Contract provisions for outsourcing

3.1   We have already considered a range of express contract terms for supply contracts, in Chapters 7 and 8 of this Course Book, and many of these will be equally applicable to outsource contracts. We will use this section to highlight and/or recap terms which are particularly important in an outsource context, and to explain how they can be developed to the outsourcer's advantage and to minimise risk. Obviously, in response to an exam case study scenario, you will have to select and adjust terms to suit the identified issues and risk factors.

Confidentiality

3.2   Confidentiality clauses are designed to protect either party, in cases where they need to give the other party access to information about their operations, in the course of the contract. A confidentiality clause should define 'confidential information' (eg information that would appear to a reasonable person to be confidential or is specifically stated to be confidential); and should provide that the other party will take all proper steps to keep such information confidential.

3.3   In certain cases requiring stricter confidentiality, one party may require the other to sign a separate 'non-disclosure agreement', to be appended to the main contract.

3.4   A simple confidentiality clause might appear as follows:

'The contractor shall not disclose, and shall ensure that its employees, subcontractors and agents shall not disclose, any information of a confidential nature obtained by the supplier by reason of this contract or any other contract between the parties.'

Intellectual property protection

3.5   Businesses often expend considerable time and money developing ideas, processes, designs and other intangible assets that will enable them to generate profits. Once they have done so, they are naturally concerned to ensure that they reap the benefits without disturbance from others. The law assists them in this by providing a range of legal measures to protect such 'intellectual property'.

3.6   Technological inventions may be protected by the law relating to patents. Products carrying a distinctive design may be protected by the law relating to registered designs. The goodwill attaching to a particular mark or logo used by a business may be protected by the law of trade marks and service marks. Other protection is afforded by the law of copyright. In the UK, much of the protection is statutory – contained especially in the Copyright, Designs and Patents Act 1988.

3.7   It is important for the buying organisation to ensure that adequate protection is included in outsourcing contracts where these matters are likely to arise. A relatively simple intellectual property clause might be formulated as follows.

'All Intellectual Property Rights in all documents, drawings, computer software and any work specifically prepared or developed by the Contractor in performance of the Contract shall vest in the Client.

'Copyright in all documentation and Intellectual Property Rights in all other items supplied by the Client to the Contractor in connection with the Contract shall remain the property of the Client to the extent they are in the ownership of the Client.

'The Client hereby grants the Contractor a non-exclusive, non-transferable licence to use all the Intellectual Property Rights owned (or capable of being so licensed) by the Client required by the Contractor or any of its employees, subcontractors or agents to provide the Services. Any such licence is granted for the duration of the Contract solely to enable the Contractor to comply with the obligations of this Contract.'

Transfer of assets

3.8   Significant assets may be transferred from the buying organisation to the supplier as part of the outsourcing arrangement, including: plant and machinery; premises; information systems; and data and proprietary information. Contract terms should clearly establish:

- The value (or valuation) of assets transferred to the supplier, and how depreciation or appreciation in value will be dealt with
- Arrangements for the return to the buying organisation, or other disposal, of assets transferred to the supplier, upon termination of contract
- Arrangements for the return of files, data and proprietary information to the buying organisation, upon termination of contract
- Ownership of assets developed or created in performance of the contract
- Responsibilities for insurance, maintenance and management of the assets.

Employment terms of transferred staff

3.9   Express provisions should be made for the disposal of existing staff providing the service:

- Establishing any undertaking by the supplier to adopt the contracts of existing staff
- Reminding both parties of their obligations under the Transfer of Undertakings (Protection of Employment) Regulations 2006 (TUPE), as amended in 2014. This is discussed in detail in the following section of this chapter.

10

Indemnities and insurances

3.10   An indemnity clause is designed to secure an undertaking from the supplier that it will accept liability for any loss arising from events in performance of the contract, and will make good the loss to the injured party (the buying organisation and/or third parties).

3.11   An indemnity clause might include costs or debts (eg reimbursement of rectification costs or legal claims incurred as a result of breach of contract terms); loss or damage to the buyer's property as a result of negligent or defective work; or injury to staff, customers or third parties (eg visitors) caused by the negligence of the supplier's personnel – especially if they are performing work at the buyer's premises (eg in the case of a cleaning service) or at a customer's premises (eg in the case of outsourced service delivery).

3.12   A general indemnity clause, designed to protect a buyer, might be as follows.

'The supplier indemnifies the buyer against all costs and claims incurred by the buyer as a result, direct or indirect, of the contractor's breach of any obligation contained in this contract.'

3.13   A buying organisation will usually wish to confirm that the supplier has the ability to pay compensation in the event of any legal claims arising against it, and will usually make it a requirement of the contract that the supplier has the necessary insurances to cover them. The type of insurances most generally relevant to outsource contracts, as discussed in Chapter 7, are: employer's liability insurance; public liability insurance; professional indemnity insurance; and product liability insurance.

Subcontractor approval rights

3.14   Since buyers have a key interest in assuring the quality of services performed by suppliers, they will generally not want the supplier to hand over the work to a third party – at least without the opportunity to pre-qualify and approve the subcontractor.

3.15   A subcontracting and assignment clause may be used to prevent any assignment or subcontracting without prior written consent. A typical clause might be as follows.

'The supplier shall not assign or transfer the whole or any part of this contract, or subcontract the production or supply of any goods to be supplied under this contract, without the prior written consent of the buyer.'

Performance management

3.16   A range of clauses may be used to support performance management, to ensure supplier performance of specific KPIs and critical success factors. Here are some examples.

- A rights of inspection clause, giving the buying organisation rights of access to inspect the supplier's premises, processes or performance to monitor compliance
- A schedule performance clause, making it a condition of contract that certain tasks (eg systems maintenance or data back-up in an IT outsource contract) be performed according to a defined schedule, or within defined timescales or response times
- Penalties for specific non-performance (eg liquidated damages), and incentives for performance or improvements (eg gain sharing arrangements, bonus payments)

Liquidated damages

3.17   If a contract clause provides for a fixed sum of damages on breach of contract, and if the clause is a genuine attempt at estimating the loss in advance of the breach, it is defined as a liquidated damages clause, and will be valid and enforceable by either party – regardless of the actual damages suffered as a result of the breach. This was discussed in Chapter 7.

Dispute escalation and resolution

3.18 Outsource contracts will often include clauses setting out the methods that will be used to settle disputes between the parties (eg stipulating the use of mediation or arbitration before resort to litigation through the courts), and how they will be 'escalated' (taken further or to a higher level) if necessary.

3.19 Because of the disadvantages and costs of litigation, it is increasingly common for buyers and suppliers to treat court proceedings as a last resort, and to stipulate in their contracts that disputes must first be referred to arbitration: an 'arbitration clause'. It is also usual for the arbitration agreement to contain *time limits* during which the arbitration must begin, in the event of a dispute.

3.20 Similarly, a 'mediation clause' in a contract may stipulate that in the event of a dispute:

- The parties will meet in a good faith effort to resolve the dispute, within a defined period (eg 10 days) of a written request by either party
- If the dispute is not resolved at that meeting, the parties will attempt to settle it by mediation in accordance with the CEDR Model Mediation Procedure (or similar)
- Neither party may commence any court proceedings or arbitration until it has attempted to settle the dispute by mediation and *either* the mediation has terminated or the other party has failed to participate in the mediation

International outsourcing contracts: applicable law and jurisdiction

3.21 It is essential to know the applicable law governing an international commercial contract, and which country's courts have jurisdiction (or power) in any subsequent dispute. The UK's Contracts (Applicable Law) Act 1990, based on the EC's Rome Convention, allows the parties to the contract to agree on which law will be applicable. They may do this by an express clause in the contract – and this is certainly the safest option – even if it is difficult to negotiate. Any stipulation as to applicable law must always be undertaken via negotiation, and with the express agreement of both parties.

3.22 If the applicable law is not expressed in the contract, and questions or disputes arise, it may be inferred from the nature of the contract and the prevailing circumstances. The general rule is that the choice of law should be the law with which the contract is most closely associated: generally, the law of the country in which the contractual work is to be performed.

Contract variation and price adjustment

3.23 A feature of long-term contracts for services is that requirements change over time. Sometimes this results from external pressures: for example, new legislation on health and safety might mean that certain activities become more costly than expected. In other cases, the needs of the user department simply evolve over time. For a large or complex contract, or a situation where a number of service level agreements (SLAs) are covered, a formal document management procedure is critically important.

3.24 It is particularly important that variation or addition of requirements, post-contract, should be carefully controlled. Formal authorisation procedures will be required to ensure that only those new requirements that can be justified in business terms are added to the contract.

3.25 **Change control procedures** should be included in the contract. The respective roles and responsibilities of both parties in the change control process must be clearly identified, along with the procedures for raising, evaluating, costing and approving change requests.

3.26   A single change control procedure should apply to all changes, although there may be certain delegated or shortened procedures available in defined circumstances (eg delegated budget tolerance levels within which a contract manager would not have to seek senior management approval). Flexibility should be built into this procedure to deal with emergency variations (eg additional, urgent requirements, or an agreement to pay instalments in order to support a supplier in cashflow difficulties).

3.27   The special case of **contract price adjustment clauses** was discussed in detail in Chapter 8.

4   Regulations affecting terms of employment

Transfer of Undertakings (Protection of Employment) Regulations 2006

4.1   The UK's TUPE Regulations 2006 came into force in April 2006, and have been amended subsequently – most recently in 2014. They are intended to preserve employees' rights to employment protection, terms and conditions in the UK:

- When a business or undertaking, or part of one, is transferred to a new owner. This type of transfer (including mergers) is referred to as a **business transfer** and it means that the staff (and their contracts of employment or service) are also transferred to the new employer.
- When a **service provision change** takes place. This includes cases where fundamentally the same service activities are outsourced, insourced or reassigned by a buying organisation from one supplier to another. Examples include contracts that provide services such as office cleaning, catering and security. It may also cover situations where one supplier, such as an advertising agency or law firm, takes over a buying organisation from another: the new firm may be under an obligation to take on the staff who were working on the account for the previous firm.

4.2   The Regulations do *not* apply to:

- The outsourcing of service provision on a one-off basis of short-term duration
- Transfers of a contract to provide goods or services where this does not involve the transfer of a business or part of a business (eg the outsourcing of service provision on a one-off basis or of short-term duration)
- Transfers of assets only (eg the sale of equipment – although the sale of a going concern *including* equipment should be covered)
- The supply of goods for the buying organisation's use (eg supplying food to its staff canteen – although the running of the canteen *for* the buying organisation would be covered)
- Transfers of undertakings situated outside the UK (although in some cases these may be covered if certain of the employer's staff are situated abroad).

4.3   One of the first things to consider, therefore, is whether a transfer falls into the category of a 'relevant transfer' for the TUPE Regulations. A 'relevant transfer' will involve situations where the ownership of the undertaking changes (eg where the undertaking is sold, or is the subject of a merger transaction or a change of supplier). If in doubt as to whether the Regulations apply to a given situation, the transferor (the seller or incumbent supplier) should, to be on the safe side, assume that they do.

Transfer of employment contracts

4.4   The Regulations have the effect that employees who are employed when the undertaking is transferred, or changes hands, **automatically become employees of the new employer**, on the **same terms and conditions**, preserving their contract rights and their continuity of service.

- The new employers must take over the contracts of employment of all employees: they cannot pick and choose. Any attempted changes arising principally from the transfer are void.
- Dismissing employees solely because of the transfer is automatically unfair dismissal *unless* there is a sound economic, technical or organisational (ETO) reason entailing changes in the workforce,

including a change to the workplace location (from 2014): in this case, dismissal would be defined as redundancy, and the usual rights and procedures would apply. Otherwise, the dismissal will be deemed auomatially unfair by an Employment Tribunal, leading to costly claims for unfair dismissal.

- If a dismissal on ETO grounds takes place immediately *before* the transfer, any liability remains with the transferor (*Secretary of State v Spence, 1986).*
- The new employers take over and are bound to honour all rights and obligations arising from the employment contracts, *except* some provisions for old age and invalidity, and the pre-existing debts to employees of an *insolvent* transferor (eg statutory redundancy pay, pay in arrears or holiday pay). They also usually take over any collective agreements made on behalf of the employees, which were in force before the transfer. From 2014, such agreements may be registered after 12 months, provided that overall the contract is no less favourable to the employees.
- The Regulations provide some freedom for either party to agree variations to contracts of employment before or after a transfer, where the sole or principal reason for the variation is a reason *unconnected with the transfer* (eg the unexpected loss of a large order), or a reason connected to the transfer which is an 'economic, technical or organisational (ETO) reason entailing changes in the workforce', provided (since 2014) that both employer and employee agree.

Consultation

4.5   Representatives of any employees affected by the transfer (eg recognised trade unions or staff associations) have the right to be **informed** about the transfer, and **consulted** about any proposed measures concerning the employees, including potentially valid changes to contracts of employment. The transferor (the seller or incumbent supplier) has responsibility for initiating this process.

- Collective redundancy onsultation should address the time of the transfer, reasons for the transfer and how it will be implemented.
- It should ideally take place 28 days or more before the transfer, but there is no statutory requirement on this, when the incoming employer is planning to make 20 or more redundancies and the outgoing employer agrees (2014 change). Failure to consult may make the transferor liable to pay affected workers up to 13 weeks' pay: they do not have to demonstrate financial loss in order to be eligible for this compensation.
- It should include all workers – including those on maternity leave, sick leave and secondment (otherwise the transferor may be liable under sex or disability discrimination legislation, for example).
- Since 2014, businesses with fewer than 10 employees are not required to invite the election of employee representatives for consultation if no existing arrangements are in place.

Information

4.6   In addition, the Regulations place a duty on the transferor (old employer) to provide information to the transferee (new employer) about the transferring workforce, before the transfer takes place. This is called **employee liability information**, and it includes:

- The identity and age of all the employees who will transfer; the information contained in their 'statements of employment particulars'
- Details of any disciplinary action or grievances in the previous two years
- Details of actual or potential legal actions brought by the employees in the previous two years.

Provision of this information will have to take into account privacy issues (eg under the Data Protection Act and Human Rights Act): it will be essential to obtain the consent of individuals affected by the exchange of information.

4.7   The requirement is for this information to be provided 'at least 28 days before the completion of the transfer' (until 2014 it was two weeks). The transferee can make a complaint to an Employment Tribunal if the transferor fails to provide this information, and the Tribunal may award compensation for any loss which the transferee has incurred as a result of the failure.

10

Redundancy law

4.8 The TUPE Regulations cover the transfer of staff from one organisation to another. However, there may well be situations where an organisation wishes to outsource without using existing staff, and in such cases it must consider and comply with redundancy law – and take into account the costs of redundancies in evaluating the business case for outsourcing.

4.9 Under the **Employment Rights Act 1996** a person is defined as 'redundant' if their dismissal is attributable wholly or mainly to the fact that:

- The employer has ceased or intends to cease to carry on the business for the purposes of which, or in the place where, the employee was employed, permanently or temporarily; or
- The requirements of that business for employees to carry out work of a particular kind, or in a place where they were so employed, have ceased or diminished or are expected to cease or diminish, permanently or temporarily.

4.10 If the employer wishes to alter the terms on which the work is done, that is not a case of redundancy unless there is a fundamental change in the type of work which becomes the reason for the dismissal of the employee.

4.11 The place where a person is employed means in this context the place where they are habitually employed and any place where, under their contract, they can be required to work. There will not, therefore, be a redundancy situation where the transfer of location is reasonable or where the contract gives the employer an express or implied right to move the employee in question from one place to another.

Selection for redundancy

4.12 The selection of employees for redundancy must be undertaken in a fair, reasonable and consistent manner, based upon objective criteria, such as 'Last in First Out' or performance-based points systems. Some criteria for selecting employees for redundancy are considered to be automatically *unfair dismissal*, including: pregnancy, childbirth and maternity or paternity leave; participation in the activities of a recognised trade union; and age.

Redundancy pay

4.13 There are two categories of redundancy pay, for which an employee may be eligible.

- Statutory redundancy pay, which is set down in law as the minimum amount that must be paid. This is calculated by reference to age, length of service and final remuneration, with a maximum cap.
- Contractual redundancy pay, which may be payable if the employer has a redundancy scheme in operation. This information will be set out in the contract of employment.

4.14 A redundant employee will be disqualified from receiving a redundancy payment if he unreasonably refuses an offer to renew his contract or to re-engage him on the same terms as before, or an offer of alternative suitable employment. An employee who is dismissed by reason of misconduct has no right to a redundancy payment.

Consultation and notification

4.15 The Trades Union and Labour Relations (Consolidation) Act 1992 (TULRA) places a duty upon the employer to consult with representatives of employees to be affected by redundancy. The consultation must include such matters as:

- Reasons for the proposed redundancies
- Number of employees involved
- Proposed methods of selecting those to be made redundant

- Timing of the dismissals
- Ways of avoiding redundancy (eg offers of alternative employment)

4.16 The employer must consult with the union at the earliest opportunity and, in any event:

- At least 90 days before the first of the dismissals take effect (if there are to be 100 or more redundancies within a period of 90 days or less);
- At least 30 days before the first of the dismissals take effect (if there are to be 20–99 redundancies within a period of 30 days or less).

4.17 Consultation does not mean 'negotiation', and employee representatives have no rights to insist on negotiation over the numbers of employees that are to be made redundant or the selection process.

4.18 If the proposed redundancy will affect ten or more employees, the employer must also notify the Secretary of State, including such matters as:

- Numbers to be made redundant
- Proposed date(s) of the dismissals
- Identification of any trade union with which consultation is necessary.

4.19 For all redundancies covered by the Employment Rights Act 1996, the employer also has a duty to disclose certain information to the affected employees. If notice is not given to any employees being made redundant, they are entitled to a protective award representing the notice they should have been given.

Alternatives to compulsory redundancy

4.20 Redundancies cost time and money, and have a negative impact on employer brand, reputation, morale and employee relations. Redundancy imposed by an employer should always be a last resort after other potential avenues have been explored, including:

- Natural waste: eg a freeze on recruitment, allowing resignations and retirements to reduce the work force naturally
- Retraining or relocation and redeployment of staff. (The employee can choose not to accept any alternative employment, but if he refuses 'unreasonably', the employer may avoid liability for a redundancy settlement.)
- Loaning or seconding staff to other units or organisations with labour or skill shortages
- Incentives to take voluntary redundancy or early retirement (subject to cost constraints, and compliance with discrimination laws)
- Revised working arrangements (such as part-time working or job-sharing).

5   Establishing exit plans

5.1 One significant risk with outsourcing arrangements is that if the contract breaks down, the fallback positions are not ideal. The buying organisation has the following options.

- Award the contract to the second-choice provider from the previous sourcing exercise or re-tender the contract (if too much time has elapsed since the previous tender). Either way, there will be costs, transition and handover issues, and learning curves to get through, with potentially serious disruptions to business continuity.
- Bring the work back in-house (insourcing). This is often expensive and difficult, because the organisation may have lost in-house plant, equipment, capability and expertise to perform and manage the activity.

5.2 Contingency and business continuity plans should be developed for either eventuality, in order to manage the risk of disrupted services. These may be seen as 'exit plans' or 'exit strategies': in other words, plans for unravelling and getting out of outsourcing arrangements, if there is a need to do so.

10

5.3   It is worth emphasising that the breakdown of an outsourcing arrangement may not only be due to failure of the supplier, or incompatibilities and conflicts of interest affecting the relationship. Core competencies change with competitor activity, customer demand and changes in the critical success factors of the market. Business requirements may change over the life of a long-term service contract. More innovative solutions and suppliers may emerge in the market. The cost comparison between in-house provision and outsourcing may change (eg due to the buying organisation's development of new technology or acquisition of new premises, systems or skills). Or the supplier may become insolvent.

Contractual provisions for review and non-renewal

5.4   A contract would normally expressly state a **duration** period, especially in the UK public sector (where maximum contract durations are set by the EU Procurement Directives, in order to promote competition and value). For long-term service contracts, a termination date encourages review, re-negotiation or re-tendering of the contract – which may be important if the contract proves unsatisfactory for either party, or if ongoing improvements in terms are desirable. If a contract is drawn up *without* a specified term, both parties are at greater risk of early termination by the other.

5.5   A **duration clause** might set out the contract period, with a specified commencement and expiry date. For example: 'The contract period shall be from 1 January 20XX ('the commencement date') until 31 December 20XX ('the expiry date') inclusive.'

5.6   If the parties wish to keep open the possibility of continuing under the same contract, after the end of the original term of contract, they might include an **extension or renewal clause**, giving them this option. This would be particularly valuable in contracts for long-term service requirements, where contract performance is satisfactory to both parties (and/or where continuous improvement measures have been built into the original contract), because it saves the time and expense of re-letting the contract. A renewal clause may also act as an incentive to the supplier to maintain high levels of performance, if renewal is not automatic but made a 'reward' for good performance.

5.7   Provisions for renewal of contract may include:

- The initial duration of the contract
- The availability of an extension period, if any
- Criteria for qualifying for extension
- Procedures for terminating the contract
- Procedures for handing over to a new supplier, where relevant.

Contractual provisions for early exit

5.8   It is important for a clause to be expressly written into a contract concerning the timing, circumstances and methods by which the contract can be terminated by either party, if required. This enables each party to 'get out of' a contract which is no longer satisfactory – while protecting the rights of the other party.

5.9   A **termination clause** might set out the circumstances in which either party may terminate the contract immediately upon written notice to the other party (eg in the case of going into liquidation, or in case of breach of a vital term of the contract).

For example: *'Without prejudice to other remedies, the buyer may terminate the contract for material default if, upon written notice, the supplier, in the case of remediable breach, fails to cure the matters set forth in said notice within 30 calendar days from the date of said notice.'*

Contractual provisions for emergency 'step in'

5.10   A **step-in clause** may be inserted, expressly allowing the buying organisation to temporarily re-assume responsibility for the work in the event of serious breach of contract or service failure. Such a clause should provide for:

- The buyer's right to step in, in specified circumstances: for example, circumstances constituting, in the reasonable opinion of the buyer, a situation of 'emergency'; circumstances constituting, in the reasonable opinion of the buyer, a serious risk to the health or safety of persons or property or the environment; or a breach of a statutory duty by the supplier or its subcontractors.
- The provision of notice to the supplier of intention to step in (in the form of a step-in notice), and discussion on fair and reasonable terms of how this will affect the contract
- The buyer's right to suspend the right and obligation of the supplier to provide all or any of the services or requirements involved in the contract
- The buyer's right to have access to, and the right to use, assets and documents used in the performance of the contract, in order to provide for alternative provision
- The duty of the supplier to co-operate fully with the buyer, and provide all reasonable assistance (including access to or copies of technical information)
- The duty of the buyer to reimburse the supplier for all reasonable additional costs incurred by the supplier in assisting the buyer
- The provision of notice of the buyer's intention to reinstate the supplier's obligations and rights ('a step-out notice'); any conditions that attach to re-commencement (eg compliance with improvement targets or risk mitigation measures); and the date on which provision should recommence.
- The buyer's right, if not satisfied, to terminate the contract in accordance with appropriate termination provisions.

Contractual provisions for transition

5.11   An express **transition clause** aims to ensure a smooth transition from the current supplier to any new supplier who may be awarded the business for a new contract period (if the existing contract is not renewed), or on contract termination due to breach or insolvency.

5.12   Such a clause should stipulate that the outgoing supplier will co-operate during the handover arising from the completion or earlier termination of the contract: giving access to documents and other information; returning or re-selling assets (at appropriate valuation); and taking no action to disrupt the handover.

Planning for supplier switching

5.13   Buyers need to be aware that switching outsource supplier (whether to in-house or alternative external providers) causes upheaval and cost – because strong relationships will often have been established, and relationship-specific plans and investments made. Some of the costs and risks of switching are summarised in Table 10.2.

5.14   Even if there is a strong business case for switching or insourcing, there may be barriers. The time and effort invested in developing long-term supplier relationships and integration can cause a psychological 'lock-in' to the current supplier. The existing provision, especially where a satisfactory and proven relationship exists, could lead to future competitive advantage through continuous improvement over time, or co-investment in innovative supply solutions.

5.15   If switching or insourcing does take place, some key issues for buyers will include the following.

- The need for early **flagging of contracts up for renewal**, so that buyers can discuss renewal and switching options with key stakeholders (including users who may have feedback on the impact of supplier performance and risk)

- The need to **capture and document** the knowledge bank, policies, systems and procedures of the existing supplier (if these do not already exist): user manuals, policy statements, procedure flowcharts and so on – for the use of the incoming supplier
- The updating of **specifications, SLAs and draft supply contracts**, to cut down on work at the switching stage
- The proactive preparation of **contingency transition plans**, and related contract terms, detailing the risks and responsibilities of both parties in the changeover process, including the identification and ironing out of unforeseen problems or issues
- Readiness of stakeholders, systems and infrastructure for the implementation of the new contract. Staff in both organisations need to be aware of the new arrangements, and their responsibilities within it. Customers may need to be made aware of any implications for quality or delivery.
- The proactive planning of **changeover approaches**.
- A trial period or pilot programme, for example, allows the buyer and new supplier to test their readiness, identify issues and iron out problems prior to acceptance or full implementation.
- Direct or phased implementation may be used, depending on whether there are discrete sub-sets of the service that can be phased in incrementally.
- Some variation of parallel running may be used, where the outgoing supplier's activity is progressively reduced or 'ramped down' while the incoming supplier's is 'ramped up'. A ramp-up/ramp-down phase gives all parties a chance to adjust with minimal disruption (and the chance to measure the new supplier's performance against the old).
- **Contract management and review**, to ensure that: co-operative working relationships are built with the new supplier; shortfalls on agreed specifications or service levels are followed up; any early changes to contract terms are systematically documented and managed; and continuous improvements are built into supplier performance over time.

Table 10.2 *Costs and risks of supplier switching*

RISKS OF SUPPLIER SWITCHING	COSTS OF SUPPLIER SWITCHING
The new supplier may fail to perform (eg if it made exaggerated claims to win the contract...)	Identifying and qualifying alternative suppliers
Process incompatibility (eg if integrated systems and relationship-specific modifications were made with the previous supplier)	Initiating and administering tendering exercises or other sourcing and contracting processes
Cultural or inter-personal incompatibility (eg where patterns of understanding and behaviour developed in the old relationship)	Settlement of work in progress projects with the outgoing supplier; settlement of outstanding claims; payment of 'exit' (eg early cancellation) fees
Loss of knowledge (eg where collaborative processes with the outgoing supplier were undocumented)	Change of internal systems and processes to align with the new supplier
Learning curve: time for the new supplier to achieve peak performance, teething problems	Familiarising and training the new supplier in policies and requirements
Exposure of intellectual property, confidential data (without trust having yet been built up)	Contract development and contract management (often with more intensive monitoring and contact in the early stages of the relationship)
Problems of adversarial hand-over from the old supplier to the new: trouble accessing designs, documents, assets, work in progress etc.	Risk mitigation measures (eg insurances) and corrective measures (eg re teething problems)
De-stabilisation of the workforce, through multiple transfers of service provision.	

Maintaining performance from the 'outgoing' outsource supplier

5.16   In any change of supplier, there is a risk that the current supplier may attempt to disrupt the transfer of business to new suppliers, or may simply lose motivation to provide the required service levels.

5.17   Constructive relationship management should underpin any change in supplier. The buying organisation may offer the outgoing supplier helpful feedback on the reasons for non-renewal (enabling it to plan improvements). Where possible, the door should be left open for renewal of the relationship in future: the contract may be revisited at the end of the contract period, for example, or there may be new contracts for which the supplier will be invited to bid.

5.18   Additional incentives may be used, in the form of loyalty or performance-related bonuses or positive supplier rating, to motivate the supplier to provide quality service right to the end of the existing contract.

5.19   Where necessary, however, sanctions may be applied to enforce the terms of the contract and service level agreement for the full duration of the contract. Model contracts often include clauses to ensure smooth transition, so that any disruption caused by the outgoing supplier is interpreted as breach of contract, opening them to legal damages. An example of such a clause may be as follows.

The Supplier shall co-operate fully with the Buyer during the handover arising from the completion or earlier termination of the Contract. This co-operation, during the setting up operations period of the new Supplier, shall extend to allowing full access to, and providing copies of, all documents, reports, summaries and other information necessary in order to achieve effective transition without disruption to routine operations.

> ## Chapter summary
>
> - A key factor in the outsourcing decision is a comparison between the costs of internal and external provision. It's important to remember that fixed costs relating to internal provision will not necessarily go away if we outsource.
> - Another key factor is that the decision must be aligned with the overall strategic objectives of the organisation.
> - To get the decision right, it is important to follow a structured decision process, beginning with a feasibility study and development of a business case.
> - An outsourcing decision can only be a sensible option if potential suppliers have been thoroughly pre-qualified. And once the contract has been awarded, it remains important to manage the supplier's performance.
> - Specific terms of an outsourcing contract will cover confidentiality, intellectual property protection, transfer of assets, employment terms of transferred staff, indemnities and insurances, subcontractor approval, liquidated damages, dispute resolution, and contract variation.
> - Staff transferred from the buying organisation to the supplier are protected by regulations preserving their employment rights.
> - The buying organisation must be prepared for the contract to come to an end. It is important to formulate an exit plan right at the beginning.

 ## Self-test questions

Numbers in brackets refer to the paragraphs where you can check your answers.

1   Explain the importance of the marginal cost of in-house provision when considering an outsource contract. (1.7)

2   List reasons why an organisation might consider outsourcing. (1.13)

3   List stages in an outsource procurement process. (Figure 10.1)

4   List typical contents of a statement of source requirements. (2.9)

5   List Carter's 10Cs of supplier appraisal. (2.14)

6   Describe actions that will be necessary as part of post-contract management. (2.28, 2.29)

7   What are the implications of outsourcing for relationships with suppliers? (2.30)

8   Suggest wording for (a) a confidentiality clause and (b) an indemnity clause in an outsource agreement. (3.4, 3.12)

9   In what circumstances do the TUPE Regulations apply? (4.1)

10   What are a buyer's possible fallback positions if an outsource contract breaks down? (5.1)

11   What is a step-in clause? (5.10)

12   What is a transition clause? (5.11)

Subject Index